Company of Pianos

Finchcocks – Home of the Finchcocks Collection.

Company of Pianos

for Malcolm

Richard Burnett

Richard Burnett

with Glossary and Keyboard Chronology by William Dow

Company of Pianos

Richard Burnett

with Glossary and Keyboard Chronology by William Dow

© 2004 Finchcocks Press

First published in 2004 by

Finchcocks Press,

Finchcocks,

Goudhurst, Kent, TN17 1HH

www.finchcocks.co.uk

in association with

Third Millenium Publishing Limited,

an imprint of

Third Millenium Information Limited

Farringdon House

105-107, Farringdon Road

London EC1R 3BU

www.tmiltd.com

ISBN 1-903942-35-7

DESIGN Paul Cooper Design

ORIGINATION & PRINT Colorprint Offset (Hong Kong)

Contents

Instruments of the Finchcocks Collection, as they appear in the text, are listed in italics.

Preface

The prime purpose of this book is to act as a companion to the pianos as found in the catalogue of the Finchcocks Collection. To this end, therefore, I have tried to bring to life the various instruments by describing in a certain amount of detail their physical and tonal characteristics, their influence on eighteenth and nineteenth century piano music, and problems of interpretation that arise when playing the classical masters. At the same time I thought I should discuss the careers of some of the more famous builders, and to deal with the background to their work and certain aspects of social life which seemed to me to be of interest. I also felt that I should not ignore those antecedents of the piano which influenced its development, and I have therefore included a number of earlier instruments of the collection. But I do not pretend to have written a detailed history of the piano, which is a complex subject. For those interested, a bibliography lists a selection of the many exhaustive (if, in some cases, exhausting) studies of that kind.

Throughout the text I have made a point of employing the common modern English terminology for pianos, e.g. 'piano', 'pianoforte', 'grand piano' or even just 'grand' etc. One of the most frequent questions that I get asked at Finchcocks is 'What is the difference between a pianoforte and a fortepiano?' The short answer is that there is no essential difference. For many years no-one seemed able to decide whether these instruments should be called 'softloud' or 'loudsoft'. In England, the tendency was always to call them 'pianofortes', whereas in Vienna in the early days they were known as fortepianos (or in common German speech 'Hammerklaviere' or, specifically for grands, 'Hammerflügel'). Since London and Vienna in the late eighteenth and early nineteenth centuries were the most famous centres for piano building, and since their respective instrument production methods varied considerably, so musicians have frequently used these two terms for Viennese (or Viennese-type) and English (or English-type) instruments. The current usage for today's instruments is of course 'piano', 'pianoforte', etc. except in the slavonic countries, where 'fortepiano' is still employed. Just to confuse the issue even more, however, the term 'fortepiano' is unfortunately often employed by musicians and concert promoters, to denote any early piano (usually an instrument without iron reinforcement) in contradistinction to a modern one, whether or not this was the term used by its maker.

Pitch notation

Acknowledgements

Many people over the years have helped me in various ways in the preparation of this book. I am particularly indebted to Dr. William Salaman, educational consultant, who has painstakingly read and commented on the contents. His great experience in musical publications has certainly helped me to avoid many pitfalls. I am also immensely grateful to David Steed, who, like William Salaman, is a trustee of the Finchcocks Charity, and to Dr. Alastair Laurence, whose unrivalled knowledge of English pianos has been invaluable. John Collard, who is descended from the famous firm, and Peter James, a direct descendant of Robert Stodart, have both given me much useful information. I must also thank David Robinson of the Broadwood Archive, who assisted me in my research, and Geoffrey Simon for his account of the Broadwood firm at the present time. Peter Bavington has been of great help to William Dow in the preparation of the glossaries, for which I am most grateful. I am grateful too for the account of Clementi's dealings at Kentwell Hall, kindly given to me by Patrick Phillips, and to Charlotte Ellis, for introducing me to the account of the downfall of the American square piano.

Others who have steered me on to the right track, or who have made generous contributions to the contents, include the instrument restorer and builder, David Winston, the pianist Virginia Pleasants and Gerry Gregory, senior lecturer in Education, Brunel University. I would also like to thank those who have provided me with helpful books, articles and monographs. They include Andrew Benson-Wilson, Martyn and Phyllis Clarke, Martha Clinkscale, Michael and Warwick Cole, Margaret Cranmer, Clemens von Gleich, Lady Glubb, Christo Lelie, John Henry van der Meer, Kenneth and Mary Mobbs, Bart van Oort, Nicholas Plumley, Sandra Rosenblum, Kerstin Schwarz, Ernst Self, Nigel Simeone and Deborah Wythe. There are also many other people who have helped in other ways. It is virtually impossible to list them all, but I would like to thank the many musician colleagues who have enriched my understanding of the early piano both by their performances and also by their comments. To mention just a few: my erstwhile partner at Finchcocks, Derek Adlam, the tenor, Nigel Rogers, who was my contemporary at King's College, Cambridge, and who introduced me first to the possibilities of the early piano during his years in Munich with the Studio der Frühen Musik, the clarinettists Alan Hacker and Lesley Schatzberger, the oboist and composer Edwin Roxburgh, the viola player Alan George and other members of the Fitzwilliam String Quartet, the violinist Daniel Spektor and the cellist Christine Kyprianides; the tenor Ian Partridge, the soprano Poppy Holden, and fellow pianists such as Lorna Fulford, Mary Sadovnikoff from Providence, Rhode Island, David Ward from the Royal College of Music, and Sally Fortino from the Fritz

Neumeyer Collection, Bad Krozingen. Above all, I would like to thank my two colleagues at Finchcocks, William Dow, the curator of the collection, and Steven Devine, the assistant curator. Steven Devine has been instrumental in helping with the problems of putting the book together, and William Dow, quite apart from his own contribution in providing the technical glossaries, has given invaluable assistance in the analysis of the various instruments under discussion. Tim Smithells, another colleague from Finchcocks, has helped as proofreader. In addition to those I have mentioned I must express my gratitude to my wife, the writer, Katrina Hendrey, who has assiduously helped and encouraged me throughout.

Quite apart from the debt I owe to those who have helped me jump the writing hurdles, the book could never have been born without the existence of the many and varied instruments, pictures, musical ephemera etc., that comprise the Finchcocks Collection. I would like therefore to take this opportunity to extend my grateful thanks to the many people or institutions, who have either made generous donations or who have helped me make acquisitions or improvements to the contents of the collection. They include in particular the tenor, the late John Kerr, who has given enormous assistance over many years, and also The Musical Museum of Brentford, Middlesex, The Horsham Museum, and Gerry Higgins, Dr. Alastair Laurence, Julian Machin, Jean Phillips, Gerald Pointon, Mrs. Szkoda, the late Adam Johnstone of the Broadwood Trust, the late Mrs. Hart Still, and the late Joan Harding. There are also many who have given their services at Finchcocks in different ways. It would be impossible to list them all, but I should like to thank especially the conductor, Michael Foad, the clavichord builder, George Veness, the pianist, Sandra Carlock and Christopher Clementi, a direct descendant of the composer, Muzio Clementi. Finally, I am very grateful to Gef Lucena, who brought so many of the instruments alive through his record company, Saydisc. Under his classical label, Amon Ra, and at his own instigation, he made with his colleague, David Wilkins, some thirty-five CDs at Finchcocks in nearly thirty years.

PHOTOGRAPHERS
Juliet Coombe, Steve Davey, Alexander Dow, John Freeman, Geoff Partner, Andrew Sydenham, Alexander Welsh, Michael Wheeler, Jeremy Whitaker.

Part 1 – The Instruments

Cristofori and some precursors of the piano

Possibly the most fascinating and varied of all the families of keyboard instruments is that of the piano. At Finchcocks we have to date some sixty historical pianos of many different types and styles. And yet we still do not possess all the varieties common in the past. The richness of their attributes is astonishing. When unused, they sleep, but when played they come alive, and like people they bear family characteristics. The head of the firm is the father, and through generations the firm's character and idiosyncrasies tend to be retained. As in a real family, each instrument has its own personality, quite distinct from its sibling, yet each bears the imprint of its maker. Some siblings are steady and reliable, with relaxed and mellow voices. Others have neurotic traits – they sound irascible and are not always in tune with themselves. And occasionally of course there is the black sheep of the family, constantly causing trouble, and in the end of little use to anybody.

The earliest piano in the collection dates from 1769, and was made only a few years after pianos were first produced commercially in England. To look at such an innocent little thing, it is hard to reconcile it with one's preconception of how a piano should be, let alone to think of it as being in any way connected with a Steinway concert grand. Yet this small rectangular object, built in London by Zumpe and Buntebart, two emigrant Germans, is as much a genuine piano as the modern grand and in its own way every bit as serious a musical instrument. To understand though how the piano evolved, and how it came to be the most ubiquitous of keyboard instruments throughout the western world, we have to visit Italy at the beginning of the eighteenth century.

When Bartolomeo Cristofori around 1700 built a harpsichord with which it was possible to achieve a range of dynamics through finger touch, he singlehandedly and at a stroke revolutionised keyboard playing in the home and in the concert hall for the following three hundred years. Throughout the seventeenth century instrumentalists had tried to imitate the cadence of the human voice. Since the plectrum of a harpsichord, operated from the keyboard, cannot vary the volume of a note, this was scarcely possible for the player of such an instrument, save by subtlety and guile, or by the somewhat cumbersome use of gadgets whereby more than one string was sounded for each note, thereby acquiring different layers of volume. For many years builders had tried without much success to devise ways of making slight changes in volume possible, but the attempts were halfhearted and sporadic, for paradoxically the very disadvantage of a harpsichord in this respect acted as a kind of challenge, inviting players to use their initiative in finding ways to overcome or avoid the problem.

Cristofori (1655-1731) was a harpsichord builder at the court of Ferdinand de' Medici in Florence. His production of a harpsichord col piano e forte ('with soft and loud') was a remarkable achievement, since he hit upon an action design that was not only not seriously improved for over a century, but could be said to be the prototype of the pianoforte of today. Yet the invention was slow to take on, even though Cristofori himself continually worked to refine his invention throughout the remainder of his life. First, the novel touch made it awkward to play, if, as was the case, you were unused to such a thing. Secondly, the action, in which the hammers strike the strings, is far more complicated and difficult to make than a plucking mechanism. Thirdly, the instruments were not much louder than a large harpsichord, so offered little advantage as far as volume was concerned. And finally, they were almost without exception grand pianos (in the shape of long thin harpsichords), and those who had similar looking instruments were people of means, who had spent a great deal of money on a beautifully crafted harpsichord and who couldn't care less about a new-fangled machine for which in any case no music had as yet been written. Acceptance of the piano was therefore reluctant for several decades after Cristofori's time. However, the third quarter of the eighteenth century saw a tremendous upsurge in piano building all over the continent, and also in England.

Through much of the late seventeenth and eighteenth centuries the most common English keyboard instrument was the bentside spinet. These delightful baby harpsichords

ABOVE **Spinet attrib. Cawton Aston, London, circa 1700** The attribution of this spinet to the English builder, Cawton Aston, is derived from the letters C A, which are written in ink upon the lowest key lever. The instrument is made of walnut, with a spine of spruce – a type of composite construction that appears characteristic of some northern European instruments of the seventeenth century and later. Other examples built in this style include English virginals and some early French harpsichords. The spine is the part of the instrument that was normally placed next to a wall, so the use of a different (and cheaper) wood would not be noticed. The interior of the instrument, veneered in cypress, with a panelled front board and profiled key cheeks, gives an Italian appearance and provides a pleasing contrast to the dark walnut of the exterior and lid. The natural keys are ebony and the accidentals solid ivory. These former have gothic trefoil decoration (known as 'arcades') in stamped paper, painted black, on the ends of the levers. As is usual with English instruments from this period onwards, the soundboard is varnished. This contrasts with contemporary European instruments which are left untreated. When the spinet was acquired by Finchcocks it came with a stand made in the late eighteenth century. This was fitted with a rudimentary lid swell. The remaining evidence for this is a hole bored through the wrestplank, which housed the rod that lifted the lid, and a leather pad which acted as a bearing surface glued to the lid. During restoration this stand was removed and a new one provided, which was copied from an anonymous late seventeenth century instrument in the Russell Collection, Edinburgh.

were pretty and simple to play. They were also cheap. Many things musical in the past were prohibitively expensive. A large eighteenth century harpsichord could cost anything up to seventy pounds (or even more), thus putting itself quite beyond the reach of the average citizen. But a spinet could be purchased for five or ten pounds. The English bentside spinet was originally an Italian concept, designed by the harpsichord builder, Girolamo **1** Zenti, who came to London in 1664 to work here.[1] Until his arrival the normal domestic harpsichord was the larger and rectangular virginal (or 'pair of virginals' as they were often referred to) of which there may have been a considerable number around; for in his account of the great Fire of 1666 Pepys describes

> *the River full of lighters and boats taking in goods, and goods swimming in the water; and*
> *only I observed that hardly one lighter or boat in three that had the goods of a house in, but*
> **2** *there was a pair of virginalls in it.*[2]

From this one can imagine that many such instruments were consumed in the conflagration. Possibly, though, this disaster acted as a catalyst for a change in fashion, since the virginal for use as a domestic instrument was soon to be displaced by the little spinet, and Pepys himself bought such a one in 1668.

Today only a handful of original English virginals survive. Spinets are more plentiful, but still only relatively so. Spinets traditionally had separate trestle stands on which the instrument proper rested quite loosely. Unfortunately original stands are now seldom found. The reason may be due partly to the fact that the instruments are so light you can pick them up on their own, and so the stands could easily be separated and subsequently lost. Unfortunately, too, the most insatiable lovers of spinets have been not human beings, but woodworm. Insects appear to be irresistibly attracted to spinets, particularly the walnut of the stands. The Finchcocks spinet of circa 1700, attributed to Cawton Aston, is typical in that the stand is a modern reproduction.

The spinet, then, dominated music making in English homes through the latter years of the seventeenth and the major part of the eighteenth century. The word became so synonymous with small keyboard instruments that in modern times it has often mistakenly been used by antique dealers to refer to square pianos, while in the United States of America, where English-type spinets were produced in the eighteenth century, it has become a common term for a mini-upright piano.

NOTES
1. Zenti took up an appointment as a harpsichord builder for King Charles II. Apparently, however, he remained in England for less than a year, and his position was taken by a certain Andrea Testa, a former colleague of his.
2. Diary of Samuel Pepys, 2nd September 1666.

The piano's arrival in England

A round 1740 occurred an event of considerable importance. A Cristofori-type grand piano was brought to England from Italy by a wealthy dilettante and traveller, Samuel Crisp. The instrument had been built by a cleric – a certain Father Wood[1], of whom nothing whatsoever is known, apart from the fact that he was apparently a friend of Crisp. Crisp subsequently sold the instrument for no less than one hundred guineas to the English aristocrat, Fulke Greville, who had previously taken under his wing the young Charles Burney. This truly enormous sum – considerably more than the cost of the most expensive harpsichord – can only be explained by the novelty value of the instrument. An account of this transaction is given by Dr. Burney himself in the early nineteenth century Rees's Cyclopaedia under the heading 'Harpsichord', in which he relates that the piano *remained unique in this country for several years*. Unfortunately, the fate of Father Wood's piano has never been learnt. From Burney's accounts it would seem that the touch was fairly sluggish, and it could well be that the instrument was purloined by a Roger Plenius, a Dutch craftsman, resident in London, to whom Greville had lent the instrument, and who had undertaken to make a copy, presumably with the intention of improving the action. Plenius, however, went bankrupt, having built the copy, and it has been suggested that the original instrument disappeared into the oubliette of Plenius' belongings, which were sold at auction. The reputation of Father Wood's piano would appear to have instigated the production of grand pianos in England, which commenced some twenty years later.

To begin with, though, the type of piano that really took England by storm was the little rectangular instrument, commonly known as 'square piano' or 'table piano'. These became immensely popular when a group of German craftsmen began to settle here in the 1760s, and to produce in large numbers these lively little instruments, that were both simple, practical and cheap, and with which you could get a range of volume by finger touch.[2] They began to appear in the houses of the aristocracy as cute little

Square Piano by Zumpe and Buntebart, London, 1769

toys to complement the grander instruments, and added cachet was provided by the fashionable John Christian Bach (the 'English Bach'), J. S. Bach's youngest son and tutor to Queen Charlotte. In 1768 J. C. Bach gave in London the first ever solo performance on a piano. This was part of a concert with other artists in the well-known Thatched House Tavern in St. James's Street. He played a tiny square piano by Johannes Zumpe (1726-1790), the most famous of these German settlers. The early 1760s saw a great wave of foreign musicians and craftsmen visiting England, many of whom were of German extraction. Of these Zumpe was certainly one of the most important, for it was his pianos that were first designed for the general public, and he thus laid the foundation for the commercial development of the instrument. The arrival of the English square piano, therefore, usurped the position of the spinet as the common domestic instrument, just as the spinet had replaced the virginal one hundred years previously.

Dr. William Crotch, aged 3

The earliest surviving Zumpe pianos, of which there are only two, date from 1766. One of them, now in the Landesmuseum Württemberg, Stuttgart, was built for Dr. Crotch, the eminent English musician, who was an astonishing child prodigy. In the eighteenth century, however, keyboard instrument playing in refined society was by and large the prerogative of ladies, not gentlemen. The Finchcocks square was made in 1769 in conjunction with Gabriel Buntebart, another German builder who became a friend and business partner of Zumpe. Typical of Zumpe, to keep the cost down, the instrument is extremely simple and plain. Although in appearance it resembles a clavichord more than any other keyboard instrument of the time, it is built far more sturdily in order to take the stress from thicker wire, and the action is much simpler than the sophisticated designs of Cristofori. This makes the instrument at first somewhat awkward and clumsy to play, but with a little practice much can be achieved, and with a full five octave compass even the whole of the first sixteen of Beethoven's thirty-two piano sonatas can be performed on it (though the results might occasion surprise). As pianos go, it is certainly diminutive, but the tone is beautifully clear and quite pungent, so it can sound surprisingly effective even from some distance away. As was the tradition with eighteenth century English square pianos the instrument has a sustaining mechanism operated by hand levers, the purpose of which was somewhat different from

Ladies at a cabinet (tall upright) piano

TOP **Concert at Dr Burney's home** Dr. Burney chats to a lady during a performance by well-known musicians. BOTTOM **Recital in Farmer Giles' parlour**

the pedal of a modern piano, for, since hand levers cannot be moved quickly (the hands presumably being busy at the keyboard), they had to be employed for longer sections of a piece of music, providing colour and aiding volume through the echo-like effect of a series of undamped strings vibrating in sympathy. The wash of sound thus produced was to become a feature of all English pianos, and this will be discussed at some length in the second part of the book. Unlike Zumpe's earliest squares, the piano has two hand levers for the sustaining mechanism, one for the bass and one for the treble. This became a common feature of many squares of the time, and the idea was also incorporated, though in the form of a divided pedal rather than hand levers, into some later grand pianos, including the Finchcocks Broadwood of 1823, described later on. The purpose of two levers was to allow a more sophisticated and precise use of the dampers, so that, for example, the melody could be clearly heard, rising above a sonorous bass. It has to be said, though, that good as the idea may be, there seem to be remarkably few places in contemporary music where it is of the slightest benefit. A more useful idea is the buff stop. This, inherited from the harpsichord, is a gadget which presses leather pads up against the strings to shorten the sound, and a lever to operate this was added to Zumpe pianos. The buff lever on the Finchcocks instrument exaggerates the natural astringency of tone colour, and provides a bold contrast to the sound of the undamped strings. It can also of course be used in conjunction with the sustaining levers, which has the effect of partially muting the reverberation.

For fourteen years Zumpe's piano business flourished, to such an extent indeed that he apparently never considered the need to advertise (thus keeping his costs down), except insofar as he put his address on the nameboards of his instruments – an idea subsequently much copied. The business only ceased when he decided to retire, and, after amicably severing his partnership with Buntebart, started dabbling in real estate – something which many a wealthy piano builder in later years was given to doing.

LEFT **Square piano by W. & M. Stodart, London, 1807**

After Zumpe there was no holding back the English piano. By 1800 so many craftsmen were building so many squares and grands that the entire family of plucked keyboard instruments had all but been eclipsed, and were not to be seen again until Arnold Dolmetsch revived the cult of the harpsichord at the end of the nineteenth century. Dr. Burney, who was brought up on the harpsichord, but who was every inch a modernist, rather rudely summed up the prevailing opinion when he wrote:

3

The harsh scratching of the quills of a harpsichord can now no longer be borne.[3]

For some fifty years after the arrival of Zumpe, square pianos dominated domestic music making in England. They owed their popularity partly to their convenience as musical instruments, but also to a factor which rapidly dawned on the makers – they could be designed as attractive and practical pieces of furniture. Their oblong shape – never square, a typical English misnomer – enabled them to double up as sidetables for the small urban parlours of the time. The loose trestle stands were then soon discarded in favour of framed stands, and shelves were added to hold books or music.

The beautiful 1807 square by W. & M. Stodart with painted decoration on a veneer of satinwood is a fine example of this. When the fall that covers the keyboard is lifted, a music rest can be raised, allowing the table top body of the lid to remain closed. However, if more volume should be needed, the entire lid can be opened up, and an alternative music rest is then provided.

By the end of the eighteenth century pedals had generally replaced hand levers, since their operation was far easier, as well as giving one's legs something to do, and the Stodart has one pedal to operate the dampers, which is, perhaps rather surprisingly, housed on the left side of the instrument rather than the right. This, though, is characteristic of several of the early pianos at Finchcocks. For some reason, if given a choice, the makers plumped for the left. There appears to be no technical purpose in this, though. Possibly the fact that hand levers were positioned on the left encouraged knee levers and pedals to follow suit. Whatever the point at that time, it certainly seems that players today do not take naturally

4

to this arrangement.[4]

Another square piano with a single pedal is of a much earlier period and built by Adam Beyer, a contemporary of Zumpe, and probably a compatriot, since, although nothing is

**Square piano by
Adam Beyer,
London, 1777**

known of his ancestry, 'Beyer' has no English overtones, but is a common name in Germany. The instrument is larger and more powerful than the Zumpe, as one would expect, since it was made eight years later in 1777, and the casework is more finely wrought. Like the Zumpe, it has two hand levers for the sustaining mechanism, which would be used to lift the dampers off the strings before playing, thereby creating the rich, full cascade of sound, which was becoming so much the taste of the time. It also has a hand lever for the buff, but one wonders in this case whether it was ever used much, for the mechanism has a disconcerting tendency to send the instrument out of tune, since pressing pads of leather against the strings on this piano has the effect of pushing them slightly upwards, and this succeeds in disrupting the tuning. For a small instrument such as the Zumpe, the buff works very effectively, particularly in combination with the sustaining mechanism, by which one can create resonance without obscuring the texture of the music. The buff mechanism on the Beyer is essentially a faulty design for such an instrument, and was probably added simply to complete the instrument in accordance with tradition. The pedal mechanism however is an excellent adjunct; it controls the volume very effectively by the simple expedient of raising the right hand part of the lid to let more sound out. Known as the 'nag's head swell', the device, which had previously been incorporated in a number of harpsichords, was a recent addition to square pianos and became very popular indeed throughout the latter part of the eighteenth century. However adept one is, control of dynamics is certainly tricky with early English squares. But even though contrast in volume is so limited, the novelty of such an instrument at that time caused great excitement, and players wanted to do as much as possible with it. For this purpose, the nag's head swell is a splendid aid[5], and the device is perfectly straightforward to use, so long as one is careful not to let the lid crash down.[6]

As the word 'swell' implies, it can aid crescendos and diminuendos, as well as generally increasing the volume over lengthy passages. As much of the music performed would have been originally written for the harpsichord, the swell could effectively be used like a harpsichord register for sequential passages. By far the most ubiquitous musical instrument in those days was the human voice, and here again the swell mechanism would have come into its own, since the need for more powerful pianos was only too obvious when accompanying a singer. For the next hundred years there was to be a constant desire for greater volume and dynamic contrast, which were assiduously sought after by the manufacturers.

NOTES

1. It was not unknown for clergymen to have involved themselves in making keyboard instruments. An intriguing example is the Lazarist priest, Theodoric Pedrini (1670-1745) who was sent to China in 1702 to be a court musician to the emperor K'ang Hsi. As well as teaching members of the Imperial family, he made harpsichords and organs.

2. The English musicologist, Edward Rimbault, (1816-1876), in his book 'The Pianoforte: its Origin, Progress and Construction' (London, 1860), refers to these London domiciled German makers of square pianos as 'The Twelve Apostles.' When, where, why and by whom this nickname was coined has not yet been discovered. Although for long known to be inaccurate (William Dale in 'Tschudi, The Harpsichord Maker', published in 1913, asserts that there were far more piano builders of German extraction in business at that time) the catchy title has become so established that there seems to be no reason to discontinue its use.

3. Rees's Cyclopaedia. 1802-1819

4. Probably a crazy idea, but I have wondered if people in those days tended to be not only more right-

handed but more 'left-legged' at the same time. To be both is apparently perfectly possible, but sadly no-one up to now has brought me any enlightenment on this matter.

5. Strangely, the nag's head swell has been much derided in recent years: Edwin Good in 'Giraffes, Black Dragons and Other Pianos', (Stanford University Press, California, page 102) and Michael Cole in his authoritative 'The Pianoforte in the Classical Era' (Clarendon Press, Oxford, page 76) both seem surprised that the device was ever incorporated into pianos. Michael Cole suggests that pianists at that time were so unaccustomed to their instruments that they used a harpsichord technique, employing the nag's head swell alone in order to vary the volume.

   I doubt myself that this was so. A more likely scenario, in my opinion, is that the early pianists were so pleased with the possibilities of their novel instruments that they tried to create as much variety of volume as they could. And for this reason the swell mechanism proved very useful, enabling them to achieve what the instruments were otherwise unable to provide. As pianos became ever more powerful and more capable of greater dynamic range, so swell mechanisms became less and less necessary and by the nineteenth century had mostly died out. Due to its single action the Finchcocks Beyer has a very limited dynamic range just by finger touch. A very light touch on a key will often produce no sound at all, whereas if one presses too hard the hammer can rebound, thereby producing an unwanted repeated note. The nag's head swell is a gentle and efficient corrective to these disadvantages of the instrument.

6. Helen Rice Hollis, in her book 'The Piano' (David & Charles, West Vancouver, BC, 1973, page 75), relates how the mechanism was used by a young lady to get cannon effects when she played battle pieces on her square piano. This would hardly have been helpful for maintaining the instrument in tune and would probably have loosened the hinges on the lid.

Rivals

Fashions in those days changed with astonishing rapidity, and Dr. Burney's scathing remarks about the harpsichord might well make one think that the instrument had long since been abandoned. But such was not the case, and at least until the 1780s harpsichords were being produced in large numbers as rivals to the upstart piano. The reason for this is that harpsichords were both more pungent and louder than pianos by Zumpe and his contemporaries, and the only reason for their almost total disappearance from the scene by the end of the eighteenth century was that by then they had finally lost their dominant position in this respect. They were often very beautiful too. The 1756 Kirckman harpsichord in the collection, with its lovely burr walnut veneering and elaborate marquetry, is a fine example of an instrument to grace an elegant drawing-room, and would surely have cost more than seventy pounds. Yet, typically, since the owner had decided the instrument was to stand against the wall, the maker had been instructed to leave the long side quite unadorned – a nice case of aristocratic cheese-paring. Yet, although far more glamorous than the diminutive square piano, the harpsichord co-existed and the upper classes and people of means retained both types of instruments for their homes, and tended to treat the little square as a delightful and amusing plaything.

The Kirckman has a particularly sweet and attractive tone colour. Rather more severe, both aurally and visually, is another large double manual harpsichord, made in London in 1744 by Thomas Blasser. The instrument is veneered in a striking though somewhat sombre mahogany panelling and crossbanding, and is an early example of the use of mahogany in English domestic musical instruments. The interior is veneered in figured walnut with holly stringing. The sound of this harpsichord has a more astringent and baroque quality to it than that of the Kirckman, as befits its earlier date. Who was Thomas Blasser? No-one knows. The name strongly suggests (once again) a German origin. The harpsichord appears to be the only instrument by him to have survived, though from its high quality one would suppose that he had produced many another during his working life. This is unfortunately often the case with early harpsichord builders, and there are a surprising number of important builders of whom only one example is extant.

Much later than these English instruments, the beautiful Portuguese single manual harpsichord by Joachim Antunes (1731-1811), made in Lisbon in 1785, can be said to represent at Finchcocks the final flowering of the harpsichord before its subsequent rapid decline. Although harpsichords continued to be produced, though in ever decreasing numbers, throughout the 1790s, they had virtually died out by 1800 (apart from the rectangular Italian virginal, which would seem to have remained popular for some time,

Harpsichord by Jacob Kirckman, London, 1756 This instrument is a fine example of the more elaborate and expensive type of English harpsichord. The use of walnut, rather than the more fashionable mahogany, gives it an appearance which must have looked somewhat old-fashioned at the time, and this is heightened by the stand with its strange combination of turned and carved elements. Burr-walnut veneer is used for the panels on the body and lid, and there is marquetry decoration on the keywell and interior vertical surfaces. The oak, of which the carcase is mostly made, can be clearly seen if one looks at the unveneered spine. The interior of the lid, which has been protected from light and wear, displays the colour of the wood almost as it must have been when new, as well as the non-glossy varnished or polished surface. The marquetry decoration, based on abstract plant forms, but incorporating two eagles, is carried out in holly and various other hardwoods on a walnut ground, and this design would seem to be the negative of a similar instrument in the Russell Collection, Edinburgh, in which the woods are reversed.

Harpsichord by Thomas Blasser, London, 1744

perhaps because it resembled a square piano). There is though a suggestion of a piano about the Antunes. The broad cantilevered hitchpin rail looks superficially like Cristofori's design, but a closer examination shows that the extra double row of guide pins, which on Cristofori's pianos would have increased tuning stability, are absent. Instead, there is a single row, of doubtful effectiveness, for the lowest twenty-one strings. It seems that the width of the rail had been chosen purely for cosmetic reasons, to make it look like a piano. A genuine grand piano of 1767 by Manuel Antunes, Joachim's elder brother, was sold in 1990 by Sotheby's. The Sotheby catalogue for this sale informs us that in 1760 Manuel had been granted by King Joseph I a licence for the manufacture and sale of pianos. The piano is now at the Shrine to Music Museum in Vermillion, South Dakota, U.S.A. The instrument is signed only with the surname Antunes, and it is thought therefore that the brothers, who shared a workshop in Lisbon, probably built the piano together. In design and construction the instrument shows remarkable similarities to our harpsichord.

Harpsichord by Joachim Antunes, Lisbon, 1785 This striking rarity is, so far as is known, the only 18th century Portuguese harpsichord in this country. In common with other Iberian instruments it has a plain painted exterior (now a dark green, but originally a much brighter colour, which is visible in various places), combined with an exotic veneered interior, which would seem to be tulip wood. The wrestplank and the jacks are also made from South American wood, which is not surprising, in view of Portugal's hegemony over Brazil. The decorative lid seems to have come from an earlier and smaller instrument, for joins are visible, especially on the bentside and tail. The registration is changed not by the hand stops which were more common at the time, but rather by means of pedals. Although these pedals had disappeared by the time that Finchcocks acquired this instrument, the fittings for them still remained, and they were therefore reconstructed during restoration.

The small Italian single manual harpsichord by Elpidius Gregori is an example of a working musician's instrument built during the eighteenth century. It is dated 1697, but this is undoubtedly a deception, since there is clear evidence that the six had at some time been inked in over a seven, which had been obliterated by scratching. The reason for this, of course, was an attempt to increase its value by making it appear one hundred years older than it was. In other respects, too, the instrument has been altered, and both the exterior decoration and the cabriole stand probably date from the end of the nineteenth or the beginning of the twentieth century. Fortunately however the instrument proper is in very good condition, and possesses a tone quality that captivates with its clarity and freshness.

In contrast to the Gregori, the Italian virginal of 1668 by Onofrio Guarracino is the earliest member of the harpsichord family in the collection and is in astonishingly pristine condition. The stand is modern, but this hardly counts, since the instrument may not have been built to be fitted with a stand but to be placed on a table top or some other support. The exterior of the instrument is remarkable for its 'marbling', the imitation in paint of stone inlay work.

Harpsichord by Elpidius Gregori, Italy, 1697(?) This is an example of what can happen when a straightforward musician's harpsichord passes through the hands of a late nineteenth century dealer. Originally it would have been quite a plain instrument, possibly unpainted, with probably a simple turned stand, which was later to be replaced by the present cabriole legged example. The painted decoration, with its Pannini-esque lid picture and 'arte povera' rococo exterior, was also carried out at this time, probably during the 1890s. The date, which has been tampered with, may possibly be as late as 1797, but is likely to be somewhat earlier, if only because of the circumscribed keyboard compass of four octaves from C with a 'short' bass octave. The case is of poplar and fir with a cypress interior, which creates an illusion of an instrument in a separate outer case (cf. the Guarracino). The keys are covered with the boxwood usual in Italy, but the accidentals are more decorative than the plain ebony-capped examples which are normally found; instead they are covered with a veneer sandwich made of bog oak and holly.

Virginal by Onofrio Guarracino, Naples, 1668 This outstandingly well preserved virginal shows what is now usually considered to be the typical style of keyboard instrument design in Italy for the best part of three centuries – a lightly constructed instrument kept in a separate decorated outer case. The case of our instrument is finely painted on the outside with trompe l'oeil marbling, or, more precisely, imitation hard stone inlays ('pietra dura'), in which several different types of marble are accurately represented. The lid interior is decorated with an apparently incomplete architectural fantasy, devoid of human figures, and set in a landscape which is only roughly indicated. The instrument itself has sides made of cypress wood, dovetailed together. The keyboard, partly recessed and placed to the left, is an example of a type which seems to have appeared in Naples sometime in the sixteenth century. Instruments of this design are relatively uncommon. The more familiar type of Italian virginal is usually polygonal, sometimes oblong, but with a more or less centrally located keyboard that projects completely. Both bridges are placed on the soundboard, and the narrow wrestplank is to the right. The Neapolitan style, as exemplified in the Guarracino, reverses this, with a wide wrestplank, bearing one of the bridges, placed to the left. As only one bridge is on the soundboard the acoustic behaviour of a virginal of this design is similar to a spinet or the usual type of harpsichord – 'usual' because there exists a small number of Italian harpsichords with both bridges on the soundboard. Two examples suffice to demonstrate how long this type was in evidence: the Victoria and Albert Museum's Giralomo da Bologna made in Rome in 1521, and the Roberto and Federigo Cresci made in Livorno in 1778, in the Germanisches Nationalmuseum, Nürnberg. The fir soundboard has a finely wrought rose or soundhole decoration made from laminations of veneer and parchment, cut with a knife and punches of various sizes. This layered, rather organic looking arrangement is also very commonly found on guitars of the period. The colour of the ivory and ebony keyboard makes a pleasing contrast with the sand-coloured cypress which surrounds it. It is probably true to say that the classic Italian style of the sixteenth to seventeenth centuries produced the most visually refined of all keyboard instruments. The instrument seems to have been untampered with until the 1930s when some unnecessary modifications were made to the action. The aim of the recent restoration was to reverse this and to restring it in accordance with historical precedence.

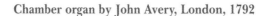

Chamber organ by John Avery, London, 1792

However, another type of keyboard instrument for the home, and one too with the longest and most distinguished pedigree of all, was not eclipsed by the piano, and indeed remained in constant use for some time. This of course was the chamber organ. Although chamber organs were expensive, if you could afford them they had some advantages over both the harpsichord and piano. The chamber organ in the collection by John Avery (1738-1808) was built in London in 1792. Although a relatively modest instrument, it was designed to look fairly tall and imposing. The keyboard is tucked away behind a panel and simply drops forward when this is lowered. Until needed, then, the instrument can remain concealed within an apparently grand piece of furniture. In fact the whole of the upper half of the instrument is simply a bookcase of three shelves, divided by a central partition, with the pipes contained below.[1] The organ is very simple, with just three pipes for each note at 8', 4' and 2' pitches (that is to say, normal pitch, one octave and two octaves higher), and sound is produced by pumping on the single pedal (which can easily be removed if one wants the instrument to remain fully concealed).

There seem to be few extant chamber organs by John Avery, though as a builder he was very highly regarded in his lifetime. Like many instrument makers of the period, however, he was apparently often in financial straits. Sir John Sutton, of Jesus College, Cambridge, who was described by his friend Canon Dickson, as leading the life of a recluse[2], prissily describes him as a shocking drunken character and a person not in any way to be depended upon, being generally drunk and often in prison for debt, but was nevertheless an excellent workman when he was once set to work.[3] Nonetheless, many clearly did depend on him, as is evident from the many important organs throughout the country that he was involved with, including those at Winchester and Carlisle Cathedrals, and King's College, Cambridge.

The Avery organ is very clear and sweet toned and not a bit like most people would expect an organ to sound.[4] It seems somehow to need to be treated more like a piano, and the advantage in this respect is that, although not very loud and lacking the dynamic resources of a piano, it is certainly more powerful than any piano or indeed harpsichord made at this period. It also has the enormous advantage of not needing to be tuned, or at any rate once a year at most. For these reasons, little domestic instruments of this nature continued to be made until well into the nineteenth century.

A far grander chamber organ is the instrument by John Byfield, the second in a family line of four organ builders, all of whose Christian names were John. Little of Byfield's work appears to have survived, though a fine example is the splendid church organ of St. Mary's, Rotherhithe, London, SE 16. The present instrument was built in London in 1766 for the 'common dining-room' of Castle Grant, the home of James (later Sir James) Grant near Grantown-on-Spey in Scotland. Dignified and magnificent, it stands 12½ feet tall, yet it is hardly more sophisticated than the Avery.

ABOVE **Chamber organ by John Byfield, London, 1766.** BOTTOM PREVIOUS PAGE **Suggested stop combinations for the Byfield organ, written by the maker himself.**

There is no pedal board (pedal boards are very rare in English chamber organs) and again, it can be played almost like a piano. A problem however is its size. It is far too big for the air intake to be operated by the player, so a hand pump is connected to the side of the casework. Since a servant standing at the side and pumping away might well appear a distraction, provision had been made for a hand pump to be connected with the rear of the instrument, so that, with the organ placed against the wall and a hole drilled through it, music could thereby be produced as if by magic.

The Byfield organ is of historical importance, since it is one of the best preserved of all surviving English chamber organs of the eighteenth century, with its mechanism and pipework virtually intact. The remarkably pure tone colours obtainable from the instrument provide a vivid tapestry of sound. As a piece of furniture it is very beautiful, if somewhat austere, as befits the Scottish castle whence it came. The dignified case of solid mahogany is decorated with fine applied limewood carvings of acanthus scrolls and swags, all in nearly pristine condition. These are protected by glass-panelled doors, the glazing bars arranged in the 'Chinese' manner. The gilded display pipes behind the two central doors are dummies, but these are flanked by two groups of three speaking pipes.

Byfield shipped the instrument up by the North Sea to Castle Grant (which still stands today), with written instructions concerning its installation in the dining-room, and the organ remained there until the twentieth century. Some of the correspondence in connection with the organ has fortunately survived, and is kept in the Scottish Record Office, Edinburgh. From this we learn that James Grant's agent, a certain Thomas Mackie, oversaw its arrival at the castle. He it was, too, who dealt with the financial negotiations.

The case of the instrument was apparently the work of John Adam, the brother of Robert Adam, since he was responsible for the furniture at Castle Grant, and there is a reference in a contemporary letter to a 'Mr. Adams' (sic) as having designed the casework. Byfield himself was paid £200 in advance for the organ, and another final payment of £50 when the instrument was consigned to Scotland. Mackie wrote about this to Mr. Grant on the 4th of August 1767:

> *I have paid him the fifty pounds and taken the receipt in full. The sum you advised me remained unpaid, and indeed I promised to pay it how soon the organ was shipt. He is very hungry, and I hope you will approve the paying it.*

After Sir James Grant died, the organ appears to have been neglected. As a result the pipes were not altered to conform with nineteenth century pitch, which was at least a quarter tone higher than the pitch of this instrument, which is about $a^1=420$Hz – very near to the pitch of Handel's tuning fork, $a^1=422.5$Hz. The tuning temperament, which is almost, but not quite, one-fifth comma meantone temperament, is also original. Although built in the reign of George III, the Byfield organ is,

Anonymous English chamber organ circa 1680

like Finchcocks itself, for its date, quite old-fashioned. A true Handelian instrument, it has a baroque musical character, with bold and contrasting tone colours, that can be mixed together as an artist might do with his palette. The importance of these tone colours can be gauged by the list of suggested combinations of the stops, pasted on each side of the keyboard on the stop-jambs. In spite of its grandeur, the organ is basically quite simple, and one can imagine its bold sounds being used as background music in the dining room of Castle Grant.

In striking contrast to the Byfield, the anonymous little English instrument, demurely encased in dark oak, is the smallest and oldest domestic organ in the collection. Although undated, it is unlikely to have been made much later than 1680. The casework is only partly original, for the lower half, housing the feeder and reservoir, has been rebuilt to a certain extent, and the top, containing the pipework and soundboard, has been extended at the back. Musically, however, the instrument has been well preserved, which is fortunate, since very few similar instruments of this period have survived. Although one of the three registers is no longer present, the other two, a stopped 8' and an open 4', both in pine, are in excellent condition. The four octave keyboard, in common with many of this era (cf. the Cawton Aston spinet on page 15) is particularly attractive. The oak natural keys are covered with snakewood, a highly figured exotic from South America, and have, in addition, on their fronts a decoration consisting of an ogival arcade carved directly into the wood – an atavistic feature often found in the sometimes rather conservative repertory of the pre-nineteenth century keyboard instrument maker. The accidentals are of solid ivory. As is so with the Avery, a convenient pedal supplies the wind, thereby obviating the need for the distracting presence of a second person operating the bellows.

In the nineteenth century chamber organs slowly lost popularity as the piano took ever firmer hold on people's imagination. However, the pipe organ was soon to be replaced for domestic use by small free reed organs, and, during the latter half of the century, harmoniums, as they were generally called (other common names being seraphines, euphonions and melodeons), became the only serious keyboard rival to the piano for home use. By the end of the century the harmonium too was on its way out. Partly this was due to the global competition of piano production, which resulted in ever more affordable prices; partly because surprisingly little fine music had by this time been composed for it; and partly because harmoniums were either, on the one hand, not very good instruments, or, on the other hand, good instruments but difficult to play well.

For a time, however, the harmonium was regarded as a serious musical instrument, particularly in Paris, where harmonium courses

Harmonium by Alexandre Père et Fils, Paris, 1858
The casework of this harmonium is veneered in rosewood, and presents a relatively plain appearance., relying on mouldings and turned balusters below the keyboard for decoration. It was built at the time of the industrial exhibitions, and a gilt brass medallion advertises the success of the firm in 1855. The instrument is an excellent example of the finely made products of this famous maker.

Miniature harmonium This instrument is veneered in rosewood and decorated with wave mouldings, which returned to favour in the nineteenth century, having first made their appearance three centuries earlier. It is completely portable and weighs only 10 kgs. The stand of grained beech, with bamboo-style legs, may be a later replacement. Underneath the pretty rosewood veneer is a simple case made of poplar, which would seem to indicate a French or possibly Belgian provenance.

were given in music academies, and composers such as César Franck and Lefébure-Wély made significant contributions to its repertoire. One of the most distinguished of French harmonium builders was the Parisian, Jacob Alexandre (1804-1876), and the collection's harmonium of 1858 by Alexandre Père et Fils (Alexandre's son Edouard had recently become a partner) is a good example of what can be achieved musically by such an instrument. A notable feature of harmoniums of this type is that volume can, if desired, be controlled by wind pressure, operated by one's feet on the pedals. In this respect the harmonium has the edge over conventional pipe organs, where a variation of wind pressure can disrupt a given pitch. Although clearly a useful musical device, it has to be said that it is also extremely awkward to operate effectively, and many players become too disheartened to devote sufficient time to mastering the technique.

Contemporary with the Alexandre harmonium in the collection is an anonymous miniature free reed organ of four octaves and a mere sixty-one centimetres wide. The keys of this tiny instrument are very small and narrow and therefore difficult for an adult to control. It may have been intended for a child to play, in which case it could well be an example of a 'marmotine', which was a harmonium designed for children and patented by Debras in France in 1859. Musically, the instrument is a delight, with a clear and piquant tone colour. It is just a pity that one needs to be less than ten years old to play it well.

A few years before Zumpe commenced his immensely successful business, attempts were being made to establish the grand piano as a serious keyboard instrument. But the English grand made a somewhat hesitant start, compared to the square, in public esteem. The most important early builder of these instruments in London was another émigré, Americus Backers, whose origin is not known, though probably Dutch or German. Backers' influence on later English builders was very great, and the design of his pianos became the foundation of much subsequent piano technology. Backers died in 1778, having made grands for about ten years, at the rate of some seven a year, so he hardly had time to establish himself. Only two of his grands have survived. One of these, dated 1776, is in London at Fenton House, Hampstead. The other, built in 1772, is part of the Russell Collection at St.Cecilia's Hall, University of Edinburgh, and is believed to be the oldest extant English grand piano.[5]

Although Backers' instruments were highly regarded, they were expensive, probably more so than a harpsichord, and far more than a square. Also the sound was not, it would seem, quite so enticing as that of squares. In the final analysis, people simply liked square pianos, and it took a long time before other types of piano succeeded in overtaking them in popular appeal. The English square soon began to make inroads abroad, especially in the New World, which beckoned many makers of these little instruments to set up shop there. For the following hundred years, the square piano, based on early English designs, became the favourite domestic keyboard instrument in the U.S.A. Even after it had become obsolescent, shortly before the end of the nineteenth century, such were the fond memories of it, that a music critic in America some twenty years later found himself able to assert that the square piano had been

> *a more direct descendant from the precursor of the modern pianoforte than either the grand or the upright; it is of purer strain, so to speak.*[6]

The size and expense of the early English grand piano induced some makers to try their hands at producing cheaper instruments that hopefully would combine the superior quality of the grand with the intimacy and dimensions of the square. The transverse piano of 1779 by Crang Hancock[7] in the collection is an example of one such endeavour. In appearance it looks like a large bentside spinet, and rather surprisingly sounds a bit like one too, but since its inventor called it a 'portable grand pianoforte', we can consider it to be such. Strangely enough, it lacks many of the requisites of both squares and grands, since it has neither sustaining mechanism nor any other device. This certainly makes the instrument highly portable, for it rests loosely on its stand, and one (very strong) person can lift it off and carry it unaided. Although it looks quite small, its size is a little misleading, since the position of the keyboard at the side rather than at the end allows the instrument to be much shorter than if it were a normal grand. It is a delightful instrument to play, since the action is light and responsive, and the sound is beautifully clear and attractive. The lack of a sustaining mechanism can be seen to be a disadvantage when playing eighteenth century piano music, and this acts as an inducement to the player to pretend it is a real spinet and to concentrate on the harpsichord repertoire.

NOTES

1. Although the Avery's falling keyboard appears to be unusual in English chamber organs, concealment of instruments was not at all uncommon at this period, and piano mechanisms were sometimes hidden in large pieces of furniture, sometimes cupboards, with the keyboard appearing when a certain drawer was pulled out. A good example of this is the innocent looking mahogany sofa table of the collection, the front drawer of which enables a keyboard to appear, which operates the striking of bars of blue glass. This musical table was built circa 1815 by the well-known London firm of publishers and piano manufacturers, Chappell and Company, which had only a few years previously, probably about 1810, been founded by Samuel Chappell (1782-1834) in association with two partners, one of whom was the composer and pianist John Baptist Cramer. The instrument, a keyboard crystallophone, was usually known as a 'pianino' and a similar one of the same period is to be seen in the Victoria and Albert Museum, London. It makes the puniest of noises, but at least it never has to be tuned.

2. Andrew Freeman, 'Father Smith' (Positif Press, Oxford, page 51)

3. Sir John Sutton, 'A Short Account of Organs Built in England from the Reign of King Charles the Second to the Present Time' (London, 1847, page 86)

4. Sir John Sutton would no doubt have agreed with this. Avery instruments follow the style of delicate sweet voicing, characteristic

Keyboard Crystallophone by Chappell & Co., London, circa 1815

of the work of his contemporary, Samuel Green, whose instruments were described by Sutton as emulating the tone of a musical snuff box rather than that of an organ. Ibid. page 82.

5. In fact, the Edinburgh instrument may be the only surviving instrument. According to Warwick Henry Cole, 'Americus Backers, Original Forte Piano maker' (Harpsichord and Fortepiano magazine, 4/4, October 1987) the authenticity of the Fenton House piano is highly dubious.

6. Henry Krehbiel, in 'The Musician,' 1911.

7. Confusion appears to reign over the name of Crang Hancock. The organ builder, John Crang, came from Somerset and in the earlier eighteenth century became apprenticed to the Loosemore family of organ builders. He achieved considerable success and apparently considerable wealth, and since he came from farming stock, he invested in farms and other real estate. In later years he joined up with his brother-in-law, James Hancock, the firm then becoming known as Crang Hancock. John Crang never married, but his name was incorporated into the Hancock family, since two children of James Hancock, who continued with the instrument building trade, were called John Crang Hancock and James Crange Hancock, (Crange being a family variant of Crang). According to an article by a descendant, Meg Crang Botting ,'A Tuneful Family History; Crang and Hancock, Organbuilders' (Country Life, 6 November 1980), John Crang, in association with James Hancock, started building transverse pianos such as the one at Finchcocks, and reference is made to one by this partnership in the Colt Collection, dating from 1782. However, the book about this collection, 'The Early Piano', refers to an advertisement of December 4th 1791 in The Observer, which commences as follows: John Crang Hancock, No. 32 Parliament Street, Patentee of the Grand and small piano forte, with spring key touch, etc. The article in 'The Early Piano' assumes that the instrument in the Colt Collection was indeed built by John Crang Hancock, and not by the Crang Hancock partnership, even though on the instrument the Christian name is omitted. The Finchcocks piano, however, does not have a spring key action, and this, coupled with the fact that it dates from the previous decade, implies that it may indeed have been built by the brothers-in-law. Against this, however, is the fact that an advertisement of 1786 put in by 'Crang Hancock' in the Morning Post refers to 'he' rather than 'they' being the inventor of the 'Portable Grand Piano Forte'. To add to the muddle, the article 'Crang & Hancock' in The New Grove Dictionary of Music and Musicians, Second Edition, states that James (rather than John) Crang Hancock was living at no. 32, Parliament Street, and that John was possibly a brother (rather than a son) of James Hancock. What appears to be beyond dispute, however, is that the founder of the firm, John Crang, retired in the 1780s, and that the instrument business by the family carried on until about 1820.

Transverse grand piano by Crang Hancock, London, 1779

CHAPTER FOUR

Vertical pianos

While, at the end of the eighteenth century, the square piano was being produced in vast numbers and the grand was beginning to catch up, the upright piano, the instrument that was soon to become so ubiquitous, was scarcely known. Uprights in various forms certainly existed throughout much of the eighteenth century, but for several decades until the 1790s no maker appeared to be very interested in developing the concept. It would seem that uprights were squeezed out between the popular square and the burgeoning powerful grand.

The little upright piano at Finchcocks by Robert Woffington must be one of the earliest examples of its type to be found today. It is undated, but for stylistic reasons and from circumstantial evidence it is unlikely to have been made later than about 1800, and may well date from the late 1790s. Woffington was an organist and instrument maker, mainly of organs, in Dublin. An excellent chamber organ by him of the same period is to be seen in the National Museum of Ireland. His dates are not known, though he is said to have died in about 1820. He is also said to have been a pupil of the distinguished Dublin organ builder, Ferdinand Weber (1715-1784). The instrument is particularly interesting, because it must be one of the very first to have been made in the modern conventional style, with the strings rising from floor level instead of from above the keyboard, which was a method of deploying the strings until then virtually unheard of. At time of writing the instrument is unrestored, and indeed it is not entirely clear what some of the mechanisms are meant to do. Instrument production in Dublin was

Upright piano by Robert Woffington, Dublin, circa 1800

idiosyncratic and in many ways more innovative and interesting than that of the London workshops. One of the pedals operates a mechanism for obtaining una corda (the sounding of a single string) by the simple expedient of pressing pads against each of the two outer strings, a method which, as far as I can ascertain, appears to have been totally ignored by all other piano manufacturers both then and in later years.

The instrument is delightful to look at. It is veneered in an amazing combination of different exotic woods, including, amongst others, mahogany, satinwood, tulipwood, thuya and purplewood. Above the keyboard there are finely wrought ormolu grilles backed with pleated green silk. The instrument would surely have cost a good deal, which is perhaps not surprising, given that it must have been a great rarity at the time.

Upright square piano by William Southwell, Dublin, circa 1800

Contemporary with the Woffington upright is a strange instrument by William Southwell, another Irish builder, who was also for a time apprenticed to Ferdinand Weber. This is a square piano turned on to its side – an upright square in fact. This invention of Southwell's was patented by him in 1798, but, in spite of its considerable merits, the upright square never took on, and the Finchcocks instrument is one of very few still in existence. The piano is sturdier than the average square, which is true of upright pianos in general, since it is strongly braced internally. But it takes up more room than a conventional upright, since, being a square piano, the casework continues some distance to the right of the keyboard. The only practical advantage of all this would seem to be a visual one, since the extra width allows room for a great deal of decoration. Like the Woffington, considerable attention has indeed been paid to this, and since many of the details show similarities, it is possible that the same cabinet maker had been involved. The whole appearance of the piano, however, is a somewhat odd blend of sophistication and naïvety, as demonstrated here by the central painted cluster of musical instruments, of which the 'violin' to the fore is like no stringed instrument yet known.

Unfortunately, the mechanisms operated by the two pedals are missing, and one can only therefore surmise their purpose. One of them must certainly be the normal sustaining mechanism to lift the dampers, but the second is not so obvious. It cannot be a keyboard shift, since there is no room at the ends of the keyboard for any movement. The only other upright square by Southwell that I have come across which is in playing order, is part of a private collection. In this instrument one pedal works the dampers and the other operates a drum mechanism, the so-called 'Turkish Music', a device frequently used in the German-speaking regions of Europe, but which was hardly to be found at all in England. (cf. page 121 for further discussion of this.) Although Dublin at this time was the second British city, it enjoyed many links with the continent, and a mechanism such as this would not be at all unexpected. Possibly, too, Southwell's relationship with Ferdinand Weber, who was of German origin, encouraged this connection.

Because the square has been tilted vertically, but the keyboard has remained at normal playing level, the hammers are now far beyond reach of the keys, and a method had therefore to be discovered to harness them together. Southwell solved this problem by placing thin vertical wooden rods, known as 'stickers', on the keys, which engaged with the hammers above. When the keys were depressed, the stickers pushed the hammers on to the strings. A problem with an upright as against a horizontal piano is that the hammers cannot return easily by gravity, so the wooden stickers had a double function; they impelled the hammers towards the strings, but then pulled them back by their weight. This method, possibly initiated by Southwell, was at any rate patented by him for upright pianos in 1807. A similar system is to be seen in the piano by Woffington, who may well have borrowed the idea from his compatriot. Known in modern times as the 'English sticker action', this mechanism was taken up by piano manufacturers throughout the greater part of the nineteenth century. It was both simple and cheap, and therefore ideal for the many firms that started up at around this time.

A good example of a much later upright with the sticker action is the stylish Victorian upright by Brinsmead. The firm was founded by John Brinsmead (1814-1908) in 1837 and with the assistance of his two sons, Thomas and Edgar, became one of the most prosperous English piano firms by the end of the century. The Finchcocks upright was clearly an expensive instrument, with its beautiful birch veneer and elaborate fretwork panels.

This piano was previously owned by the famous music hall artist, Vesta Tilley (1864-1952), who married an M.P., Sir Walter de Frece. The piano resided in her home in Monte Carlo. One of Edgar Brinsmead's

Upright piano by John Brinsmead and Sons, London, circa 1860

advertising gimmicks was to put on entertainments for customers, some of which at the time caused raised eyebrows. One such was a performance by the Gaiety Girls. It is thought that Vesta Tilley acquired the instrument, perhaps as a gift from Edgar, during a visit of this kind.

The instrument, which is undated, was probably built between 1855 and 1865. By this time the more complicated and costly tape-check action, which allows rapid repetition and which is the basis of modern upright piano actions today, was in general use throughout the world, yet the hammers are operated by stickers, for British firms often still favoured the older sticker action. John Brinsmead outlived both his sons by two years, Thomas dying in 1906 and Edgar in 1907. John Brinsmead himself had an astonishingly long working life, remaining at the helm of the business right until his death at the age of

1. UPRIGHT IRON GRAND WORKS. 2. THE NEW HORIZONTAL GRAND WORKS. 3. ENGINE HOUSE. 4. UPRIGHT IRON GRAND FINISHING SHOP. 5. JAPANNING HOUSE. 6. GRAND FINISHING SHOP. 7. MACHINE ROOM. 8. BACK MAKING SHOP.

MESSRS. JOHN BRINSMEAD AND SONS' PIANOFORTE WORKS.

The Brinsmead factory as published in The Graphic on September 29th, 1883

ninety-two. When well into his nineties he inspected carefully every single instrument that left the factory. This took place in the 'looking-over room' and if any fault was discovered, the appropriate employee was instantly summoned down from above (the looking-over room being on a lower level) to explain himself. For this reason the looking-over room was known to all in the firm as the 'Chamber of Horrors'.

Throughout their working years the three Brinsmeads were tireless at promoting their business by every possible marketing ploy. In 1870 Edgar published his 'History of the Pianoforte' which enjoyed a large sale, and throughout which the firm's pianos are extolled to a quite astonishing extent. Although kindly, if passing, reference is made to a few other manufacturers, such as Steinway, few could have remained in doubt, after reading this volume, that 'the Palm belongs to the Pianos of the house of Brinsmead'.

In fact most of the great manufacturing firms spent a good deal of effort extolling their wares. Brinsmead's methods however were so over the top as to cause derision. Cyril Ehrlich, for example, in his social history 'The Piano' (J. M. Dent & Sons, 1976), denigrates the company, clearly regarding it as an easy target. His comment (page 148):

Advertisement for Brinsmead pianos, published in The Graphic on March 9th, 1889

Euphonicon by F. Beale and Co., London, circa 1842

that surviving instruments suggest that Brinsmead was never more than a good medium-class maker whose products were not comparable with the best German and American instruments

has been taken up virtually word for word in the article on the firm in the New Grove Dictionary of Music and Musicians (1980). The verdict is certainly dubious. The firm was outstanding and won the highest international awards, though sadly went into decline after the First World War. Surviving grand pianos in first class order are seldom found today, and there seems to be no one left with working knowledge of the firm. William Sale, whom I knew as a highly regarded tutor at the London College of Furniture, had been articled to Brinsmeads as a young man, but later joined the firm of Bechstein. In conversation with Alastair Laurence (see page 59) he said that there was little to choose between the best of Brinsmead and the finest Bechstein. Although in other respects an excellent and well researched history, Ehrlich's 'The Piano', with its uncritical approval of American firms and Steinway in particular, and its bias against English pianos, has done quite unnecessary harm.

The nineteenth century was an age of experiments in piano design, and vertical pianos in many shapes and sizes appeared from time to time, several of which are discussed in later chapters. A very recent addition to the collection at the time of writing, and certainly one of the strangest, yet perhaps most stylish of all vertical pianos, is the beautiful euphonicon, invented by John Steward and patented in 1841. The Finchcocks instrument has survived in remarkably good condition. Although not yet in perfect playing order, it possesses a sweet and tender tone colour, slightly reminiscent of a harp. These instruments were also known as 'harp pianos', presumably because of their appearance, and perhaps partly because of the sound they produce. The conventional upright piano has the wrestplank at the top bearing a more or less straight bridge, the nut, and one large soundboard with the curved bridge placed upon it. The euphonicon differs from this in having the wrestplank, of iron, at the bottom, with the nut placed on three separate soundboxes. The decorative cast-iron harmonic curve combines the functions of bridge and hitchpin rail. Although there appear to be very few extant, those that are in playing order do apparently remind the listener of a harp. The complex structure of euphonicons must have made them extremely expensive to build, and this would explain their rarity, since they could hardly have been commercially viable.

John Broadwood and Sons

The late eighteenth century saw the birth of some of the great dynasties of piano firms. John Broadwood (1732-1812) had been born and brought up in Oldhamstocks, a small Scottish market town near the English border and the East coast and on a latitude with Edinburgh. He was the eldest of three brothers, all of whom worked for a time in their father's carpentry business. As was so often the case in Scotland, however, lack of opportunity in a relatively poor environment had the effect of tempting the more adventurous members of families to seek their fortune elsewhere, and in 1761 John Broadwood set off for London, where he succeeded in joining the famous Swiss-born harpsichord builder, Burkat Shudi, as a journeyman. Broadwood was nearly twenty-nine years old and Burkat Shudi fifty-nine. Their relationship was to prove the most propitious in the history of piano building in England. Like John Broadwood, Burkat Shudi, or Burckhardt Tschudi, to give him the original spelling, was a trained woodworker, and again, like Broadwood, left home to seek his fortune elsewhere, due to lack of prospects in his home town of Schwanden. When only sixteen he arrived in London in 1718, and joined the small group of Swiss emigrants, some of whom were engaged in the musical instrument trade. He soon became apprenticed to a leading harpsichord builder, Hermann Tabel, who had settled in London at about the beginning of the century. A few years later another apprentice joined Tabel's workshop. This was Jacob Kirckman, of Alsatian stock, who was some eight years younger than Shudi. Both these young men were to establish themselves as the most prominent makers of harpsichords in England by the latter half of the century. Hermann Tabel died in 1738 only a few years after Kirckman had become articled to him. Kirckman thereupon took the advantageous step of promptly marrying his widow (a practice that seems to have been not in the least unusual in those days amongst suppliers of musical instruments).

A generation later a somewhat similar situation arose when Shudi gave his blessing to the marriage of his twenty year old daughter, Barbara, to John Broadwood. This was in 1769, when Broadwood was thirty-six years old. Shudi had had five children from two marriages. Of the two sons, one died at the age of eighteen, while the other had no interest in pianos. And at the same time as his rival, Jacob Kirckman, was forging ahead, so Shudi had no close relation whom he considered suitable to inherit his life's work. John Broadwood however proved well able to fulfill the role of a son, and two years after his marriage Shudi handed over the running of the firm to him. When, a further two years later, Shudi himself died, Broadwood thus found himself, in 1773, in sole charge of the business.

Shudi had not involved himself at all with the emergence of the piano, but John Broadwood was friendly with Johannes Zumpe, who for a time had worked in Shudi's shop, and so, after taking over control, he set out immediately to exploit the potential of this new type of keyboard instrument. In this he was so successful, that when he died in 1812 the firm had achieved a very dominant position. Growth rapidly continued, and by the mid 1830's, when Broadwoods had become the largest and most successful piano manufacturer in the world, output had reached the astonishing level of almost two thousand pianos per annum, with a workforce of approximately one for every ten instruments.[1] All of which makes the Broadwood archives, which fortunately have survived, such particularly fascinating documents, for they give us an intimate glimpse into day-to-day work experience at the commencement of what was then a relatively modest concern.

In the eighteenth century few keyboard instrument businesses were more than middling in size, and in some cases virtually one-man bands, but a feeling of intimacy was a salient characteristic of firms both large and small. A flavour of this is beautifully conveyed by Shudi's daughter, Barbara. She kept a daybook,[2] started when she was just twenty-one, shortly after her marriage to John Broadwood, on the first page of which she wrote, rather endearingly, 'This is the Book belongs to Barbara Broadwood'. From this diary one gets the impression that she acted both as a housekeeper for her husband and as a receptionist for messages and accounts. The whole book provides a vivid and touching record of the early days of the firm.

Here, everything is jumbled up as it comes in day by day, starting off with the punctilious young wife carefully making a "List of Mr Broadwood's Cloathes", which includes a number of items probably due to be cleaned, including

12 Shirts Ruffelled, 3 night caps and 8 pocket handkerchiefs.

But a few lines later business breaks in:

Dutchess of Marlborough £78.15s.

The page is too torn to reveal what the duchess paid for, but Barbara is soon back in the kitchen:

a pound of ham...Eggs...three Minced pyes...Jellered Ellels.

Barbara fills in the odd moment with an inventory:

Mrs B Cloths (9 prs of cotton stockings, 12 pr of sleeves, 5 laced Nightcaps, 5 plain ditto and 5 cloth aprins)

before returning to

turnips, potatoes and beer.

On the very day of her marriage, January 2nd 1769, she enters purchases of comestibles:

	[£	*s*	*d]*
Beer	*0*	*0*	*5*
Sallad	*0*	*0*	*1*
A pint of porter	*0*	*0*	*1¾*
An egg	*0*	*0*	*1*
An ounce of peper	*0*	*0*	*1*
Washer woman	*0*	*1*	*3½*
Half a pound of butter	*0*	*0*	*4*
A brown loaf	*0*	*0*	*2*

On August 8th 1771 a homely list of potatoes and cucumbers (0-3-1d) is interrupted by a flow of grand names, without explanation:

> *Lady Cope – Cork Street Burlington Gardens.....Lady Betty Warsley, Albemarle Street.....Mrs Hayward park st Grosvenor square opposite the golden Head.*

In 1772 Barbara is clearly in charge of appointments, including tuning:

> *Mr Gould....to tune a spinet on Monday Morning, Lady Edgecumb at two oclock Monday Morning.....Sir Charles Cocks to tune on Monday.*

On July 14th 1772 Barbara engages a servant, Jane Kennedy, who signs neatly for her quarterly wages at the rate of

> *Five pounds & Ten shillings Wages pr year & a month*

and on the 24th she receives from Mr. Broadwood £5.5.0 for her shopping accounts. The list runs on:

> *a goose a fowl 0-6-0*

and, the largest item by far,

> *a dozen of chamber pots*

at the enormous sum of £30.2.4d.[3]

Babies arrive, and there is a reference to

> *shoes for Kitty [Catherine Margaret]*

but on the 8th of July 1776 Barbara dies, at the age of twenty-seven, after having given birth to her fourth child. Death however does not stop the flow of this little book, and soon a new hand takes up the list, mingling yet again household accounts and business. Another servant girl is brought in, Elizabeth Banister. Unlike Jane Kennedy though, she is illiterate, and signs for her wages with a cross.

The style of the book changes considerably after Barbara's death, with different hands taking turns to write the entries. On one occasion a page is decorated with a profile of faces sporting twirling moustaches.

In 1782 the entries are taken up by Broadwood's second wife, the twenty-nine year old Mary Kitson. As before, household expenses feature throughout, but business entries take over more and more, in line with the ever increasing success of the firm. In 1782 pianos are mentioned for the first time:

> *sent a pianoforte to Mr Sarn*

Mr. Silvian Clearland has a

> *piano inlaid with satin purple.*

Older instruments however still remain on the books; Mrs. Castlefranks at Clapham has her "spinnet" repaired.

As the years go by so the names become ever grander. The aristocracy in particular goes in for hiring rather than purchasing pianos:

> *Duke of Devonshire for hire of pianoforte...Countess of Errol a piano on hire*

RIGHT **Mrs. Billington** and BELOW **Madame Mara** – two famous Broadwood customers. Elizabeth Billington (1765-1818) was one of the greatest sopranos England has produced. This fine print, after Reynolds, depicts the English-rose freshness for which, in her youth, she was known. Gertrud Elisabeth Mara (1749-1833) by contrast, was no beauty. A dumpy German soprano, she apparently suffered from rickets, had protruding teeth, dreadful English and no talent as an actress. In spite of these disadvantages, because of her wonderful voice, she landed, at the age of forty-two, the role of Polly, the young heroine of Gay's The Beggar's Opera, therefore demonstrating the overwhelming importance for the public of good singing over mere appearance.

and the hire of a piano for "Princess Czarro" for a dinner. The Bishop of London hires a piano on two occasions for just one night, and the Archbishop of Canterbury makes a single appearance. Musicians are regular customers, and are often lent pianos free of charge. The famous singers, Madame Mara and Mrs. Billington, receive pianos, and Mrs. Billington in fact, who was herself also a distinguished pianist, returns again and again.

4   The book finishes in 1791[4], but another contemporary account of the dealings of the firm is given in the 'Journal', begun by John Broadwood in 1771 on taking over the firm from Shudi. Here we find details of orders, and in particular prices of instruments. These varied enormously according to how expensively they were produced. The usual top price for a harpsichord (double manual) was £73.10s, but a specially elaborately decorated one could be almost £90, while a very simple single manual one could be as little as fifteen guineas. Some harpsichords were sold for a mere four guineas, but these were almost certainly secondhand or reconditioned ones. The last harpsichord built by Broadwoods dates from 1793, but well before this the decline in interest in these instruments (even though the firm maintained production during the 1780's) meant that more and more were offered secondhand. Secondhand square pianos were regularly sold for six guineas and on one occasion in 1795 a certain Miss Forbes bought two old pianofortes for ten guineas. Fifteen guineas was also the price of a

5   new but simple square piano.[5]

On May 26th 1784 the Duke of Queensborough bought a more expensive one for twenty guineas, but the most costly standard model was £26.5s. Grand pianos are first mentioned in January

6   1785 when a certain Count Brühl bought one for £52.10s.[6] The standard price was soon raised to £57.15s however. A mere six months after the first grand was sold, secondhand grands appear:

June 22nd 1785 Mr Savory for a Grand Piano-forte Secondhand £36.15s.

Although prices of grands were sometimes as high as £63, in the early days they were on the whole slightly cheaper than the most expensive harpsichords. Gradually, though, the standard price of grands increased, until by the early 1800s they were sold for £86 or more. A remarkably high price, however, was obtained for a grand piano built in 1796 for the prime minister of Spain, Manuel de Godoy. Made in the newly fashionable satinwood and elaborately decorated with Wedgwood plaques, it cost in all, including transport to Spain, £257.4s.6d. The instrument has survived, albeit with certain alterations and replacements, and can be seen today in the Museum of Fine Arts, Boston, Massachusetts.

From the Broadwood archives it appears very evident that both the aristocratic and the Bohemian worlds enjoyed fairly free rides from the firm, the former because they did not enjoy settling up accounts and the latter because they couldn't afford to. As was so often the case in those days in all trades, the wealthier the client, the more painful he found it to part with money. The Broadwood Letter Book from 1801 to 1810 deals with correspondence and customers.[7] While much of this concerns details of transport, arranging prices, advice on maintenance of instruments etc., a quite alarming proportion is concerned with bad debts:

> *Rt Hon The Lady Charlotte Campbell, Edinboro.*
>
> *Madam,*
>
> *We are particularly sorry to be obliged to trouble your Ladyship again on the subject of the payment of your account. We beg to remind Col Campbell that when he bargained about the pianoforte in May 1798 he stipulated for two years credit when we should be punctually paid. Our account however is upwards of three years and a half standing a length of credit which goes far towards eating up the profits we as tradesmen expected. We now beg the favour of your Ladyship's interference and flattering ourselves we shall soon be obliged with an answer we remain etc etc.*

An attractive feature of these letters is the very close personal involvement with customers:

> *June 5th 1805*
>
> *Mrs Andrew Cox*
>
> *Just as we were putting in this to the Post Office we were informed that you had had the misfortune to lose Mr Cox and that your affairs were much deranged we have therefore thought it useless to trouble you by drawing on you as we proposed in consequence of not having heard from you which we have been in daily expectation we hope on your account as well as our own that we have been misinformed and that it may still be in your Power as we flatter ourselves it is your inclination to pay us, Mr. Pedley paid us for the Grand Pianoforte the young lady who boarded with you in Grafton Street had of us but said he had no orders from or knowledge of you to warrant him in settling for yours we beg the favor of a line by return of packet*
>
> *We remain Madam*
>
> *Yr humble Sevt*
>
> *John Broadwood & Son*

Sometimes grief and sorrow at bad behaviour leads to worldly advice being given.

> *January 10th 1802*
>
> *Mr. Caishop*
>
> *Sir, We received your letter of the 12th inst and are sorry your health has been so indifferent – from a friend who called from you on us we find the reason you are not able to pay us proceeds from your having lent the money you received to a person who has about £400 a year and who promised to repay it in May. If so we pity you for a little acquaintance with the world is sufficient to convince one that if a person imprudent enough to spend (or borrow is all the same) one fifth part more than his income it will not be in his Power if ever so well*

inclined, to repay it without a greater sacrifice to comfort and appearance than he is willing to make. We mention this that you may not place too much reliance on the promise the lady made you – our opinion is that if you do not get the money back by 5£ at a time you never will etc.

Whether or not the personal touch is typical of Scottish firms (and I am patriotically inclined to consider this to be so) it is certainly true that John Broadwood encouraged fellow Scots to join forces with him. John had had instilled into him as a child the traditional Scottish love of learning, and the firm invariably encouraged education and the arts, first by making special discounts for teachers, and secondly, by being generous to those who played in public for a living. The last of course was not entirely disinterested, since well-known performers who used Broadwood instruments added lustre to the name. It was quite customary for musical instrument builders to lend or give instruments to celebrities, the most famous example of this in all musical history being the six octave grand piano given by Broadwoods to Beethoven. The instrument was made in 1817 and delivered to Beethoven free of charge (including a special customs clearance concession at Trieste, where it arrived by sea before travelling overland to Vienna) on June 18th 1818. Musicians working in London benefited greatly from this practice, as did the builders.

John Christian Bach's performance on a Zumpe square piano in 1768 well illustrates the benefits to craftsmen of public performance for it caused intense interest and laid the foundations for the success not only of Johannes Zumpe, (who, as has already been mentioned, was a friend of Broadwood,) but also of John Broadwood himself. It would seem that Bach bought the little square from Zumpe for this recital, for on the 4th of July, shortly afterwards, he paid him £50. For many years it had been assumed that this transaction was for one instrument, but this in fact is scarcely credible. First of all, the whole point about these simple instruments is that they were cheap, the likely price being not much more than fifteen pounds, and £50 was a great deal of money for such a thing, and secondly, the last thing Zumpe would have done would have been to sting a distinguished artist such as J. C. Bach, who had done him an enormous service by publicly advertising his wares. But Bach, as is clear from his accounts with Drummonds, the bankers, also made very substantial payments to Zumpe's partner, Gabriel Buntebart, over a three year period from 1776 to 1778. One payment on the 2nd of March 1778 was for no less than £420. The total sum paid by Bach to Buntebart was £940, plus £129 in 1779, the year after he ceased his partnership with Zumpe. Bach and Buntebart indulged in many commercial adventures together, including impresario work for concerts, and it would seem likely that a substantial amount of these sums would have been for settling up debts incurred. But Bach was also the business manager for Zumpe, and it seems likely that Bach was engaged in dealing in pianos. (After all, his illustrious father, no less, acted as a salesman in 1749 for Silbermann pianos.) Certain it is that on one occasion he provided a lady in Paris with a Zumpe square, for this is reported by Burney.[8] A possible scenario for the Thatched House concert is that Bach tried out a Zumpe square free of charge, decided that he liked it and then bought a consignment for future use. To sell a piano after previously advertising it by performing on it would have been a sensible thing to do, and a somewhat similar sales policy was in fact adopted by Broadwoods. An expensive top grade new instrument would be lent or hired out to a well-known executant on a number of occasions. This would nicely advertise the instrument which could subsequently be sold to an admirer at a small concession in price as it was now slightly secondhand. The great advantage to the firm, apart from the obvious success in selling the instrument, was that the inevitable teething troubles that all new instruments go through could be dealt with before rather than after the sale.

Entrepreneurial activity of this nature was very much the norm in England at this time. Since the arts were completely unsubsidised, musicians were only too ready to turn their hands to anything that could keep them going. This was particularly true of foreign musicians for whom England was a magnet. England in the late eighteenth century was free and chic, and there was the irresistible lure of rich pickings. If these turned out to be illusory, as was normally the case, there was at least the likelihood of adventure and fun. Foreign patronage of musicians, although unpredictable, could offer a steady income, but it tended to be dull, and in any case court musicians were to all intents and purposes merely paid servants. So the musicians flocked to England and set up their own enterprises. Many came unstuck in the process. Bach himself died in penury, after having received and spent enormous sums in concert promotion. Every now and then a musician would be tempted to embark on a commercial adventure, distinct from playing or composing, while at the same time pursuing a musical career. Again, the results were usually disastrous. Dussek, for example, who was a good friend and supporter of John Broadwood, had to leave England hurriedly in 1799, leaving behind a string of debts arising from the ill-advised music publishing business in which he was involved.

The last word on all this may be allowed the great Irish tenor, Michael Kelly, who unwisely invested in a book shop and wine business. In his vivid and amusing reminiscences, 'Solo Recital', published in 1826, the year of his death, he describes a horrible day in September 1811, and moralises on its implications:

> ...while supper was getting ready, I took up a London newspaper, and the first thing I saw struck me with astonishment; I read in the gazette, these portentious words – Bankrupt, Michael Kelly of Pall Mall, music-seller – an announcement so unexpected, confounded me. I instantly wrote to my principal man of business, who had the management of all my money transactions (his name I shall not mention for the sake of his family, part of which I know to be very respectable) to know by whom the docket was struck. Unfortunately for me, I had reposed the greatest confidence in him, and would have trusted my life, as well as my property, in his hands. He was recommended to me by a particular friend and came into my employ a poor man, but he left it amply stocked with everything; and, sans cérémonie, took himself abroad. .....When I got to town, I found the docket had been struck against me by a particular friend of his, on account of a dishonoured bill. It was certainly a planned thing; my solicitor, looking into my affairs (which I unluckily did not) found I was plunged, by my fidus Achates, deeper in the mire than I could possibly have imagined, and therefore advised me, though my property might have paid all demands three times over and though I might have superseded the commission, to let the bankruptcy take its course – and so I did – and all the property in my saloon was disposed of for one tenth of its value.
>
> To be a professional man and a trader at the same time is, I believe, impossible; but this I found out too late; for if a man be fond of his profession, it must, and ought to engross all his time and thoughts; and, therefore, he is constantly liable to be cheated by his subordinates. To a man occupied in the service of the public, his mind fully occupied with the honourable ambition of standing well in their opinion, it is perfectly immaterial at the time whether meat be four-pence or a shilling in the pound, and so on in all other things; and from want of looking into his affairs, which prudence, not nearly allied to genius requires him to do, he gets involved and sinks deeper and deeper until he is gone past recovery while those about him are revelling and fattening upon his credulity and inattention.

Michael Kelly's equable temperament in the face of adversity would seem to have brought him notoriety. A review of a book published in 1828, entitled "Seven Years of the King's Theatre by John Ebers, late Manager of the King's Theatre in the Haymarket", has the following comment:

> *Mr. Ebers seems to be a philosopher of the academy of Michael Kelly – gifted by nature with a disposition to enjoy all the good that falls in his way, and content to suffer, without much repining, the various ills which such a determination sometimes and nature always entails even upon such favoured individuals.*[9]

When John Broadwood died in 1812 he had become a very wealthy man. In his later life he had been greatly aided by his two able sons, James Shudi and Thomas. James, a son of his first marriage, was brought in as a partner in 1795, after which the business was known as John Broadwood and Son, and in 1808 twenty-three year old Thomas was also made a partner, after which the firm was called John Broadwood and Sons. Together the two brothers, whose different personalities worked so well together (Thomas, the entrepreneurial businessman, and James, the designer and technician), were instrumental in establishing Broadwoods as the leading piano firm through much of the nineteenth century.

Michael Kelly

In the late eighteenth century the rise of the middle class and the consequent demand for keyboard instruments for the home benefited all makers, and Broadwoods was no exception to this. Initially however, the influence of Shudi remained strong, and the firm produced many harpsichords until the 1790s. Shudi himself died in 1773, but the harpsichords thereafter were called 'Shudi and Broadwood.' John Broadwood lived for several years with his family over the shop – their premises in Great Pulteney Street, Soho – and there would not have been too much room to manufacture grand pianos as well as harpsichords. This, combined with the Shudi family's lack of interest in pianos (John Broadwood's brother-in-law, Burkat Shudi, remained as a harpsichord-making partner in the firm for a fairly long time), acted as a deterrent, and initially therefore production of pianos concentrated exclusively on the simpler squares. Paradoxically, however, this less ambitious course turned out to be the key to Broadwood's fortunes, for by satisfying the ever increasing demands of the public with inexpensive square pianos, revenue and profits grew rapidly, thereby giving a financial head start over rivals when eventually the firm turned to grands in 1785. By this time the business had grown greatly, and an entrepreneurial spirit was much in evidence. Maintenance of pianos in those days was a considerable problem since low tension wire goes out of tune very easily. Broadwoods therefore employed many technicians to look after their clients' interests, and also, if need be, those of other firms. They also supplied parts for all comers, both here and abroad. Instruments were exported, not just to Europe, but also to North America. All of this laid a bedrock on which to build. They kept very close contact with leading pianists and composers, experimenting empirically on suggestions to improve the performance of their instruments. They were also quite canny, in that they provided pianos for all tastes and pockets.

The little Broadwood square of 1795 at Finchcocks is a good example of a simple domestic instrument. The case, which rests on a trestle stand, is of mahogany with light and dark stringing, and the keywell is veneered in maple with dark stringing. Rather surprisingly, perhaps, there is no mechanism for sustaining the sound. This, however, was almost certainly an economy measure. Although it is not possible to produce a great deal of volume from the piano, it is lively to play, and the tone quality is very clear and bright. This is partly because the soundboard of this little square is much smaller than a contemporary Broadwood grand, and also because of a Broadwood innovation found here – the so-called 'peacock' damper (derived from the side view of the moving part), which consists of a pivoted brass lever with a fork, to hold the damping cloth at one end (the peacock's head), while the weight of the other end (the tail) holds the damper in contact with the underside of the strings. This efficient damping system showed a marked improvement on the whalebone-spring over-dampers which were in use earlier. But the method was not continued, and was soon succeeded by the more usual, and slightly less effective, type of over-damper, in which cloth is held in a small piece of wood, looking remarkably like a clothes-peg. It has been suggested that this happened for economic reasons, and there may be something in this. But instrumental resonance had by now taken root, and the public liked and expected a wash of sound from their instruments, and it is difficult to believe that a leading manufacturer would deliberately resort to this cheaper method if it did not accord with musical taste.

Square piano by John Broadwood and Son, London, 1795

Broadwood's great reputation in the early nineteenth century rested in the final analysis on their production of grand pianos. By the end of the eighteenth century the grand had really come into its own. Chamber music, written for home consumption, could be heard in an increasing proliferation of concert halls, while Beethoven and other major composers were writing piano concertos for which the more powerful grands were necessary. In responding to this need, Broadwoods succeeded in building grands that were not only flexible in dynamics, but also louder than most other makes. They were also durable and did not easily go out of regulation, a great advantage for everybody who possessed one. The grand piano of 1801 in the collection is a typical example of the type of instrument that so interested Haydn and Dussek during their sojourns in London during the 1790s. The compass is five and a half octaves (FF-c^4), the extra half octave in the treble having been introduced in circa 1790 at the suggestion of Dussek to allow for the possibility of greater brilliance in performance, and known thereafter in both grands and squares as 'additional keys'. The instrument proper rests on a separate stand, and the pedals, which appear at the bottom of the front legs, have a rather comical look about them, since they

Grand piano by John Broadwood and Son, London, 1801

are pigeon-toed in order to prevent the player having to sit in an undignified fashion with legs spread-eagled.

Another characteristic of Broadwood grands was their remarkable resonance, which added extra colour and richness. The Finchcocks grand of 1823 is a good case in point. It is powerful for an instrument of its period, and capable of holding its own in concert even with a modern orchestra. The touch is refined, and the most delicate pianissimos can easily be achieved, especially with the aid of the left pedal, the keyboard shift. Unlike that of modern pianos, the keyboard shift has two positions: a small slider at the right limits the movement of the keyboard, so that the hammers hit two of the three strings for each note (due corde). But when the slider is lifted, the keyboard is free to move further to the right, allowing just one string per note to be sounded (una corda), thus producing a strangely ethereal effect. The una corda is a delicious feature of early pianos, but unfortunately is not available, as far as I am aware, on any modern commercially produced piano. The reasons for this can be found on page 188. The sustaining pedal is split into two halves, which can be employed individually or together. This is a relic of the tradition of having two hand levers for the sustaining mechanism on the earlier eighteenth century squares. The dampers are typically very light, so that the sound is never completely absorbed by them. The resultant echo effect can be rather disturbing for modern ears if one is not used to it. But if the light dampers do mean that the sounds run into each other, nevertheless the thin, almost harpsichord-like tone colour allows everything to be heard distinctly.

By the late 1820s the introduction of iron bracing to the casework of English pianos led to a dramatic increase in volume and dynamic variation. The treble end of English grands is a weak link in their construction, since it is particularly subject to distortion, and in the early 1820s a small iron bar was usually added as reinforcement. Iron bars soon appeared along the entire length of the piano over the strings, thus enabling ever higher tension wire to be used without endangering the instrument. The difference between an English grand of the 1820s and that of the 40s is well illustrated by the large and glamorous concert grand at Finchcocks built in 1846 by Broadwoods. This magnificent instrument in amboyna wood, decorated throughout with gilded and carved limewood,

Grand piano by John Broadwood and Sons, London, 1823

apparently cost the considerable sum of £167, and was bought in 1847, when he was thirty-six years old, by the Rev. Henry James Prince. An interesting account of this notorious clergyman is to be found in Ronald Pearsall's 'The Worm in the Bud: The World of Victorian Sexuality'. Having been debarred from preaching within the Church because of his amorous proclivities, but having also made a fortune from polemical writings and helpful marriages, he had, shortly before the purchase of this piano, acquired near Charlinch, a few miles west of Bridgewater in Somerset, a large estate where he founded a religious sect devoted to free love. This was the well-known Agapemone, 'The Abode of Love', which was to last until the early years of the twentieth century, and it was to this address that the present instrument was delivered, having set off on its journey from Paddington by the Great Western Railway on the 26th of July, 1847. The Abode of Love catered for sexually repressed ladies, who apparently had their frustrations relieved at the experienced hands of Henry Prince in ceremonial gatherings of his followers. It is interesting to speculate as to what role the Broadwood grand played in all this.

Considerable power, coupled, due to sympathetic vibration, with an obfuscating sea of sound, are the salient characteristics of this piano. The dampers are light for such an instrument and quite fail to extinguish totally any notes in the bass for anything up to ten seconds, according to how forcefully one depresses the keys. Old traditions die hard[10], and the tonal wash, so relished by the first performers on English pianos, here reaches its pinnacle, before receding into the greater clarity of later nineteenth century instruments. The 1846 Broadwood thus represents in this respect the link between the classical and the modern grand.

Broadwood's square piano production reached a peak in the mid 1820s with an output of about 1500 instruments a year. After this a gentle decline in numbers set in, which indeed accelerated rapidly after 1850. The very last square ever made by Broadwoods dates from 1866.

A large square piano in the collection, kindly donated by Mr. Adam Johnstone of the Broadwood Trust, was built by Broadwoods in 1858 and used as a hiring instrument. For some eight years it was loaned on a regular basis to many different addresses in London, until finally, on May 1st 1867 it was delivered, along with several other pianos, to the Queen at Buckingham Palace, where it remained for a couple of months before being returned. In 1868 and 1869 it made further fairly lengthy visits to Buckingham Palace. On August 2nd 1870, Queen Victoria arranged to have the instrument installed in the late

Grand piano by John Broadwood and Sons, London, 1846

Collage of Broadwood advertisements

Prince Consort's Room, where it remained (still on hire) for the following thirty years, until shortly after the Queen's death in January 1901. When Albert died in 1861 Victoria kept all his studies or dressing rooms in the various royal residences in pristine condition, and also as far as possible laid out in a way that he would have recognised and appreciated. 'The Royal Albert Square' – the name given to it by Broadwoods – is a fine instrument. As a piece of furniture, however, it is uncompromisingly plain, and would seem at first to be a surprising choice for a royal apartment. But Prince Albert was nothing if not unostentatious. He was also intensely musical and a composer of considerable ability, having studied under Felix Mendelssohn

The Broadwood 'Albert' square piano, London, 1858

for several years. His rooms, as maintained after his death, were certainly not kept as mausoleums, and Victoria herself regularly used them. She wanted however to be constantly reminded of Albert's presence, and a simple workmanlike instrument, such as the Royal Albert Square, would no doubt have fitted the bill very well.

Finchcocks' 1859 Broadwood concert grand shows a marked progress in the firm's development. It is a powerful instrument, and the tone colour is both clear and incisive. The damping mechanism is now much more like that of a modern grand, and the instrument is far less reverberant than that of grand pianos made a mere fifteen years earlier. This particular model was manufactured from 1851 until as late as 1897. As mentioned above, Broadwoods were ever alert to clients' requirements, and no less than five similar, though slightly differing, models were being manufactured concurrent with the present one. The design of the Finchcocks piano was the largest and most expensive type,[11] and thus the most suitable for concert work, for which reason it was hired out when brand new to Sir Charles Hallé to be used in his famous concert series in Manchester during July 1859. At the end of this month the instrument was sold to a customer for the enormous sum of 250 guineas (75 guineas more than its nearest rival). This was the full retail price, and not reduced, presumably because of the kudos attached to its association with a well known concert series. Strangely enough, Sir Charles Hallé had considerable

The interior of the grand piano by John Broadwood and Sons, London, 1859 This, Broadwood's large concert model, has the interior bracing and hitchplate painted in two shades of brown to blend in visually with the superb quality rosewood with which the piano is veneered. The wrestplank is now shod with brass sheet. Also the keyboard compass of seven octaves, AAA-a[5], has by this time become the norm. Even at this comparatively late date, however, some details of piano construction had not been standardised; in this instance, for example, the soundboard grain lies more or less transversely, similar to that of the 1848 Broadwood grand, but different to that of the 1866 Erard, in which it lies parallel to the spine or longside.

reservations about Broadwood grands, even though he maintained a good friendship with the then head of the firm, Henry Fowler Broadwood, who was very much in charge of the design of his instruments.

Hallé, besides being a distinguished conductor, was also an excellent pianist, and in 1852 gave a piano recital in which he played first a grand by Broadwood and then one by Erard, the important London piano manufacturers, descended from the great French builder, Sébastien Erard, who established a branch in London in 1792. This event, suggested by Henry Fowler Broadwood himself to discover if any discrepancies in quality between the two instruments should become apparent in performance, came about

Grand piano by Erard, London, 1866 This is an instrument decorated to special order, since it is veneered in amboyna rather than rosewood, which would have been the standard finish. This very expensive burr-figured wood, obtained from the East Indies, was used only for high class furniture. Further features include geometrical banding and details in burr walnut, stained fruitwood and maple, and, in addition, wood mosaic inlay around the edge of the lid and ormolu trim around the lower case and lid. The use of the cast iron frame on European pianos was at this time still some way off, and the present instrument, which is straight strung, displays a composite system in which four iron bars brace the wrestplank and hitchplate.

through injured pride. The year previously, in the Great Exhibition, Broadwoods, the oldest and most revered piano business in the world, had had the Gold Medal for pianoforte manufacture snatched away from them by Erards, a relative newcomer to grand piano building in England and a French firm to boot, and Henry Fowler, full of chagrin, wanted to know why. The points made by Hallé to Broadwood in a long letter following the recital are of great interest, and can be verified by comparing the 1859 Broadwood with Finchcocks' magnificent concert grand by Erard of London, built a few years later in 1866.

The whole tradition of the Broadwood firm had been based on durability, reliability and value for money. No one can deny that these are worthy aims for any firm, but they can lead to lack of enterprise. Broadwoods by this time were perhaps starting to rely too much on their reputation, whereas Erards were more forward-looking and innovative. The Finchcocks Erard is, for its date, a very modern instrument, and, in my experience, most pianists who visit Finchcocks, particularly those who are not well acquainted with early pianos, feel very at home with it. It is exciting to play, and, like a race-horse, can be spurred to ever greater feats. The Broadwood, while by no means a plodder, certainly seems less adventurous by comparison. So, at any rate, thought Hallé, who in his letter to Henry Fowler Broadwood, made tactful comments. While praising the general quality of the Broadwood, he found the Erard gave greater flexibility of tone colour according to the requirements of the music. Hallé's strictures can equally be applied to the equivalent grands at Finchcocks. In loud passages, the Erard is remarkably clear and brilliant, particularly in the treble, whereas in soft passages it can sound almost lusciously sweet. Tonal characteristics such as these are clearly of enormous benefit to a pianist when playing in a concert hall. By contrast, the Broadwood, with its rigidly barred soundboard and short string lengths in the treble, produces a feeling of sameness however it is played.

Possibly Hallé's comments it was, that led Broadwoods to alter the pitch of an instrument such as the 1859 Broadwood so as to make it sound more sparkling. The great structural strength of the grands allowed the strings to be tuned safely at different pitches. Alastair Laurence, at one time a director of Broadwoods, and formerly head of keyboard instrument technology at Musikk Instrument Akademiet at Moss in Norway, and whose ancestor, Alexander Finlayson, a Scottish Highlander, took employment with John Broadwood in the eighteenth century, relates how his great-grandfather, Alexander Laurence, worked as a tuner with the company during the 1850s and 60s. At that time there were apparently three tuning pitches used for their grands, the highest being the so-called 'Philharmonic Pitch', which is about a quarter tone higher than concert pitch of today. In the International Exhibition of 1862 the firm issued presentational cases of the three types of tuning forks used at the time. One of these cases, issued to his ancestor, has been very fortunately inherited by Alastair, who made use of it while supervising and tuning for a CD made at Finchcocks in 1998. One item in the recording was performed on the 1859 piano, and for this piece the 'Philharmonic'

ABOVE **The Digitorium and** NEXT PAGE **advertisement for it** Actions of many Victorian pianos, such as the 1859 Broadwood Grand, were quite heavy, and the 'Digitorium' was designed to strengthen one's muscles.

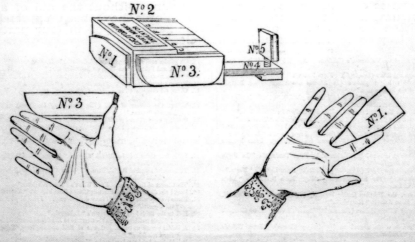

THE DIGITORIUM,

OR

MINIATURE DUMB PIANO.

(PATENT.)

THIS instrument materially assists any person to play on the Pianoforte, Organ, Harmonium, Violin, &c., strengthening the fingers, giving elasticity to the touch, and greatly assisting any student anxious to gain proficiency.

Price 15s., or with Ivory Keys, 18s. (including the exercises for practice), sent to any part of the country, carriage free, on receipt of Post Office Order.

It is invaluable for schools, saving the wear and tear of Pianoforte consequent on the eternal practice of exercises, the constant noise of the Instrument, and for practice when the Pianoforte in engaged, or whilst travelling, reading, or following any sedentary occupation.

Drawings Nos. 1, 2, and 3, are appliances attached to the sides and back of the *Digitorium*, to produce great tension of the fingers. Drawings Nos. 4 and 5 are appliances to ascertain and acquire the exact position and distance required for the Hands, Wrists, and Arms, in playing on the Pianoforte. No. 4, a slide connected with the bottom of the *Digitorium*, which can be drawn in and out at will, so as to suit all sizes of Fingers and Hands. No. 5, an appliance raised and lowered at will, on which the Wrist rests.

By a few minutes' daily practice on a *Digitorium*, heavy and unequal touch (the result of one finger being stronger than another), stiffness of wrist, execution marred by weakness, &c., can be perfectly cured.

Each hand is used separately.

Exercises are adapted to the *Digitorium*, by which the fingers move in 76 different positions, and the *exact position of the Hands and Arms (requisite in Pianoforte playing)* is acquired by its use. It is light and portable, being only SIX INCHES SQUARE. A short daily practice on the *Digitorium* will soon make up for long neglect of the Pianoforte.

No. 1. Light Touch.   No. 2. Medium.   No. 3. Strong.

TESTIMONIALS.

From CHARLES HALLE, Esq.

SIR,—I have much pleasure in stating that I believe the use of your *Digitorium* must be attended with very good results: it must give strength to the fingers, and render them independent, and I consider it a valuable invention.—I remain, Sir, yours truly, 10, Greenheys, Manchester.   CHARLES HALLE.

From SIR JULIUS BENEDICT.

SIR,—I beg to thank you for the very ingenious little instrument that you have sent me, which, by its simple construction and explanation, will prove a useful auxiliary to the musical student.—I remain, Sir, yours faithfully, 2, Manchester Square.   J. BENEDICT.

From BRINLEY RICHARDS, Esq.

SIR,—You *Digitorium* is one of the most simple and useful inventions which I have yet seen for the use of Pianoforte players, and the very portable size in which it is constructed renders it acceptable both to professors and pupils.—I remain, truly yours, 2, St. Mary Abbott's Terrace, Kensington, W.   BRINLEY RICHARDS.

From LINDSAY SLOPER, Esq.

Mr. MARKS having submitted to me his invention, the *Digitorium*, I have used pleasure in stating that its use cannot fail to result in the object sought, the strengthening of the fingers ; and that, amongst the various mechanical methods invented for that purpose, it is at once the simplest, and, from its approximation to the Instrument, the best. 70, Cambridge Terrace, Hyde Park.   LINDSAY SLOPER.

From HERR GANZ.

SIR,—I have examined your *Digitorium*, and find it very useful. I shall have much pleasure in recommending it to my friends and pupils.—I remain, yours faithfully, 15, Queen Anne Street, Cavendish Square, W.   WILHELM GANZ.

From HERBERT S. OAKELEY, Esq.

The *Digitorium* invented by Mr. MYER MARKS appears to me to be a very useful little instrument, as it is the best invention of the kind ; it should be possessed by students both of the Pianoforte and Organ.   HERBERT S. OAKELEY, M.A., Professor of Music, Edinburgh University.

---

fork was brought out. The results were fairly startling. The concert studies by Mendelssohn, which were chosen for this unusual experiment, sound brilliant but, it has to be said, also rather brittle. While perfectly acceptable for a short while, one can easily understand how this pitch could become irritating to the ears over a prolonged period, and in fact complaints were apparently made by foreign artists who visited London and had pianos loaned to them.

The Finchcocks Broadwood was hardly a rarity in 1859. At the beginning of October that year there were, incredibly, no less than 378 new grand pianos in store at Broadwood's warehouses in Great Pulteney Street and Horseferry Road, (in Westminster, just north of Lambeth bridge). This enormous stock was kept in readiness for the Christmas market, when hopefully most of them would be sold. Production of new instruments, however, was at this time severely curtailed of necessity, resulting in many employees being laid off at the end of the summer. For this information I am indebted to Alastair Laurence, who also has related to me an account of what happened traditionally to the Broadwood workforce during this lean period, which had been told to him by a technician, who was employed as a foreman at the piano firm of Danemann until about 1984. A grand exodus from London was apparently the custom, and factory hands and their families descended on rural Kent, where they worked in the hop-gardens at harvest time, earning money and at the same time having a holiday. It is intriguing to think that the hop workers' huts, still used today a stone's throw from Finchcocks, may possibly have been occupied annually for about a hundred years by the families from the Broadwood factory.

Hop Pickers print

The 1859 is the youngest Broadwood grand in the collection. The business thereafter retained its high reputation under Henry Fowler Broadwood, who, perhaps stung by the humiliation of 1851, provided a certain impetus for a time, and at the end of the century the firm produced the magnificent so-called barless grand, in my opinion one of the finest instruments of its type made by anybody. Sadly, however, a major decline in the firm's fortunes, caused by severe competition from Germany and other countries, set in shortly after the Great War.[12] In 1985, however, a new board of directors was appointed, who set about to revive the firm's fortunes. In this, some remarkable successes have been achieved, including an upright which won the 'British Piano of the Year' award in 1987. In particular, the firm has reintroduced the concept of the barless frame, and has brought out a much admired upright model of this kind, and in 1999 a small grand, for which one of the first Millenium Awards was granted.

Broadwoods remains the oldest piano firm in the world still in business. An important legacy of the original John Broadwood has come down to us today. His love of learning and the arts is epitomized by the Broadwood Trust, founded by Capt. Evelyn Broadwood and developed by the late Mr. Adam Johnstone, the munificence of which has greatly benefited many of the musical colleges, and which has generously supported the Finchcocks Charity from 1984 until 1999.

NOTES

1. Between 1830 and 1835 the total production of new pianos by the firm averaged one thousand nine hundred and forty-eight per annum, of which nearly two thirds were squares.
2. The Broadwood Journals are now in the Bodleian Library, Oxford
3. Chamber pots have been a recurrent theme in the history of the firm. David Wainwright, author of 'Broadwood by Appointment', (Quiller Press, 1982), recounts how, in conversation with the company secretary, Leo Broadwood, he was told how very old chamber pots were discovered hidden behind the panelling of the Partners' Room of the old premises in Great Pulteney Street, vacated in 1903. Capt. Evelyn Broadwood, the doyen of the firm, who died in 1975 aged eighty-five, was very protective of these relics, and kept them carefully in his cellar. At a dinner at which I was present, I asked him why

he treasured these no doubt useful but somewhat nondescript objects, to which he replied 'Mark my words, in a hundred years time they will be valuable.'

4. Barbara Broadwood's account book (MS. Eng. misc. c. 529), from which the previous quotes are taken, is housed at the Bodleian Library, University of Oxford. The following quote from the Work Journal is also in the Bodleian Library, the reference for which is MS. Eng. misc. b. 107

5. David Wainwright in 'Broadwood by Appointment' says twenty guineas, but this is a mistake.

6. Count Brühl lived in Vienna and was an enthusiastic and influential amateur pianist. This is probably the first instance of an English grand to make its appearance there.

7. The Broadwood Archive, which includes the Broadwood Letter Book, is housed at: The Surrey History Centre, 130 Goldsworth Road, Woking, Surrey GU21 6ND

8. C. Burney, 'Music, Men and Manners in France and Italy' (1770, page 19)

9. 'Quarterly Musical Magazine' (vol. 10, page 97)

10. An example of this is provided by a curious little anonymous upright piano in the collection, made in England probably around 1865. A kind of indoor street piano, it is operated by a barrel, which plays ten tunes.

    It is a genuine baby upright, and has to be kept regulated, but it has no dampers at all and makes a most amazing racket.

11. In the Broadwood Price List Catalogue this particular model is referred to as 'The Iron Grand'.

12. A valiant effort to increase sales occurred in 1926 when King George V and Queen Mary visited the factory. To celebrate this historic event a splendid panegyric in the form of an illustrated broadsheet was produced. On the very first page the queen herself endorses the high quality of a Broadwood piano. Subsequent pages show the crowds at the arrival of the royal couple and the king and queen touring the rooms. The final page depicts the Broadwood family tree.

Barrel Piano This instrument is undated but is unlikely to have been built before the mid 1860s, if the barrel of tunes is contemporary with it, as seems likely; the reason being that one of the tunes is the well-known "Soldiers' Chorus" from 'Faust' by Gounod, which was first performed in Paris in 1859, but which did not appear in London until 1863. It is not a street instrument, as might be supposed, but a well-made and nicely finished example of an indoor type which once must have existed in large numbers. Its four bun feet suggest that it was intended to be placed upon a table, and used as amusement for domestic recreation and dancing.

"WHAT a wonderful tone !"

It was Queen Mary who paid that striking tribute to the quality of the Broadwood Piano on that memorable July 20th, 1926, when Her Majesty accompanied the King to the great Factory in the East End of London, and standing in one of the spacious departments listened to the music played on an instrument selected at haphazard.

The Queen's skill as a connoisseur of music is as well known as is her passion for it. These are attested by her frequent attendance at the opera and concerts and her natural appreciation of tone has been educated to a high pitch of excellence.

Her encomium of the quality of the Broadwood Piano cannot, therefore, be interpreted as the perfunctory desire of an exalted personage to say something gracious because it is expected.

The Queen's remark was uttered so spontaneously, so obviously without preparation or premeditation, that it was a high endorsement of value and a specific criticism of merit, carrying the weight of authority of one who knows.

The King & Queen watching the accuracy with which the Broadwood soundboard bridges are moulded.

*The Royal Standard was flown during
the visit of the King & Queen to the Broadwood factories
and immense crowds watched their arrival & departure.*

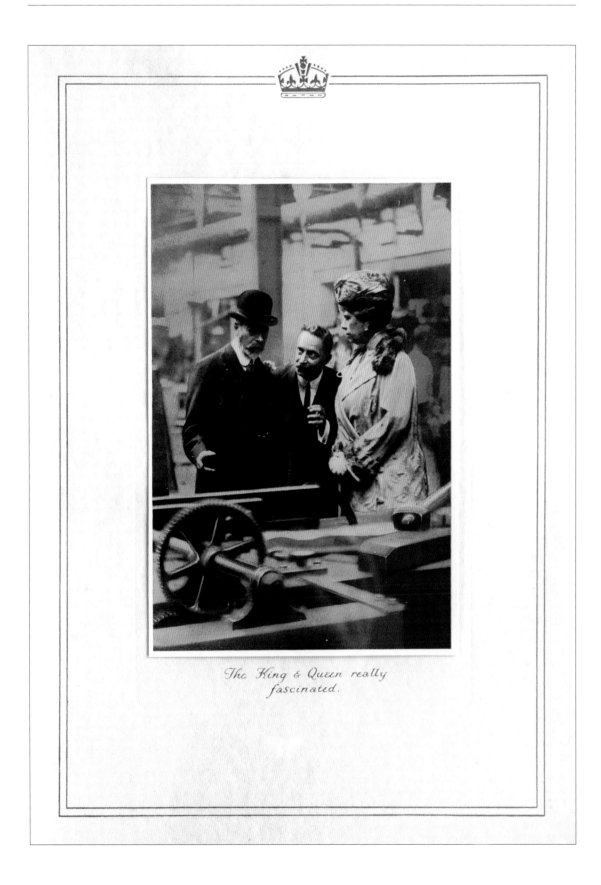

The King & Queen really
fascinated.

Clementi & Co.

A central figure in the history of English pianos, and certainly one of the most fascinating and entertaining, is that of the great Italian musician, Muzio Clementi, born in Rome in 1752. Clementi died in Evesham, Worcestershire, in 1832 at the age of eighty-one, and his career thus straddles the major development of the English piano from its earliest beginnings to the prototype of the modern instrument.

Clementi was a polymath, with an almost alarming ability to excel at whatever he touched. A great composer, arguably one who is still not fully appreciated today, and an outstanding virtuoso on the harpsichord and piano, who gave up playing in public at an early age because it was not seemly for an English gentleman to be seen to be a mere performer, Clementi was also a master of languages, both living and dead, with a life-long interest in the classics, a conductor, a pedagogue, a piano technician[1] and a successful businessman, who died an exceedingly wealthy man, having made a mint out of piano building and music publishing. In personality he was a strange mixture; sometimes quixotically generous, he was however quite ascetic and often almost pathologically mean both to himself and others, many tales of which have come down to us. But his saving grace was his wit, and his many friends apparently much enjoyed his company. He was what we would now call a card, and this side of his nature is evident in many of his letters and contemporary accounts. Paradoxically, though, it is as a businessman that Clementi is of the greatest importance for today's musician, for were it not for his business acumen there would be no Clementi pianos, and pianos built by such an outstanding musician can tell us so much about performance practice in the past.

Muzio Clementi, aged 42

Clementi was the son of Nicolo Clementi, a Roman silversmith. A child prodigy, by the time he reached fourteen he had become an extremely accomplished musician. But it was at that age that he was literally bought from his father (on a sort of hire purchase arrangement[2]) by an Englishman, doing the Grand Tour.

Peter Beckford (c. 1740-1811) was a kinsman of the notorious novelist William Beckford of Fonthill Abbey in Wiltshire. He had inherited a large estate at Stepleton (or Stapleton) Iwerne, near Blandford Forum in Dorset, and his purpose in acquiring Clementi was apparently to have a cheap musician on hand to provide music when required for friends and guests. Although primarily interested in foxhounds (he ran his own pack and produced a book, 'Thoughts on Hunting', which was to become almost a bible in hunting circles), Beckford was a man of wide cultural interests. He certainly got considerable enjoyment from music, at any rate on his travels, and the musical world owes him a real debt by his success in bringing Clementi to our shores. Beckford's musical life would seem to have reached its zenith in his twenties, for during this period he took an amazingly active part in musical promotion, putting on concerts usually for philanthropic reasons. In later life he describes the period in Italy when he met the young Clementi, and writes somewhat wryly of his musical activities:

> I was young and extravagant in those days; money, of course, was to be thrown away, and it was better spent in giving fetes than in gambling. It was also less ruinous. A concert which I gave in the Piazza di Spagna to all Rome, consisting of two orchestras and the best singers I could procure, cost little more than a hundred pounds. Another I gave on the Tyber, opposite la Ripetta, which was of instrumental music only, cost not half that sum. Ancient Romans made a trade of this courtesy. I had no other view than that of amusing, for a few moments at least, a people who were starving.[3]

A 'Memoir of Clementi' in the 1820 edition of the Quarterly Musical Magazine describes the composer's intensive musical upbringing in Rome:

> His father was a worker in silver of great merit, and principally engaged in the execution of embossed vases and figures employed in the Catholic worship. At a very early period of his youth he evinced a powerful disposition for music, and as this was an art which greatly delighted his father, he anxiously bestowed the best instructions in his power on the improvement of his son. Buroni, who was his relation, and who afterwards obtained the honourable station of principal composer at St. Peter's, was his first master. At six years of age he began sol-fa-ing; at seven he was placed under an organist of the name of Cordicelli for instruction in thorough bass; at the age of nine he passed his examination, and was admitted an organist in Rome..... He next went under the celebrated Santarelli, the last great master of the true vocal school. Between his eleventh and twelfth year he went under Carpini, the deepest contrapuntist of his day in Rome. A few months after he was placed under this master, he was induced by some of his friends, and without consulting his preceptor, to write a mass for four voices; for which he received so much commendation, that Carpini expressed a desire to hear it. It was accordingly repeated in church in the presence of his master, who being little accustomed to bestow praise on any one, said to his pupil, after his dry manner, 'Why did you not tell me you were about to write a mass. This is very well, to be sure, but if you had consulted me it might have been much better.'[4]

Very little appears to be known about Clementi's adolescent years in Dorset. It would seem that Clementi was very much left to his own devices, and there is no evidence, moreover, that any musical tuition was provided for him by Beckford. Much of Beckford's life, after his return to England, was given over to hunting matters, and probably did not allow much time for music. Besides which, a certain distrust of music had already appeared in his travel diaries in Italy:

> *Though music is a charming talent, I think more time is allotted to it than it deserves, considering the little use that is made of it afterwards; besides, it increases sensibility, particularly in a female breast, which surely is no advantage, and frequently procures a tête-à-tête that had always better be avoided.*[5]

Beckford's attitude towards music in fact well illustrates the feelings of so many educated Englishmen of the period, who approved of the art, so long as it was indulged in for innocent enjoyment, or had moral or philanthropic purpose behind it, but who regarded it as dangerous if it merely encouraged introspection.[6]

All evidence points to Beckford as a man of liberal and generous instincts, and it seems very much out of character for him to have neglected Clementi's well being. Clementi's natural asceticism is however well documented in the following account of his sojourn at Stepleton:

> *He was indefatigable in the practice of the instrument to which he had devoted himself. But his ruling principle was, that steady and regular apportionment of every moment of time to its own pre-arranged occupation, which affords the surest promise of success, whatever may be our pursuits; and without which, no great results were ever achieved either in study or in action. To this Clementi, young as he was, adhered strictly; his sleep, his meals, his relaxation, and his studies, had each their appointed time and their fixed duration; and if by the demands of his patron on his society, or his powers of contributing to the amusement of the family or guests, or by any other accidental circumstance, the order was broken, and that proportion of time which he had set apart for the study of his own profession curtailed, he drew upon the allotted hours of rest for the arrears, and would rise even in the cheerless cold of mid-winter, to read if he had light at command, or to practice on his harpsichord, if light as well as fire were unattainable. His success was equal to his zeal and assiduity: at eighteen he not only surpassed all his contemporaries in execution, taste, and expression, but had already composed (though it was not published till three years after) his celebrated Opera 2, – a work, which, by the common assent of all musicians, is entitled to the credit of being the basis on which the whole fabric of modern piano-forte sonatas has been founded; and which – though it is now, from the immense progress which manual dexterity has made in the last sixty years, within the powers of even second-rate performers – was, at the period of its production, the despair of such pianists as J. C. Bach and Schroeter, who were content to admire it, but declined the attempt to play what the latter professor declared could only be executed by its own composer, or by that great performer of all wonders, and conqueror of all difficulties, the Devil. (The Harmonicon, 1831 issue, page 183)*

At the age of twenty-two Clementi left Dorset for good and came to London, where he embarked on what was to become a highly successful musical career. At the same time, as was the case with so many professional musicians of that period, he began to dabble in commercial pursuits. But unlike many others, who rapidly came a cropper in this field, Clementi eventually succeeded, though not without mishaps on the way. His interest in the burgeoning development of the piano led him to invest in the firm of Longman and Broderip, which went bankrupt in 1798. How much he lost over this is not known, but Clementi, always close with money, would appear by this time to have amassed a fair fortune, for he took the opportunity of taking over the firm. Initially, he teamed up with

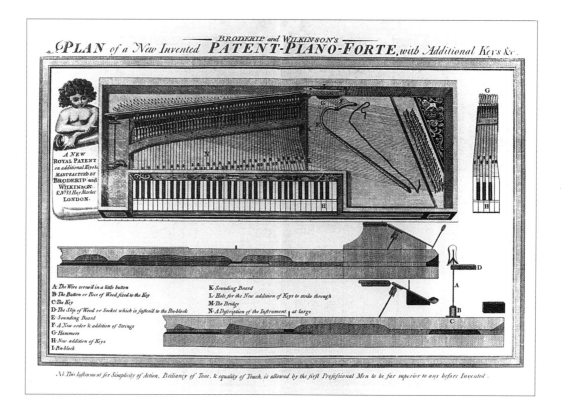

Longman and Broderip Instrument Plan. After 1798 Robert Broderip started up again with another partner, but made use of this earlier design. Notice how the name 'Longman' has been erased from the nameboard.

John Longman, of Longman and Broderip, operating from the old firm's premises in Cheapside, London, but in 1801 Longman left, and Clementi, to keep the new firm going, immediately took on several new partners, at which point the business acquired the cumbersome title of Clementi, Banger, Hyde, Collard and Davis. As the years went by, partners dropped off, and, with the accession of a second Collard, the firm settled down in 1824 (after a brief spell when it was renamed Clementi, Banger, Collard, Davis and Collard) as Clementi, Collard and Collard, or Clementi & Co., for short.

The two Collards were brothers, and they enjoyed the rather nice names of Frederick William, the elder, and William Frederick, the younger. Of the two, it is William Frederick who is the more important for us, since it was he who developed the 'harmonic swell' device, which he arranged to have patented in 1821. This invention is of the utmost importance for the understanding and interpretation of music designed for English pianos. The most prominent characteristic of early English pianos, as has been pointed out previously, is the sonic surrounding glow – the way the whole instrument seems to come alive with sound. This resonance is a permanent feature to a greater or lesser extent of every leading English make of piano in classical times, with but one major exception – Clementi. Clementi pianos have a far clearer, more 'fluty' sound than that of other English makes, a tone colour in fact reminiscent of Viennese pianos. This is perhaps not surprising, since Clementi himself was a musician with continental roots, and who retained throughout his working life a 'hands on' relationship with the products of his firm.

Empiricism was the basis of all keyboard instrument production at that time, and Clementi was one of the foremost virtuoso performers of the day. From his many revealing letters to his partners we can see how he did his utmost to make sure that all the pianos under his control expressed his own musical requirements. The pure quality of a typical Clementi piano contrasts strongly with the somewhat less pure and more nasal sound of a similar Broadwood instrument. But Clementi did not want to eschew totally the English tradition of resonance. With the introduction of the harmonic swell mechanism in 1821 he succeeded in getting the best of both worlds, for the resonance can be controlled by the player and turned on or off at will.

The full name of this mechanism is 'Harmonic Swell and Bridge of Reverberation' and it is to be found in a number of Clementi grands and square pianos. It works as follows: the strings that are struck and resonate between the nut and the soundboard bridge continue for a little while before passing over a second soundboard bridge, after which they are fastened down as normal on to the hitchrail. The string length between the two bridges is covered by a long damping bar, which can be operated by a pedal mechanism. This extra string length is not tuned and remains unaffected, directly, by the hammers hitting the strings. Indirectly, however, they resonate in sympathy when their own damping bar is raised. The more that different notes are played, the more these extra string lengths vibrate in sympathy, which of course increases the volume – hence the term 'harmonic swell'. The device was not a cheap one, since it required an enlarged chassis to accommodate the extra width of soundboard, an extra bridge, a second damping bar, and attendant pedal and trapwork. So the device is by no means common in Clementi pianos. Nonetheless, one assumes that Clementi set great store by it all, because his grand pianos often have an unnecessarily large width between bridge and hitchrail, the only ostensible purpose of which is to enable a harmonic swell to be installed as an optional extra if the customer so desired.

The harmonic swell can be used in a number of ways. Because all manufacturers then were aiming to achieve the maximum volume from their instruments, the mechanism helps greatly in this respect. But the extra resonance, when used delicately, can produce a beautiful impressionistic effect if need be.[7] The idea behind the harmonic swell was not an entirely novel one, since Erard, the great French builder, had been flirting with something similar some years before, but the fact that Clementi was prepared to go to such expensive lengths to incorporate the device is circumstantial evidence of the importance of the use of sonic resonance as a colouring effect in music played on English pianos. For fuller discussion of this, see the section on Resonance, chapter 14, page 169.

After Clementi's death the Collard brothers took over the firm, and dispensed with the harmonic swell. This had little to do with the merits of the device, but everything to do with the fact that by this time piano building had become so highly competitive that manufacturers simply could not afford inessential or luxury items, and William Frederick Collard's excellent invention was one such casualty.

Close up of harmonic swell

When Clementi re-established the firm of Longman and Broderip under his own wing he was forty-six years old and still in the prime of life. He was by that time a distinguished musician and composer with the great majority of his works already behind him. His abundant energy and drive had by no means dried up, and indeed would seem to have been inflamed by the release of his innate commercial instincts. From 1798 onwards, therefore, Clementi devoted much of his time to his business and rather less to practical music-making. This of course had the effect of putting him into good odour with the British establishment, which entertained scant regard for working musicians. From his letters it appears that Clementi maintained a close and affectionate, if at times somewhat critical relationship with his partners, and in particular the Collard brothers. While the younger Collard was the boffin of the firm, the elder was the managing director. Clementi travelled much and used every opportunity to promote sales. He also when abroad kept in close contact with the firm over all matters dealing both with the business side and the technical side of pianoforte production, and one gets the impression that Frederick William Collard's defences were at times somewhat buffeted by the busy Italian dynamo. While on tour he wrote long and often admonitory letters to his partner. Such a one from Dresden (17th August 1803) typically complains

...I shall wait your prompt answer, which I hope will be less stingy than what you sent me at St. Petersburg. You say I hate long letters – true, when they contain nothing – but I rather believe Master Collard meant to say he hates writing long letters.

Although by this time rather less of his energies were given to composition, Clementi nonetheless took every opportunity to promote his previously published works. A passage in this same letter is concerned with the sale of an instrument to a certain Mr. Davidoff:

.......Mr. Davidoff wants a grand P-F with additional keys above, plain, neat case; the tone excellent but not what is called clear, sharp or silver but <u>thick</u> and <u>sweet</u>..... Remember once for all that the Russians in general possess good ears for <u>sound</u> tho' they have none for <u>sense and style</u>. Put in the P-F case my Practical Harmony and my op. 9th, 12th, 33d, 34th, my Waltzes, 2 books and the op. dedicated to Gombertz & my 40th <u>and charge them</u>...

This seems rather rough when you have not ordered the music and are being billed for an expensive new instrument.

But Clementi was nothing if not a tough businessman. A splendid story to illustrate this was furnished me by Patrick Phillips, owner of

Lady Elizabeth Russell The tambourine, by no means an easy instrument to play well, became at this period the only type of drum frequently played by ladies. Young girls were encouraged in its use.

Savoyards of Fashion — or the Musical Mania of 1799

The bands of itinerant musicians from Savoy, who visited England in the eighteenth century, instigated a fashionable cult amongst the amateur music makers of the upper classes, who enthusiastically performed on tambourines, triangles and other folk instruments.

Kentwell Hall, the magnificent moated Elizabethan mansion at Long Melford in Suffolk. The house boasts a beautiful limewood avenue, which had apparently been noted by Clementi around 1820, when the trees were in their prime of life. Lime was an essential timber for the construction of pianoforte keyboards and Clementi thought therefore to acquire them for his firm. Richard Moore, the then owner of Kentwell Hall, had been going through a bad patch at that time. His wife had recently eloped with the steward of the Hall, causing much scandal, and Moore himself, who seems to have been something of a spendthrift, had become seriously in debt. He was thus only too happy to sell Clementi the trees. After the deal had been completed, Clementi arranged to have them felled. It was shortly after five trees, closest to the house, had been cut down, that Richard Moore's mother became aware of what was going on. Furious, she demanded the trees back. Clementi initially refused to consider this, but after persistent requests, agreed to do so, though at a price vastly in excess of the original bargain. To finance the repurchase, the family had to sell a farm at nearby Lavenham.[8]

Music and commerce might seem uneasy bedfellows, yet so many musicians of this period practised both arts, though scarcely any with such determination as Clementi. But the strange mixture of the materialistic and the poetic in his nature is perhaps the reason why even today his stature as a composer has not been fully appreciated. Long lonely hours of study throughout childhood and adolescence, and a formidable intellect, gave rise to a number of works, which, though lean and sometimes austere, rank amongst the finest of the classical era; and the best of this music combines in perfect balance the extraordinary dichotomy of his nature – asceticism on the one hand, and worldly zest for life on the other. Unfortunately, in much of his output the two strands part company in a fairly disastrous way, giving rise to compositions which are either extremely severe and dull, or else superficially effervescent, and it is these that have tended to demean his reputation.

A good example of the latter are the collections of simple piano waltzes (first published with accompaniment of tambourine and triangle – a combination of drawing room instruments much resorted to at that time). I have to confess that I personally find them enjoyable and good fun, though no one I think could pretend that they are great music. However, these little pieces caused outrage in certain quarters when they first appeared in print, nowhere more so than in Vienna, when a rather humourless critic, who could not believe that they were really the work of a distinguished composer, gave vent to his righteous indignation:

> *It is indeed gross impudence to misuse the name of a living composer in such an outrageous way, and to ascribe to him the work of some scrawler in Vienna; for even a fleeting glance at this miserable hackwork will convince one that it is nothing more than pitiful rubbish, which Clementi's own servant could have done better.........*[9]

As a pedagogue, though, Clementi's reputation has always remained secure. His huge and magnificent work, Gradus ad Parnassum, (delightfully sent up by Debussy in 'Doctor Gradus ad Parnassum' from 'Childrens' Corner') rightly remains one of the most important aids to pianism ever written. It appeared in three volumes between 1817 and 1826, and consists of ninety-eight works of varying complexity and difficulty, but written with the definite purpose of furthering the technical dexterity of the serious performer. At the same time the finest of these piano pieces are thrilling compositions in their own right and show the composer at the peak of his form.

Long before Gradus ad Parnassum appeared, however, another teaching manual had been published. By the end of the eighteenth century Clementi was in great demand as a teacher, but involvement with instrument production had forced him to curtail the time given to individual tuition. Astute as ever, he quickly found a way of getting the best of both worlds, for in 1801 he produced his highly successful Introduction to the Art of Playing on the Piano Forte, a treatise for complete beginners. Although the popularity of the piano had encouraged others to publish similar manuals, Clementi's was different, in that the second part of the volume was given over to a copious and varied selection of simple arrangements of graded pieces by diverse composers – pieces often originally written for every type of keyboard instrument. The cunning purpose of this was to demonstrate that the purchase of a piano could open for the tyro, with only the modicum of perserverance, the gateway to a whole new world of great music (see fig. 6.1).

It was his fame, too, as a teacher that, earlier on still, helped lay the foundations of Clementi's success as a piano manufacturer, for it was in 1793 that he took on the young Irish prodigy, John Field, as his pupil. Field had arrived in London that year with his father, a theatre violinist. He was eleven years old, and already well-known in his native Dublin. It had long been thought that Robert Field, John's father, paid Clementi the large sum of one hundred guineas as an apprenticeship fee, but this has now been shown to be by no means certain. Whether true or not, there is no doubt that Clementi took a special interest in the gifted boy, and during the seven years of being in charge, helped him

Fig. 6.1 Clementi: Introduction to the Art of Playing on the Piano Forte op. 42.

greatly. It has also been generally accepted that Clementi made use of Field's pianistic talents to demonstrate pianos to prospective customers in his showrooms. That however could hardly have been the case through most of these years, since Clementi's firm did not commence until 1798. Still, ruthless exploitation of young acolytes was very much the order of the day, and many a young and alluring singer, for example, had had her voice destroyed by over-exposure. In the early days, though, Field showed considerable loyalty to his master, and we can reasonably assume that he did in fact play a useful part in the sale of instruments. It would seem also certain that Field's idiosyncratic style of composition, which had such a strong influence on later composers, was nurtured by the type of improvisations that he indulged in during these sessions. But these showroom demonstrations could only have continued for a short time, for in the summer of 1802, by now twenty years old, he accompanied Clementi on a tour abroad and was not to revisit England until thirty years had elapsed. Although the official tutelage was now over, a definite master and pupil relationship still existed, quite clearly cemented by the fact that Clementi was wealthy while the young Irish pianist had scarcely any financial resources. They travelled to Paris and thence to Vienna, but the main destination was St. Petersburg, where Clementi had arranged for a consignment of his pianos to be delivered, and where he intended to inaugurate a trade.[10]

As soon as the pianos from England arrived, Field was set to work once more demonstrating them to potential clients. It would seem that Clementi was not exactly generous to his protégé during their stay in St. Petersburg, although it is likely that the many stories of their time together had been embellished over the years, since they mostly appear in accounts of Field's life, published at the time of his death in Moscow in 1837. One such was all about a hat, which Field sadly lost, shortly after their arrival in St. Petersburg in the late autumn of 1802. Since Clementi refused to buy him another, and since he was entirely reliant on him for sustenance, he had to endure weeks of the Russian winter before Clementi eventually relented.

Their rooms in the Hotel de Paris were the cheapest that Clementi could obtain, and his parsimony was such, that he and Field did their own laundry by hand rather than sending them out to the washerwoman. Field was also kept on very short commons and was not invited to take part in any of the social occasions and dinners to which Clementi was invited. It is said though that he managed to top up his rations by making friends with one of the waiters.

In June 1803 Clementi left St. Petersburg, but Field remained. It must have been something of a relief for him to part company. By this time, too, he had built up a considerable reputation as a pianist, and however painful the spartan treatment he had undergone may have been, Clementi at least put him in touch with people of influence before his departure, thus enabling him to take the decision to further his career in Russia. There would seem also to be no doubt that relations between the two men remained reasonably amicable from then on, and Field's subsequent fame as a virtuoso undoubtedly played a part in the success of Clementi's business.

Besides pianos, Clementi also provided customers with other types of instruments, including harps, wind instruments – clarinets in particular – and certain kinds of musical furniture such as canterburys, for example. How much these were the product of his factory is not certain. More likely they were manufactured by other hands and marketed under the Clementi label.

But Clementi also published music, and very early in the nineteenth century, when he embarked on long continental journeys, this became an important sideline of the new business. The publication of his own music naturally featured strongly, but the really big catch was that of Beethoven. Beethoven was notoriously difficult with publishers, and for several years Clementi's efforts to interest him proved unavailing. But Beethoven much admired Clementi's piano compositions, citing their passion and exuberance. In fact the elder composer exerted a significant influence on Beethoven's creative output, and it seems probable that this played a part in Clementi's success in eventually persuading Beethoven to allow him to have his works published. At any rate, by early 1807, Clementi's firm had set themselves up as the leading publishers of his music in England. News of his conquest of Beethoven was sent to Collard by a letter written in Vienna on 22nd April 1807, the first quarter of which is perhaps worth quoting, since it demonstrates so vividly Clementi's coruscating personality:

> By a little management, and without committing myself, I have at last made a compleat conquest of that haughty beauty, Beethoven: who first began at public places to grin and coquet with me which of course I took care not to discourage: then slid into familiar chat, till meeting him by chance one day in the street – 'Where do you lodge?' says he; 'I have not seen you this long while!' – upon which I gave him my address. Two days after I find on my table his card, brought by himself, from the maid's description of his lovely form. This will do, thought I. Three days after that, he calls again and finds me at home. Conceive then the mutual ecstasy of such a meeting! I took pretty good care to improve it to our house's advantage, and therefore, as soon as decency would allow, after praising very handsomely some of his compositions – 'Are you engaged with any publisher in London?' – No, says he. 'Suppose then, you prefer me.' 'With all my heart.' Done – What have you ready? – I'll bring you a list. – In short, I agreed with him to take in MSS form three quartettes, a symphony, an overture, a concerto for the violin which is beautiful and which, at my request, he will adapt for the pianoforte with and without additional keys; and a concerto for the Pianoforte: for all which we are to pay him two hundred pounds sterling.

The final decades of Clementi's life were given over partly to business and partly to the promotion of his music, in which however he was only partially successful. Clementi had long wanted to rival Beethoven as a symphonist, but although he achieved a certain succès d'estime, his many essays in this field never achieved lasting approbation. After the age of fifty he wrote very little piano music, though he did publish three big sonatas in 1821. These were his op. 50, of which the third, the famous Didone Abbandonata, was his final major composition for the piano. This sonata is one of the finest in the canon, and its reputation today has greatly increased. But in 1821 Clementi the composer was rapidly going out of fashion. His works did not attune with the taste of the time, being regarded as both old fashioned and severe. Nonetheless Clementi remained as indefatigable as ever in promoting his music, and, as luck would have it, the op. 50 sonatas did receive an ecstatic review in the prestigious London periodical, the Quarterly Musical Magazine (vol. IV page 483). The reviewer clearly could not get over the excitement of what he had met with:

> These Sonatas display so much genius, such consummate art, and such profound scientific knowledge, that we deem it incumbent on us to enter into an elaborate analysis of their construction; not only for the purpose of doing justice to the great talent which has produced them, but of laying before the competitors for musical fame such materials for their reflection and study, as the works of few authors have ever exhibited in such ample abundance as that which is now before us. It is a web of such inimitable texture as to render delicacy compatible with strength, variety with simplicity and splendor with purity – in which, parts that are the most remote from each other are connected with such art as almost to escape detection, and yet in their very minuteness serve the more strongly to work out the masterly design of a great whole...

... and so on for no less than eighteen pages!

It was not unknown for musicians in those days to laud their own merits in print, and it takes little imagination to guess the name of the author of this panegyric.

Clementi retained all his business acumen and energy to the last years of his life, and it was only in 1830, when he was seventy-eight years old, that he finally retired and handed over the firm to the Collard brothers. He died on the 10th of March 1832 and was buried at Westminster Abbey. The stone on the floor of the cloisters reads:

MUZIO CLEMENTI CALLED THE FATHER OF THE PIANOFORTE HIS FAME AS A MUSICIAN AND COMPOSER ACKNOWLEDGED THROUGHOUT EUROPE PROCURED HIM THE HONOUR OF A PUBLIC INTERMENT IN THIS CLOISTER BORN AT ROME 1752 DIED AT EVESHAM 1832

Today there are many direct descendants of Clementi, some of whom occupy prominent positions in public life. Clementi was married twice; the first time in 1804 when he was fifty-two years old to an eighteen-year old German girl, Caroline Lehmann. But Caroline died the following year in childbirth, though the infant, Carl, survived. Clementi was grief stricken and it was not until seven years later that he remarried, this time to an Englishwoman, Emma Gisborne, who gave him four children, two girls and two boys. One of these boys, born in 1816, survived to the twentieth century. He was the Rev. Vincent Clementi, who emigrated to Peterborough, Ontario. On August the 20th 1895, in reply to a nephew who was enquiring after his illustrious father, he wrote as follows:

Dear Cecil, I greatly regret that it is utterly out of my power to furnish you with the information you seek respecting the Clementi family. My father never appeared to take the slightest interest in his children, scarcely even speaking to us. When in the house he spent almost his whole time in his study which was kept locked up to prevent the entrance of intruders. The room had a fireplace in it, & contained his small Wellington-like bedstead, his pianoforte of course, 1 or 2 chairs (no easy one) & a table. The walls were quite concealed by book-cases, faced with cane & reaching from floor to ceiling. He had a beautiful library consisting partly of all the best editions, large paper copies of the classics, handsomely bound. When, occasionally, very seldom, I was allowed a brief entrance to the room I usually found him sitting at his instrument, his fingers at wonderfully rapid exercise, with a vol: of Greek or Latin, generally a play of Euripides or Sophocles on the desk before him instead of a music book.........

And then, after this marvellous pen-portrait:

But all this you will doubtless regard as mere twaddle. I only wish I could have made it less uninteresting.

NOTES

1. 'A piano technician' – It has to be admitted that this is certainly a debatable assertion on my part. The general assumption has been that Clementi, being a wealthy musician, became involved with instrument building as a business venture. That he took great interest in the production of pianos under his name and endeavoured to make sure that they turned out the way he wanted them, has not been in dispute, and the letters to his partners confirm this. I think, though, that there was a lot more to it than that, and, while there appears to be no concrete proof of this, circumstantial evidence strongly suggests that he was much involved with the nuts and bolts of piano building. To begin with, his family background would have encouraged him to have a 'hands on' approach to the trade, and secondly, it was simply not in his nature to be involved with anything by halves. (This is apparent in his music, where an obsession with past theories of composition occasionally mars his output.) Although of written evidence there is little, what there is does however seem indicative.

   Much of Clementi's life was taken up with travelling, for both business and musical purposes. In a letter to his partner, Frederick William Collard, from St. Petersburg, dated June 9th 1806, he reveals his intense interest in the details of piano production:

How goes business? How do you all do? I have but one longing; which is to see again my old friends, &
my concern, especially the instrument manufactory, having plenty of ideas for correction & improvement;
besides the notion of a grand effect which I am almost sure of producing by an invention of mine, which I
shall disclose as soon as I have the satisfaction of seeing my partners again.

(What the 'grand effect' was we may unfortunately never know. One suspects it may have been the
'harmonic swell' device – see pages 70 and 71 – which was not however patented till some fifteen years
after this letter was written.)

Perhaps the most convincing evidence of Clementi's technical ability comes from the Quarterly
Musical Magazine of 1820, and the article on Clementi in this publication was repeated word for word
in Sainsbury's Dictionary of Musicians of 1825:

....to the year 1802, he remained in England, pursuing his professional labours with increasing
reputation; and wishing to secure himself sufficient time for the prosecution of his studies, he raised his
terms for teaching to one guinea per hour. His fame, however, was so great, that this augmentation of price
rather increased than diminished the candidates for his instruction. The great number of excellent pupils,
of both sexes, which he formed during this period, proves his superior skill in the art of tuition; [but
then....] About the year 1800, having lost a large sum of money by the failure of the well-known firm of
Longman and Broderip, 26, Cheapside, he was induced, by the persuasions of some eminent mercantile
gentlemen, to embark in that concern. A new firm was accordingly formed, and from that period he
declined taking any more pupils. The hours which he did not thenceforward employ in his professional
studies, he dedicated to the mechanical and philosophical improvement of pianofortes; and the originality
and justness of his conceptions were crowned with complete success.

A very similar account appears in 'Memoir of Muzio Clementi', page 184 from the 1831 edition of
The Harmonicon, in which 'construction' is substituted for the word 'philosophical':

...A new firm was quickly formed, at the head of which was Mr. Clementi's name; and from that period he
declined taking any more pupils, but dedicated the time which was not demanded by his professional studies
or mercantile engagements, to improving the mechanism and construction of the instrument, of which he
may be said to have first established the popularity.

None of the above would be of much significance if Clementi had been either an instrument builder
or a composer. The combination of the two, however, is of immense importance for the interpretation
of much of the repertoire of classical piano music.

2. According to Leon Plantinga ('Clementi' page 3) Peter Beckford arranged quarterly payments to
Nicolo Clementi – the sum not specified – for seven years until Muzio reached the age of twenty-one.

3. A. Henry Higginson, 'Peter Beckford Esquire. Sportsman, Traveller, Man of Letters. A Biography'
(London: Collins, 1937, page 81)

4. Higginson relates that Beckford heard a performance of this mass, and was thereby inspired to
negotiate with Nicolo Clementi over the 'abduction' of his son. Ibid. page 84

5. Ibid. page 88

6. The typical English music phobia continued in some quarters until well into the twentieth century, and
reached its apogee, as far as I personally was concerned, in the august figure of Sir Claude Aurelius
Elliott, headmaster of Eton College from 1933 to 1949. Although in many ways a fine administrator,
Elliott was not only totally unmusical but positively antagonistic to music in principle. Since Eton was
the nursery of the country's leaders, and since music was degrading and liable to corrupt a youth and
turn him into a milksop or worse, so music had to be discouraged at all costs. So, at any rate, thought
Sir Claude, and he exerted what influence he could bring to bear to circumscribe the activities of the
Precentor of Music, the much loved Dr. Henry Ley, who apparently on occasion was suborned by the

headmaster into conniving with him to cancel or curtail certain concerts. Extensive coverage of all this is found in 'Slow on the Feather' (Michael Russell Publishing Ltd., Salisbury 1986), the entertaining autobiography of the late Wilfrid Blunt, senior drawing master at Eton, who provides a wholly riveting account of Eton before and during the time I was there half a century ago. Blunt makes it quite clear that Elliot represented merely the tip of the iceberg, for the whole ethos of Eton at that time was, whether covertly or no, loaded against the arts, which included not only music but painting and sculpture, and even, oddly enough, theatre.

In his book Blunt expresses surprise that painting was considered somewhat less dangerous than music.

> *I find it strange that, in general, music seems to be more suspect than the visual arts; for at least there are no nudes in the symphonies of Beethoven. An Old Etonian, unknown to me personally and well before my time, wrote to me after reading Married to a Single Life [Blunt's earlier autobiography] 'In one of my reports, m'Tutor [his housemaster] wrote – "All his many shortcomings must, I suppose, be attributed to his musical temperament" '; and Lord Harewood, who when at Eton helped me with my gramophone concerts at the Drawing Schools, likes to quote the remark made by his uncle (the Duke of Windsor): "It's very odd about George and music. You know, his parents were quite normal."*

Claude Elliott might well have said exactly that (Ibid page 129).

I think, however, that it was not music itself that was the problem, but the performance of it. For the composition of music, like painting and writing, tends to be a private occupation, but music, when created, lends itself to public performance. And while devotional music, and choirs or orchestras full of a large number of fairly anonymous people were broadly accepted, soloists, whether singers or instrumentalists, were a different matter altogether. For soloists show off, indeed flaunt themselves in public, and even, to add insult to injury, seem to expect themselves to be applauded for doing so! Such people were clearly effete, and probably homosexual, and to be avoided at all costs. (Blunt quotes from a letter to him by an Etonian

> *I did not know until I read it two years ago that among the upper classes during the first years of the century to describe someone as 'musical' implied that they were probably homosexual. [Ibid. page 125])*

This attitude towards public performance does appear to be a trait embedded in the English psyche, and goes back a long way, certainly till the early eighteenth century, when a whole host of foreign musicians invaded London, including in particular coloratura sopranos who gave highly embroidered performances of operatic arias.

These were certainly not to everyone's taste, and the enormous success of Gay's 'The Beggar's Opera' of 1728, with its catchy, down-to-earth English folk tunes, bears witness to this. The average Englishman's lack of interest in serious music, and the woeful standard of amateur music making, was often savagely attacked by satirists (see illustration page 81).

In the nineteenth century things got even worse. The proliferation of large concert halls encouraged ever more public performances by soloists and these provided a catalyst for the increasing distrust of music amongst certain leaders of British society, reaching a climax during the first half of the twentieth century, before happily gradually evaporating after the Second World War. Amongst the upper classes in Beckford's day, music was fine if it served a celebratory purpose, or was engaged in for social reasons. Hence Beckford's musical activities in Italy and his 'purchase' of Clementi to entertain his guests. Hence too the popularity of The Noblemen and Gentlemens' Catch Club, founded in 1761, in which the upper classes, together with professional musicians, met socially to sing madrigals together, and which has remained popular throughout the twentieth century.

It is truly ironic that Higginson, in his biography of Beckford, applauds him for turning away from music to sport (which was to culminate in the publication of his classic volume 'Thoughts on

"A Little Music" or — the Delights of Harmony

Hunting'), when today only the stone deaf can be sure of avoiding music altogether and when political correctness dictates that foxhunting is taboo.

7. The influential Quarterly Musical Magazine, in its 1821 no. XI edition, was pleased to bestow its approval in a lengthy review:

From the long and deep attention there has been bestowed on the structure of Piano Fortes, and the eminent success with which every hint for their improvement has been pursued, we were not prepared to expect any invention that might add to the general powers of the instrument, although among the prodigious assistances mechanics are able to lend to art, we should not have doubted that there might be yet some particular parts susceptible of a superior construction. – The object of Mr. Collard's invention is however general, and it imparts not only a new and richer degree of tone, but it submits a choice of fresh varieties and degrees to the player, which can hardly fail to call forth novel and beautiful effects in performance........ The final part of this review is given over to an excellent analysis of the harmonic swell, and reminds one again of the British love of "continuity of sound": *The improvement.... is an additional bridge on the sound-board, not for the purpose of regulating musical intervals (the string lengths between the two bridges remain always untuned), but of augmenting the duration of the vibration, and consequently increasing and beautifying the tone. This bridge, which he calls 'the bridge of reverberation', is placed at a regulated distance on the sound-board; and the important advantage resulting from it is, that the motion given to the principal part of the string by the impulse of the hammer is kept up by the bridge of reverberation, instead of being suddenly checked by an attachment to an unyielding substance. The prolonged vibration produces an extraordinary purity, power, and continuity of sound somewhat resembling the richness of an octave below.*

From this essential improvement the Patentee's second invention is derived, which is as follows:

On the old plan of passing the strings directly from the side of the case to the original bridge on the sound-board, it became necessary, in order to prevent the jarring noise of those portions of the wire which lie between them, not only to place some soft substance on the top of the moulding, but also to weave a piece of cloth between the strings (known today as 'listing'). *The second improvement, which the patentee calls the Harmonic Swell, substitutes a novel action for those portions of the string which lie between the two bridges, yielding most sweet and melodious tones. The performer, by lifting a valve, is enabled to elicit those harmonious sounds through a well-known sympathetic relation between accordant strings, without touching those portions of the strings which produce them. The augmentation of sound caused by this means resembles in some measure the effect of lifting the dampers, but without producing the same confusion, since every note on the body of the instrument is regularly damped as the performer lifts his finger. By this apparatus a threefold power of augmenting the sound is acquired; whereas instruments of the common construction have but one caused by lifting the dampers.*

The first augmentation of power is by lifting the harmonic swell.

The second – by dropping the harmonic swell and raising the dampers.

The third – by raising the harmonic swell and the dampers together.

...........The improvements, as simple in themselves as their effects are striking, enable the player greatly to extend the variety of his performance, and are acknowledged by the first professional judges to have given a new character to the instrument of the most effective kind. That which we heard appeared to us to produce the kind of prolonged tone which arises in a room of fine resonance, and the power was certainly vastly augmented. Upon the whole, the inventor seems to have accomplished far more than could have been expected after the very high state of improvement the piano forte had already attained.

8. I am grateful to Patrick Phillips for this account, which I understand is based on the papers of Elijah Davey, cleric and local historian, and which is part of The Harley Collection at the British Library.
9. Es ist doch in der That eine ungeheure Unverschämtheit den Namen eines noch lebenden Künstlers so unerhört zu mißbrauchen, und ihn dem Werke irgend eines Sudlers in Wien vorzusetzen; denn daß dies nichts mehr als jämmerliche Sudeley ist, die Clementi's Bediente besser muß machen können, lehrt der flüchtigste Blick auf dies elende Machwerk....... (Allgemeine Musikalische Zeitung, 15 May 1799).
10. In this he did indeed have considerable success, and the reputation of Clementi instruments spread over Russia to such an extent that they greatly influenced the subsequent design of Russian makes.

CHAPTER SEVEN

The Clementi Pianos

When surrounded by old keyboard instruments one is hardly aware of the absence of furniture, for they are often not only beautiful articles of furniture in their own right, but are sometimes deliberately designed to take the place of tables, sideboards and cupboards. At Finchcocks there are nine pianos by Clementi's firm, which is more than that of any other maker apart from Broadwood. It is evident from many passing remarks in Clementi's voluminous correspondence that he set considerable store by the appearance of his instruments, and many of those here are

Square piano by Clementi and Co., London, circa 1815

Upright grand by Clementi and Co., London, circa 1804

particularly beautiful. An example of this is the square piano on six turned legs, built circa 1815. Although as an instrument it is unexceptional, the case is lustrously veneered in figured Brazilian rosewood (not easily obtainable today, since the tree is under preservation), and edged with another Brazilian wood, gonçalo alves (there does not seem to be an English equivalent of the name). The attractive dustcover is grained in imitation of rosewood, and decorated with small flowers in gold leaf.

Of the five grand pianos, four are horizontal and one vertical. The vertical one is indeed an upright grand piano, and not just a very tall upright. When the two doors are pulled open the shape of a grand can be clearly seen. Although there seems to have been little interest in the idea of a vertical piano during the eighteenth century, vertical harpsichords ('clavicytheria') had been made for several centuries, and were still being made in Dublin after the square piano had become fashionable. Since the clavicytherium is a horizontal harpsichord on end it was natural to extend the idea to horizontal grands. Such an instrument was patented by William Stodart in 1795, who termed it 'upright grand pianoforte in the form of a bookcase'. The Clementi upright grand has indeed this double function, which was so popular in those days, for the shelves on the right can take a considerable amount of sheet music, or indeed books.[1] It also, when the doors are decorously shut, looks to be a handsome and, at nearly 8½ feet tall, important article of furniture. The piano is not dated, but was almost certainly made not later than 1805. The beautiful case is veneered in mahogany with satinwood banding and light and dark stringing. Silk panels, with pleats radiating from a central tassel, cover the doors, and enable the sound to emerge without them having to be opened. Should more volume be required, then of course the doors can remain open during performance. Musically speaking there is no disadvantage in a vertical as opposed to a horizontal design, and also there is one definite advantage, in that the sound is projected forwards instead of up into the air (which is why the direction in which the lid on a grand is pointed is so important for the listener). Upright grands, such as this, were made until the 1820s, but only in modest numbers, for the obvious disadvantage of such an instrument rapidly dawned on manufacturers; the wasted space under the stand meant that it could only fit under tall ceilings, and so sales were severely circumscribed.

The conventional upright, therefore, which commenced production at the start of the nineteenth century, soon overtook the more expensive and less convenient upright grand

‘Cottage’ cabinet piano by Clementi and Co.,
London, circa 1825

in popularity. Very often, though, like the
upright grand, these instruments were
surprisingly tall, sometimes as much as
seven feet. They were invariably known as
‘cabinet pianos’, the term ‘upright’ being
but seldom used.

Small cabinet pianos of Clementi's
firm were usually termed ‘cottage pianos’
and the pretty little instrument illustrated
is of this sort. Again, the piano is not
dated, but would have been made towards
the end of Clementi's life, probably
between 1825 and 1830. It has the normal
sticker action and two pedals – keyboard
shift and sustaining. Unlike grand pianos,
though, the keyboard remains still when
the left pedal is depressed. Instead, the
stickers are simply angled to the right so
that the hammers, housed on top of them,
strike either two strings or one string per note instead of the full complement of three.
Because the keyboard does not move, there is no slider to prevent a single string being
struck, such as English grands of the period have, so a certain amount of practice is needed
with one's left foot in order to gauge the amount of pressure needed to choose between
due corde and una corda.

The four horizontal grands of the collection, of which only one is dated, are all both
very stylish and very different from each other in appearance. The earliest was made
shortly after the turn of the century and is especially elegant with its mahogany veneered
case decorated with satinwood banding and "dog-tooth" stringing. The lid is solid
mahogany and treated in the same way. The interior of maple lightens the whole aspect of
the instrument, as does the maple keywell with purple wood crossbanding, and the display
of roses, sweet peas and convolvulus painted on the nameboard. The instrument has the
normal five and a half octave compass from F to C (FF-c⁴) and is now in full playing order,
having been restored by David Winston of Biddenden, Kent, who had been for a time a
member of the team of craftsmen at Finchcocks. The tone colour is remarkably clear and
incisive, and the damping is more immediate than one would expect from an English
grand. A rather strange thing, though, about this piano is its surprisingly narrow trestle
stand. There seems no reason to suppose it is not original, yet it appears to have been
made for a five octave instrument. During the rather tortuous period between 1798 when
Longman and Broderip went bankrupt, and 1801, when Clementi was in a position to start
his own company, it seems likely that there might have been a quantity of unused stock,
and that the stand had originally been destined for an earlier model altogether.

Another grand dates from the second decade of the nineteenth century, and was
probably made about 1815. It is rather more elaborately decorated than the earlier one.
The exterior is veneered in mahogany with rosewood cross-banding and brass stringing,

Grand piano by Clementi and Co., London, circa 1800

and the lid of solid mahogany is similarly treated externally, but the cross-banded part is inlaid with stamped brass decorations of a stylised vegetable type. The inside of the case is, again, veneered in maple with black stringing. The unusual stand is of a type known as 'sabre leg' or 'scimitar leg', since it was supposed to imitate the shape of a cavalry sabre. It is in two separate parts. The keyboard end has a trestle with four incurved legs capped with hollow brass balls and hairy lions-paw castor mounts. The tail end has three similar ones fastened back to back. The legs are veneered in mahogany and rosewood. The compass is six octaves, FF-f⁴. Of the five grands in the collection, this is the only one with the far more useful range to the high f, rather than to the c, a fourth below. Although this lower compass is to be found quite frequently in other English makes of the time, it seems to be especially common in Clementi pianos.

'Sabre-leg' grand piano by Clementi and Co., London, circa 1815

The last two Clementi grands are contemporary with each other, and can therefore be regarded as twins, though not identical ones. One of them is dated 1822 and has the number 156 stamped on it. This is the serial number for this particular model. Another number – 17626 – is written in ink on the wrestplank. This is the cumulative instrument number, i.e. the 17626th instrument to have been built by the firm. The other grand has the number 132, from which one concludes that it is slightly earlier in date. However, it is unlikely that it was made before 1821, since that is the date of the patent for the harmonic swell, and both these grands are equipped with this mechanism. The 1822 grand is the better preserved of the two, and is a fine performing instrument, with considerable power, and the clarity that one comes to expect from this make, which stems largely from the construction of the soundboard. Soundboards are the souls of musical instruments, and Clementi's firm paid a lot of attention

Grand piano by Clementi and Co., London, 1822

to soundboard design. While in many respects Clementi pianos copy Broadwoods (stringing lay-out, striking points, action design), their soundboards are of a different quality. The soundboard of the 1822 grand, for example, which is approximately the same thickness as a contemporary Broadwood, is freer and more resilient. It is very lightly barred and the bars themselves are wide and flat and more like straps, whereas Broadwood bars are heavier and more like girders. An interesting feature of these two pianos is that they both have labels on them, to explain the operation of the harmonic swell. Strangely enough, though, each label gives a different purpose behind the employment of the mechanism. The 1822 grand has three pedals – from left to right, keyboard shift to una corda, sustaining and harmonic swell. The label recommends combining these last two devices:

> *By using the Harmonic Swell and the Damper Pedal at the same time, this instrument gains the whole body of tone caused by the Harmonic Swell, beyond that which Piano Fortes on any other construction can produce.*

The second, undated, piano has the same three devices – keyboard shift, sustaining and harmonic swell. The difference here, though, is that the label on the inside of the instrument gives a suggested usage for all three devices simultaneously. In view of the fact that this is likely to cause problems, if, as it is assumed, you only have two feet available, so an extra pedal, the second from the left, has been added, in order to release the keyboard shift, after the left pedal, which on this piano locks into a due corde position, has finished being used. This rather complicated situation is summed up as follows:

> *The first pedal to the left shifts the mechanism on two strings and fixes it there; so as to leave the feet of the performer for the alternate or simultaneous use of the Harmonic Swell and the Damper Pedal; by which a singularly beautiful and harmonious effect may be produced.*

In these two instruments, then, we find important ways of employing resonance, first by increasing volume through the sympathetic vibration of undamped strings, and secondly by achieving an atmospheric wash of sound.

On Clementi's death in 1832 the Collard brothers took over the helm, and the firm from then on became known simply as Collard and Collard. Throughout the latter half of the nineteenth century the firm remained successful under the control of two nephews of the brothers (one of whom continued the family tradition of being named Frederick William), and was eventually taken over in 1929 by the piano firm of Chappell, which continued to produce instruments until 1969, when they in turn were taken over by Polygram. Some time later Kemble and Yamaha became involved, and Collard pianos are still today available from Yamaha-Kemble. Of the several instruments in the collection by Collard and Collard mention should be made of a fine upright dating from around 1865, and generously donated to Finchcocks by Mrs. Szkoda of Paddock Wood, Kent. The instrument is a perfectly routine domestic piano, but paradoxically it is its very ordinariness that makes it so interesting, for it is unusual for such instruments to be looked after so carefully and to have survived in such pristine condition. Apart from the loss

Upright piano by Collard and Collard, London, circa 1865

of the candle supports on the inside of the keyboard cover and the silk behind the fretwork panel it is something close to its original state, although a small amount of fading of the beautiful rosewood veneer has occurred on the sides. It was fortunate that enough traces of the original silk remained to enable a suitable replacement to be made. An instrument such as this makes a welcome addition to the collection, since it illustrates the very high quality of a standard upright of the mid-Victorian period.

Grand piano by Collard and Collard, London, circa 1840

Grand pianos by Collard and Collard are notable for their robustness and reliability, and the collection has an exceptionally stylish instrument from around 1840. The piano is lavishly embellished and appears to be a very early example of the rococo revival which was to become more important during the course of the nineteenth century. The case is decorated with an elaborate marquetry of various exotic woods upon a ground of bird's eye maple. Frames of rococo-like scroll and tendril enclose maple panels on the side of the instrument, whilst three compositions of fruit, flowers and musical instruments etc. are inlaid on the lid, which itself is edged with a carved gadrooned decoration in maple. The stand is surprisingly high, and consists of a frame and six cabriole legs, all carved in maple with flowers, shells and scrolls. Similar decoration is to be found on the lyre and on the outside of the key cheeks.

Collard and Collard pianos are difficult to date because of the Bond Street fire in 1964 that engulfed Chappells, and which destroyed all records of the business. Throughout history fires have been the bugbear of piano firms. In 1856 a vast fire destroyed the Broadwood factory, and incinerated around one thousand instruments. Half a century earlier, Clementi himself suffered a similar severe setback, which was reported in the London 'Times' on Saturday 21st of March 1807:

> *About five o'clock yesterday morning a fire was discovered on the premises of Messrs Clementi & Co., musical instrument makers, Tottenham Court Road. In the course of an hour the conflagration threatened the destruction of the whole of the adjoining neighbourhood. Happily the prompt arrival of the engines, and the timely exertions of the firemen prevented the calamity spreading; but exclusive of the front of the building scarcely a vestige remains standing of this once extensive manufactory. A similar accident took place on these premises about ten years ago.*

The Broadwood firm rallied round to help Clementi after this disaster, and this kind gesture was reciprocated in 1856 when the Collard brothers provided equipment and tools for the Broadwood workforce. This was especially generous since five years previously on the 19th December 1851 Collard and Collard had themselves suffered a grievous loss, when more than two hundred finished instruments were destroyed in a fire which took place in their headquarters in the Oval Road, Camden Town. This building, as reported by the Times the following day, had been erected within the previous twelve months, and was in the form of a complete circle on five floors, and approximately ninety feet high and seventy-five feet in diameter. The premises, according to The Times, were utterly consumed in the fire, which

2
> *illuminated the whole of London, until daybreak*[2]

The illustrations, from a pictorial record of the firm printed circa 1920, show the premises after renovation and one of the circular rooms with instruments under construction.

All Collard and Collard pianos have serial numbers stamped in them, but these numbers refer only to the output of the various models, and can no longer, for reasons just mentioned, be dated. However, a separate number, quite distinct from the stamped number, is often found within the instrument. This is invariably in ink, and for this reason has unfortunately frequently become indecipherable over the years. The number is a cumulative one, given to every instrument that left the factory, of whatever type. Although few instruments are dated, nonetheless a sufficient number have been discovered to allocate certain numbers to certain years. From this it would seem evident that the

The Collard and Collard factory in Oval Road, Camden Town The aim of the circular design of the rooms was to maximize the light at all points for the workforce. This however was sometimes self-defeating, as apparently in winter the craftsmen sometimes boarded up the windows to keep out the cold.

Finchcocks instrument was built in the early 1840s and possibly in 1844. The nameboard is marked 'Collard & Collard', while underneath is written 'Late Clementi, Collard & Collard'. Another fairly similar grand by Collard and Collard in the collection, in a straightforward rosewood case, has an earlier stamped number (1029 as against 3339) and a somewhat shorter compass (six octaves, FF-f⁴ instead of six octaves and two notes, FF-g⁴). This indicates that this instrument is of a slightly earlier date. Corroboration of this is provided by the fact that the wrestplank is stamped 'Clementi & Co.', which implies that old stock was not being wasted.

These two pianos are both excellent instruments and retain the fresh clarity that is such a marked characteristic of all Clementi pianos. Both instruments are bichord, and, since there are only two strings for each note, the keyboard shift invariably produces a very beautiful una corda. Trichord instruments of this period have keyboard shift mechanisms which, unlike pianos of an earlier period, move only to due corde, for reasons explained in chapter 15, page 188.

The compass of both instruments is restricted, and small instruments of this type were usually referred to as 'cottage grands'. An odd feature, indeed, of many grand pianos in the early years of the nineteenth century is their compass. When the portly Bohemian pianist and composer, Jan Ladislav Dussek (1760-1812), settled in London at the end of the 1780s, he fell in love with Broadwood pianos, finding them an ideal medium both for his playing and the lyrical effusions of his compositions. His first major work written on English soil is the lovely sonata in B flat op. 23, in which the composer clearly relishes the richness and sonority of his instrument as he explores the full range of effects from the different compasses. Dussek could claim to be the first of the travelling virtuoso pianists, and possibly even the first of the romantic composers, at any rate as far as his use of the keyboard was concerned. But right at the start of his stay in London he felt constricted by the piano's compass, and it was for this reason that he prevailed on John Broadwood to arrange to have it extended up a fifth from f³-c⁴. Thus, on the title page of the first edition of the sonata op. 23 we find the following warning:

for the grand and small pianoforte with additional keys.

In other words, this piece could not have been performed on most of the pianos currently in use at the time of publication in 1793. This was commercial suicide, and is a pointer to the sad end of Dussek's sojourn in London. In 1792 he married the singer, pianist and harpist, Sophia Corri, and together they performed regularly in recitals. Unfortunately, as previously mentioned on page 50 he was tempted into business, and so joined up with Sophia's father, Domenico, to found a publishing company (Corri, Dussek & Co.), which of course published his own music. Probably Dussek would have stayed in England for good, were it not for the fact that the business went bust, but he fled abroad in 1799, never to return. His unfortunate father-in-law was jailed for bankruptcy, and Dussek failed to meet up ever again with his wife and their daughter.[3]

A few years previously, also possibly at Dussek's instigation, John Broadwood began to build pianos with a six octave range. The earliest extant Broadwood piano with this range was made in 1796 and is now in the Museum of Fine Arts, Boston, Massachusetts. For these six octave instruments Broadwood lowered the bottom note to CC and kept the top note the same. This would have seemed a natural arrangement since it followed the lay-out of his firm's larger harpsichords which were then only just at the end of their production. Another reason for extending the compass downwards rather than upwards may have been due to the likelihood of the sonorous tone quality of the bass benefiting from the increased area of soundboard rather more than the treble would have done. Whatever the reason, though, it was hardly a good idea. No composer at the time wanted more notes in the bass, but they very much wanted more notes in the treble. Therefore, although in theory pianos with the compass CC-c^4 were six octave instruments, in practice they still remained 5½ octave ones. But this applied only to the British Isles. On the continent, and particularly in Germany and Austria, they preferred the higher range, FF-f^4, and this was indeed the compass used by so many of the greatest composers, including Beethoven and Schubert, when writing for the six octave instrument. In point of fact, Broadwood, amongst other firms, did make a few six octave grand pianos with the continental compass, and many square pianos had this range too, presumably because the 'English' compass necessitated an increase of long strings in the bass register and therefore an extended width of the case. The fact though that a few six octave grands with the higher compass were being built by Broadwoods during the first few decades of the nineteenth century makes it quite extraordinary that the firm sent out to Beethoven a piano with the lower compass, CC-c^4 It is particularly astonishing, since Thomas Broadwood actually visited Beethoven at his home in Vienna in August 1817, and would, one should have thought, have taken the trouble to find out what Beethoven needed for his music.

In England, the top F of the compass (f^4) only became common when 6½ octaves were made. The earliest extant Broadwood grand with this compass dates from 1820. Thereafter in England 6½ and 6 octave grands were made concurrently. Because the top note of English pianos varied so much, it became normal for composers in England to write alternative versions at a lower pitch when the music rose above c^4. This was not always the case, however. Another outstanding emigré musician in London, a good friend of Clementi and sharing many of the same interests, was the German-born pianist, composer and teacher, John Baptist Cramer (1771-1858). As a boy of twelve, Cramer had studied under Clementi for a while, and the latter's influence remained with him throughout his career. Along with Dussek and Clementi, he may be said to make up a triumvirate of the finest and most influential pianist-composers in England at the end of the eighteenth century. Younger, and with a life ahead of him lengthier even than Clementi, Cramer dominated English music as a piano teacher, commanding high fees, and was generally referred to by his pupils as 'Glorious John'.

Like Clementi, Cramer went in for music publishing and piano manufacturing. In 1824 he joined up with two partners, Robert Addison and Thomas Beale, and Cramer pianos continued for the following 140 years until the firm was taken over by Kemble & Co. By 1824, pianos with a compass of 6½ octaves were becoming quite common and Cramer's music, although mainly written for the lower compass, sometimes at this period reaches to top f^4. In 1825 he produced for his pupils a delightful album of piano studies, with amusing titles.[4] The pieces vary a lot in difficulty. No. 23, 'The Gilded Toy', makes neither pianistic nor instrumental concessions (see fig 7.1 page 99).

Clementi, right to the end of his life, eschewed the higher compass for his piano music. In the early nineteenth century he concentrated on large scale symphonic compositions, and only returned to writing for the piano at the end of the second decade. In 1821 he published his three op. 50 sonatas, and a group of Monferrinas, an Italian dance that had become for a time immensely popular in Regency London. These twelve little pieces keep to the compass CC-c^4, yet continually hug the topmost notes, as if the composer were longing to climb higher.[5] At this time, too, Clementi was much involved with finishing 'Gradus ad Parnassum'. In 1804 and 1810 Cramer had published his famous sets of studies for the piano (eighty-four in all), and Clementi probably undertook his pedagogical works so as not to be outdone. Although Gradus was not completed until 1826, and although the last of the three volumes contain pieces requiring considerable virtuosity, the compass remains consistently between CC and c³, and can thus be played on any piano. Gradus ad Parnassum contains much beautiful music, and it is understandable that Clementi wished these compositions to be available to all pianists.

Less easily to understand, however, is the compass of Clementi pianos of that time. Clementi was very much an international artist with strong links to the continent. It seems quite natural, therefore, that the 1815 grand at Finchcocks has a compass of FF-f⁴, for it is perfectly suited to all music written in the early nineteenth century by the great continental composers. But the two Finchcocks grands of 1821 and 1822 revert to the lower six octave compass. This is quite surprising, as both instruments are clearly of high quality and would have been very expensive to buy. Clementi's final spate of piano composition in the early 1820s was to a certain extent an attempt to regain favour with the public. His symphonies, on which he had been working for many years, had not succeeded in entering the orchestral repertoire, in spite of respectful accolades in the press, and his piano works were beginning to seem outmoded in their rather severe classicism – at any rate in England, although on the continent he was still regarded as one of the greatest living composers. We have seen that Clementi habitually sent out copies of his music to clients who had just purchased one of the firm's instruments, and it is quite clear that his very strong business sense tended to spill over into his artistic life. It also seems evident that he possessed quite a mischievous streak in his character. The compass of the two late grands is a puzzle. It would though be going perhaps too far to suggest that Clementi deliberately chose instruments with this lower range so that no contemporary music by any other important composer could be played on them...wouldn't it?

NOTES

1. The Rev. H. R. Haweis, M.A., in his delightful book of 1876, 'Music and Morals', (London, Daldy, Isbister & Co., page 409) gives advice about the proper care of the piano:

    Do not load the top of it with books; and if it is a cottage [a small upright] *don't turn the bottom – as I have known some people do – into a cupboard for wine and dessert.*

2. London "Times" Saturday 20th December 1851.

3. Before his arrival in England, Dussek had lived in Paris, and was a favourite of the French aristocracy, and it was for this reason that he came to London to escape the Revolution. After leaving London for good he travelled widely and finally settled back again in Paris, where he died. His enormous girth, coupled with alcoholism, led to his spending much of his final days in bed. In this respect he presaged John Field, who also, twenty-five years later, spent much of his time in bed. But Field, who towards the end of his life gave piano lessons to young ladies from an adjoining bedroom, took to his bed from sheer indolence.

4. J. B. Cramer's 25 New & Characteristic Diversions composed for the Piano Forte and dedicated to his PUPILS [sic]. op. 71. London: published by J. B. Cramer, Addison & Beale, 201, Regent Street, Corner of Conduit Street.

5. Two of these monferrinas are illustrated in Part Two on pages 172-175. While music as an art form was regarded in England by the educated classes in Clementi's day with a certain amount of distrust, dancing to the accompaniment of music was a different matter altogether. For dancing was healthy exercise and encouraged good deportment. Dancing masters were employed (French fiddlers were much favoured) both to train children and to teach adults, and formation dancing became highly popular (see pages 96-98).

Fig. 7.1 Cramer: "The Gilded Toy"

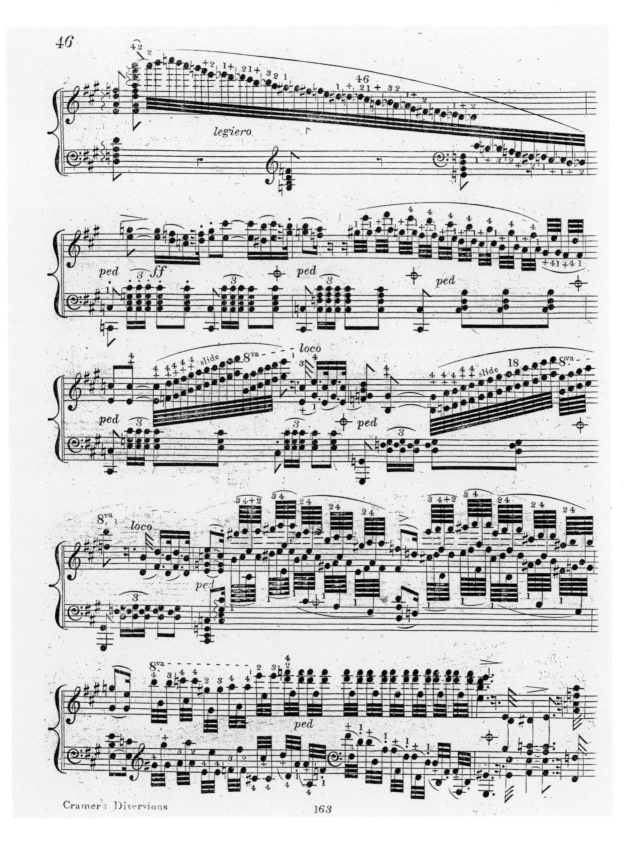

Fig. 7.1 Cramer: "The Gilded Toy" *continued*

Fig. 7.1 Cramer: "The Gilded Toy" *continued*

The Stodarts

After Broadwood and Clementi, the third most important name that we have at Finchcocks in connection with the English grand is that of Robert Stodart (1748-1831). A fellow Scot, Stodart originally joined John Broadwood as a works engineer, (having previously acquired engineering skills during an apprenticeship in Scotland) but left in 1775 to set up a rival firm. To begin with, however, there was little rivalry involved, since Stodart concentrated on grands, whereas Broadwood, due to the Shudi influence, and possibly also due to depression after the death in 1776 of his much-loved twenty-seven year old wife, Barbara, showed for some time little interest in branching out into pianos. Even square piano production was not started by him until about 1780. For some ten years, therefore, Robert Stodart had the field more or less to himself, for the first mention of a grand piano by Broadwood is in 1785. Stodarts' instruments, almost without exception grands, were modelled on Backers' designs, and show considerable mechanical ingenuity. The Finchcocks Collection has one grand only by Robert Stodart, which is dated 1787. It possesses the customary two pedals, keyboard shift to both due corde and una corda, and sustaining. As was invariably the case with very early grands, the soundboard bridge is undivided. Very shortly after this instrument was made, John Broadwood started building grands with the soundboard bridge in two separate parts, an innovation, which, since Broadwood rather surprisingly failed to patent it, was rapidly copied by rival firms, and which is still in use everywhere today.

The pitch of a piano's string depends on three factors: the length of the wire, its mass and its tension. These factors can be varied with each other. To lower the pitch the wire has to be lengthened and/or the mass increased and/or tension relaxed. If the mass and the tension remain unaltered, the length of the wire has to be doubled for every full descending octave. This means that the bottom notes of many pianos, (depending on their compass), would have to be anything up to twenty feet long.[1] The only way to counter this, therefore, is to experiment with the mass and tension of the wire. To get the best out of iron or steel, and to produce a pleasant full, rich and rounded tone colour, the wire needs to be longer than brass of the same thickness. Otherwise, with a shortened length, tension has to be reduced, and this tends to give rise to a rather uninteresting, 'tubby' sound. Brass wire was traditionally used in the bass of early pianos, because brass differs from iron in density and tensile strength, and produces a very pleasant sound when the string length is shorter than would be suitable for iron. For this reason it is convenient for the purpose of circumscribing the length of a grand piano. But brass breaks easily, and on an undivided soundboard bridge it is dangerously overstretched, while at the same time the iron wire for

Grand piano by William and Matthew Stodart, London, 1802

the lowest notes has to be kept too short. By sharing the same bridge, brass and iron wires both suffer. As a result the brass strings used to snap, which must have caused considerable annoyance, since brass wire in those days was expensive, while at the same time, there was an audible jump in tone colour between the adjacent types of material. Broadwood's divided bridge of 1788 solved this problem completely, and may be regarded as the firm's most important contribution to the evolution of the piano.

The enormous success of the production of square pianos and the wealth thereby generated would seem to have given Broadwoods a commanding position, for a mere five years after the Finchcocks Stodart grand of 1787 was built Robert Stodart decided to retire, at the early age of forty-four. He handed over his business to two nephews, William and Matthew Stodart, and returned to his country of origin. Possibly, however, ill-health may have played a part in his decision to quit, for he apparently caught malaria as a very young man during a spell in Tobago where he worked as a machinery technician in the sugar plantations. Evidence for this is provided by the fact that he stayed thereafter for a short time in Greenland, which was regarded then as a place to go to recover from the disease. All this took place before he joined Broadwoods in London in 1770 at the age of twenty-two. Nonetheless, he managed to enjoy a life of ease on his large sporting estate at Kailzie, near Traquair, Peeblesshire, bought at auction for a sum in excess of eleven thousand pounds. Whether he had a private fortune is not known, but it is difficult to think that a mere thirteen years of work could have provided him with the wherewithal for such a life. In fact the Stodart family did come into an estate through the husband of Robert's sister-in-law, a Riddel from the Borders, who died childless. In this connection it is interesting that Robert's youngest son was christened John Riddel Stodart. Whatever the truth of the matter, Robert's appearance on the Scottish scene apparently caused some comment, as it was reported by William Chambers in his 'History of Peeblesshire' that members of the local gentry were

not accustomed to seeing men of mechanical professions becoming landed proprietors.

Nonetheless it would seem that Robert became a highly respected figure in Scottish society. After selling the Kailzie estate, apparently because Robert's wife had no taste for country sports, the family eventually settled at no. 52, Queen Street, Edinburgh. Robert and his wife had their portrait painted by Sir George Watson, and it was rumoured that Robert himself had been offered a baronetcy by Pitt, which he declined.

The firm continued successfully under the nephews for some years, but suffered gradual decline by the middle of the nineteenth century. Some time after Matthew dropped out, William's son Malcolm joined and the firm became known as William Stodart & Son. Malcolm died in 1861 and it was in that year that the business ceased trading.[2]

The collection has two instruments by the Stodart nephews, the beautiful painted square of 1807, described in Chapter Two, and a grand piano dated 1802. This latter is a typical English instrument of its period, approximately 7½ feet long, with 5½ octaves – FF to c^4 and the customary two pedals – keyboard shift to two or one strings and sustaining. In essence, it is virtually identical to the 1801 Broadwood grand and the early Clementi grand, mentioned above, yet these three contemporary instruments made by the three leading builders of the day are remarkably dissimilar. All three are immediately recognisable as early English grands, yet all three are very unlike each other in tone quality. The sound of the Stodart has a tight, brittle, almost bitter taste, whereas the Clementi is quite the other way; rather sweet and fruity in texture, and very clean and clear. The Broadwood is neither as sparky as the Stodart nor is it as luminous as the Clementi. Its somewhat dull and 'woody' tone colour is however offset by its considerable resonance (see chapter 15, note 4 for further mention of 'woody').

Of the three instruments, the Clementi has the thinnest soundboard, and, like the 1822 Clementi grand discussed previously, the barring under this is also the least rigid, being secured with the flat 'rafters' so typical of this firm rather than the normal stiff vertical 'joists' of most English makes of this period. The Clementi soundboard is thus somewhat more flexible than the other two grands under discussion. The Stodart has the longest scale (string length) in the middle part of the keyboard, and the strings are eight per cent longer than those of the Clementi. This alone lends itself to a thinner, more nasal, tone quality. Also the soundboard appears to be made from a different type of wood from both the Clementi and the Broadwood – fir rather than spruce – and this too accentuates the rather harsher tone colour. The Broadwood is the only one of the three to have a tapered soundboard, the thickness of the extreme treble being approximately 8 mm compared to 4 mm in the bass. This helps to produce the characteristic brilliant treble and sonorous boomy bass of typical Broadwood grands.

Timbre is notoriously hard, in fact almost impossible, to describe in words, and this attempt on my part may well invite derision. Yet their own idiosyncratic tone colour was exactly what the early builders of pianos set out to produce, working purely empirically and experimenting with their products to achieve the type of sound they were looking for, and describing their results in exactly the same sort of way as I have just done. If these three instruments are typical of the output of their firms (I am sure that this is so as far as the Clementi and Broadwood are concerned, though I cannot speak for the Stodart, since I have not had the opportunity to hear enough instruments by this firm in first class playing order), then these are the tone qualities that were aimed for by these builders and which became the hallmark of their respective businesses.[3] By the middle of the nineteenth century, standardisation of design and ever-increasing global competition meant that differences between makes of pianos became less clearly defined.

NOTES

1. Throughout the piano's history unusual 'one off' instruments have often been built. The normal length of a late nineteenth century concert grand was 8ft 6ins and this increased by the end of the century to about nine feet. But these massive instruments would appear to have been somewhat dwarfed by the two concert grands built specially for the great American pianist, Louis Moreau Gottschalk, (1829-1869) by Chickering of Boston, Massachusetts, the most famous piano firm in the United States of America during the first half of the nineteenth century, and founded in 1823 by Jonas Chickering, 1797-1853. With these two instruments Gottschalk went on extensive concert tours, (sometimes as many as ten recitals a week in as many towns) usually by train, with a Chickering tuner in attendance. In his entertaining autobiography, published in 1881 after his death, he writes about them:

    > (Gottschalk is on the road, one mile from Harrisburg, Pennsylvania, and the time is 1 pm, June 16th, 1863. The civil war is at its height, and Gottschalk's pianos, travelling by train, have been stranded.)

    > [Gottschalk and his companions] *direct our steps towards the station, which we are assured is only a walk of twenty minutes. We find at the entrance of the depot piles, nay mountains of trunks, encumbering the way. One of the mountains has been tunnelled by a frightened locomotive. Disembowelled trunks disgorge their contents, which charitable souls gather up with a zeal more or less disinterested. The conductor points out to me as a pickpocket, an elegantly dressed young man moving quietly around with his hands behind his back.*

    > *What luck! I have just caught a glimpse of my two pianos – the cowardly mastodons – (Chickering forgive me!) snugly lying in a corner and in perfect health. These two mastodons which Chickering made expressly for me, follow me in all my peregrinations. The tail of these monster pianos measures three feet in width. Their length is ten feet; they have seven and a half octaves, and with the whole of this formidable appearance possess a charming and obedient docility to the least movement of my fingers. Chickering Sons (Chickering, the father, the founder of this great house, has been dead for some years) have, by their labour*

and constructive talent, given for some time past an immense impulsion to the manufacture of pianos. Their manufactures at Boston turn out forty-two pianos a week! Five hundred workmen are constantly employed in them. The later instruments, constructed on new models of their own invention, rival, if they do not surpass the finest European pianos.

I acknowledge my heart beat at the idea of leaving these two brave companions of my life exposed to the chances of a bombardment or an attack by assault. Poor pianos! Perhaps tomorrow you will have lived! You will probably serve to feed the fine bivouac fire of some obscure Confederate soldier, who will see with an indifferent eye your harmonious bowells consumed without any regard for the three hundred concerts which you have survived and the fidelity with which you have followed me in my western campaigns.

'Notes of a Pianist' (Philadelphia: J. B. Lippincott & Co., 1881, page 209)

2. For these intriguing glimpses into Stodart's life I am much indebted to Alastair Laurence, who has furnished me with his researches, and to Peter James, a descendant of Robert Stodart.

    A nice example of aristocratic aversion to 'trade' is provided by a well-known story concerning the Broadwood family, as recounted in Jonathan Gathorne-Hardy's 'The Public School Phenomenon (Hodder & Stoughton, 1977, page 129).

    New money, money from what was loosely termed 'trade', was despised..... I was brought up on a story about my great-grandmother, Lady Glasgow. The Broadwoods had come to the neighbourhood. After a while (they were extremely rich) Lady Glasgow said that although they were in 'trade', they must be asked to stay. But instructions were given that absolutely no one was to mention the word 'piano'. That would be in extremely poor taste. The weekend went very well. Finally, the farewells came, the embraces. At last my great-grandmother went to the window and turned with uplifted arms sadly. 'I'm afraid, Mrs. Broadwood, the time has come to part,' she said. 'Your piano's at the door.' (Reproduced by permission of Hodder & Stoughton Limited)

3. In Clementi's letter to Collard written from Dresden in 1803, quoted above, the tone colour required for his piano by Mr. Davidoff is, as we have seen, thick and sweet, rather than clear, sharp or silver. 'Thick' and 'sweet' are underlined by Clementi, and this is highly indicative, implying that this timbre was a special 'one off' and not the norm. This is certainly corroborated by the pianos at Finchcocks, both by those of Clementi's firm and by those of the Collard brothers in the 1830s, all of which retain the house style – a bell-like clarity. How the piano was made to satisfy Mr. Davidoff can only be guessed at, but alterations of hammer coverings, striking points and thickness of soundboard may all have played a part.

The Viennese piano and influences on its development

I. The clavichord

I crossed the whole kingdom of Bohemia, from south to north; and being very assiduous in my enquiries, how the common people learned music, I found out at length, that, not only in every large town, but in all villages, where there is a reading and writing school, children of both sexes, from six to ten or eleven years old, who were reading, writing, playing on violins, hautbois, bassoons, and other instruments. The organist had in a small room of his house four clavichords, with little boys practising on them all: his son of nine years old, was a very good performer.

Thus Charles Burney, writing about his experiences on the continent in 1772 ('The Present State of Music in Germany, The Netherlands, and United Provinces'). For at least two hundred years before Burney wrote the above, the clavichord had become the most ubiquitous keyboard instrument in much of continental Europe, and especially in the German-speaking lands. There were at least three good reasons for this. First, it was relatively cheap to make (if also deceptively simple, since really good clavichords are not easy to build) – a very practical advantage in a country such as Germany, where music was regarded as an essential education for people of all walks of life. Secondly, it was very quiet to play, and again, this was clearly helpful for teaching purposes in schools; while thirdly, it happened to be, and still is, the most subtle of keyboard instruments. It is this last factor, the enormous challenge it presents to players, that made it such a much loved instrument for so many of the greatest musicians.

The collection has two clavichords, both of the early nineteenth century. The smaller of the two, by Georg Friedrich Schmahl of Ulm in Germany, was made in 1807, and is a fretted clavichord. A very simple plain instrument, the case is of fir, painted a dull red, and the interior is unpainted. But it has an attractive keyboard with the naturals covered in plum-wood and with stained fruit-wood sharps. It has no stand, which was to be expected for small instruments at this time, but simply rests on any convenient table top. As is so with all clavichords, the strings, in common with the piano, are struck, but instead of a piano hammer which bounces back after impact, the striker (the 'tangent') hits the string and then remains in contact with it. The reason for this is that the tangent acts both as the implement for setting the string into vibration and also as a second bridge. Keyboard instruments need two bridges over which the strings ride, but the clavichord has only one fixed one, the second being the individual tangent for each note. The tangent therefore has a double function. The volume can be varied (usually, it must be admitted, from about pppp to pp), but the tangent must always remain in contact with the string (or strings) that it hits in order for the sound to continue, for the vibrating length of the string is the distance from the position of the tangent to the fixed bridge. Because of this permanent contact with the string while the sound continues, the tangent has another function, unique amongst keyboard stringed instruments: by pressing hard against the string it can increase its tension and thus raise the pitch. A rapid up and down shake of the fingers on the keys will therefore achieve a kind of vibrato effect similar to that which a violinist employs. Known as (die) Bebung, from the German 'beben' to shake, and a noun coined especially for this instrument, it is a much loved aid to expressive playing, and used by clavichordists to enrich lyrical passages or to emphasize individual notes. The Bebung is in fact only half the vibrato that a violinist can do, since the pitch can be raised above the note but not sunk below it.

In the case of fretted clavichords, such as the 1807 Schmahl, some of the strings (or normally pairs of strings) serve two notes rather than one, since two tangents can strike the same strings in different positions, thereby altering their speaking lengths. The notes are invariably adjacent to each other, and if both tangents strike the same strings at the same moment only the higher note will be able to sound. This does not matter too much, since in music of this period you do not often expect to hear intervals of a semitone simultaneously, and it saves space in the construction of the instrument. Economy of means does seem also to have an additional subtle virtue, since it tends to add to, rather than detract from, the efficiency of musical instruments, and small fretted clavichords are often very lively and responsive. By the beginning of the nineteenth century, however, they had begun to go out of fashion, and rather more massive unfretted instruments, in which the strings serve their own individual notes, became more typical of the period. The large Swedish clavichord of the collection, built in 1806 by Lindholm and Söderström is a good example of this. The instrument is as loud as they come, but is still very quiet compared with a harpsichord or the very earliest type of piano. Yet this type of clavichord was common in Scandinavia until the 1830's, and would undoubtedly have been used in families for many subsequent years. Although it is hard to imagine compositions for the piano, such as Beethoven's, being performed on such an instrument, the incomparable touch of the clavichord ensured its popularity throughout the centuries, with but a relatively short period of obsolescence in the latter part of the nineteenth.

Fretted clavichord by Georg Friedrich Schmahl, Ulm, 1807

In earlier times, if something was no longer in vogue, for many people it was as if it had never been. The harpsichord, totally dismissed by Dr. Burney in his Rees' Cyclopaedia article, had been made, as we have seen, in considerable numbers right up until the 1790s, but the clavichord remained popular throughout much of the

Clavichord by Lindholm and Söderström, Stockholm, 1806 This clavichord has the extended compass often seen on instruments made around 1800. From about the middle of the eighteenth century Swedish clavichords began to exceed the dimensions of their German counterparts. The adoption of iron stringing, and a more Pythagorian scaling, in which the strings double in length at the octave until quite far into the bass, produce a very long instrument, longer in fact than many harpsichords. Instruments of this date now present an austere appearance without mouldings and with plain tapered legs. The workmanship however is excellent, as a close examination of the key levers will reveal. The soundboard graining is diagonal, rather than parallel to the long axis. The combination of a painted exterior (in our instrument unfortunately not original) with mahogany veneer on the inside of the case is very usual. Sometimes the painting would take the form of a grained decoration in imitation of rosewood or mahogany, but was more often a pale blue, white or grey.

continent for a considerably longer period. Yet in England they hardly existed, so very little was known about them. Even so, one might have expected rather less floundering in the dark from the editor of a serious London annual publication devoted to musical matters. The following astonishing passage is taken from the 1829 edition of The Harmonicon:

> *The Clavichord, or Clarichord, was an instrument of which but an imperfect description is to be found in any author that we have had an opportunity of consulting. That it was in the form of a square piano-forte, is evident from a woodcut in the **Musurgia** of Luscinius; and that its tones were rendered exceedingly soft, by means of slips of cloth by which the strings were muffled, seems almost certain; but the manner in which the keys communicated with*

*the strings, was unknown to both our musical historians. As to Rousseau, and the authors of the **Encyclopédie Methodique**, they do not even mention the instrument. Both Hawkins and Burney must have read Luscinius in rather a careless manner, for the former omits his description, though he gives a **fac simile** of his wood-cut; and the latter says, in "Rees' Cyclopædia," that the Clavichord had "no quills, jacks, or hammers," though the very author to whom he refers as an authority, informs us, in speaking of various keyed instruments, (the **clavichordium** among the rest) that they are struck by **plectra**. (**Musurgiæ, lib**. 1.) The Clavichord, it may then be assumed, was a kind of square spinnet, the sounds of which were much softened by dampers in continual action. And this opinion is confirmed by what the Père Mersenne says in his **Traité des Instrumens a Chordes** (Liv. iii. prop. iv.) of which the **Manichordion**, or **Epinette sourde**, which instrument was, we feel assured, the same in all respects, the name excepted, as the Clavichord.*

1

*– **Editor of the Harmonicon**.*[1]

Cristofori's pianoforte was an attempt to improve on the design of existing harpsichords by enabling the player to achieve variety of dynamics simply and quickly. Attempts had previously been made in the seventeenth century to overcome the instrument's inability to produce rapid changes in volume, by a number of devices of varying cumbersomeness, but none had proved very satisfactory. Cristofori's astonishingly successful keyboard action solved the problem at a stroke, but it did rely on a rather tricky finger touch, and this was something Italians were unaccustomed to. The clavichord, which relied entirely on a refined and accurate finger touch for effective playing, and for that reason had become, in many countries, the essential tool of practice for all serious keyboard students, had for some reason in Italy, though once popular, fallen out of fashion by the end of the seventeenth century. Cristofori's invention was therefore to a large extent an alien concept, and may well account for the fact that it took a long time to establish itself in Italy. Eventually, as we have seen, it was taken up by grand piano manufacturers in London in the latter half of the eighteenth century.

The influence of the clavichord is evident in the musical attributes of classical Viennese pianos. Like the clavichord tangent, which is fastened to the key, the piano's hammer, which faces the player at the rear of the key, is fastened to a vertical housing, called the Kapsel. When the hammer rises with the rear of the key, a projection at the back of the hammer, known as the Schnabel (beak) hits an obstacle and the front of the hammer is then flipped up against the string. This action became known in later years as the Viennese Prellmechanik, from prellen, to hit or bump. (A description is found in the Glossary, under 'Viennese Action'.) This apparently very simple keyboard mechanism enables the player to achieve considerable subtlety of control within an admittedly somewhat circumscribed range of volume. In addition, the action imparts to the player a feeling of intimacy with the sound production, similar to that of the clavichord, the notes seeming to come out of his or her very fingers.

In the Germanic countries piano production increased rapidly in the last two decades of the eighteenth century. The type of grand piano, known as the Viennese fortepiano, started life however not in Vienna but in Germany, and appears to have been the brainchild of Johann Andreas Stein (1728-1792). Stein started an instrument building business in Augsburg in 1750, when he was only twenty-two years old, and soon made a name for himself. Because of his natural versatility he built a considerable range of different types of keyboard instruments, including organs, harpsichords, clavichords and some amazing hybrid instruments, in which, for example, harpsichords and pianos were combined into one instrument. In the early eighteenth century the leading maker of pianos was Gottfried Silbermann (1683-1753), a member of a distinguished family of organ builders. Silbermann's grand pianos were based closely on Cristofori's piano design, and Stein was conversant with his instruments. But Stein's ingenuity and innovative temperament led him to construct a type of piano far removed from Cristofori's piano design, and one which became the foundation of all subsequent pianos to which the appellation 'Viennese fortepiano' is given. Whether or not Stein actually invented this form of Prellmechanik is debatable, but it seems certain that he alone was responsible for incorporating in his grand pianos a refined version of this action, which included an efficient escapement. The instruments had the advantage of being very sturdy, and the mechanism could be pushed into or pulled out of the case with no trouble. The tone was clear and precise, and the dampers cut off the sound instantly. The first great composer for the piano that we associate with Stein is Mozart, who, in 1777 at the age of twenty-one, probably on the recommendation of Leopold his father, who was a native of Augsburg, visited Stein and was captivated by his instruments. Strangely enough, in Vienna at this time there seem to have been no indigenous piano builders. There was an abundance of keyboard instruments of various types, but the only pianos were imports. English pianos were especially prized and many squares and some grands from London found their way to Vienna. When Mozart took up residence in Vienna in 1781 at the age of twenty-five, he had recourse to a Stein piano lent to him by the Countess Thun, but a few years later he acquired a piano by Anton Walter (1752-1826). Walter was the first important builder of pianos in Vienna. His instruments made some significant improvements to those of Stein's and it could be said indeed that he established in Vienna the whole style of piano design that we associate with the Viennese school. The date of Walter's arrival in Vienna is not known but is believed to be around 1780. At about the same time many other builders set up shop in the city and by the 1790s piano building in Vienna had become a thriving business.

II. The pantalon

Just at the time that Cristofori was developing his harpsichord 'col piano e forte' a weird and wonderful stringed instrument made its appearance in Germany. This was a kind of giant dulcimer, apparently nine feet long, and boasting nearly two hundred strings, which had to be sounded by the performer striking them with hammers of various sorts. The inventor of this instrument, Pantaleon (or Pantalon) Hebenstreit (1667-1750) was a virtuoso executant, and apparently electrified audiences wherever he went by the astonishing variety and richness of sounds he produced, and also by the circus-like antics he indulged in, as he leaped around while playing. The instrument was christened 'Pantalon' by Louis XIV, who was very taken with it when Hebenstreit played in Paris in 1704, while the elector of Saxony, August II, gave him a court appointment on a large salary. Hebenstreit died in 1750, a wealthy octogenarian, but after his death his invention, in spite of a number of interested musicians, rapidly faded into oblivion. The pantalon, though, was basically just a large dulcimer, and the dulcimer, found in various guises all over the world, is, and was, in Europe purely a folk instrument, the present most famous type being the Hungarian cimbalom. Throughout history, folk instruments have a habit of coming into fashion for a time, and then disappearing back into the streets again. Thus Burney, in a paragraph about the dulcimer for Rees' Cyclopaedia, saw fit, somewhat portentously, to write:

> The instrument has not the honour to be admitted into concerts, and is seldom used, except at puppet-shews[2], and by itinerant musicians.

But Hebenstreit's invention, coupled with his skill at playing it, exerted a most profound influence on piano builders, out of all proportion to its purely instrumental importance. To begin with, the strings were quite undamped, which allowed Hebenstreit to achieve astonishing cascades and washes of harmony from his huge instrument. In addition, varying tone colours could be produced by the several hammers that Hebenstreit employed to strike the strings, the heads of which were either of plain wood or covered in a soft material. The effect of all this was novel and exhilarating. It then occurred to a number of instrument makers in Germany that this extremely difficult instrument might be made accessible to the average performer if a keyboard were added so that the hammers could be operated mechanically rather than by hand. The resulting instruments, which were often advertised as 'pantalons', superficially resembled pianos, but unfortunately had none of the refinement of Cristofori's invention. Nor could the player hope to emulate the subtle effects that Hebenstreit is said to have produced, since the touch of these keyboard versions was crude and unwieldy. Like Hebenstreit's giant dulcimer, though, the strings were undamped, so that all the notes ran together, and they usually incorporated a plethora of gadgets to produce different types of sound. These Neanderthal-like instruments died a natural death during the eighteenth century, but their legacy is to be found in the various tone colour devices that are such a feature of the classical 'Viennese' piano, the most important of which is the so-called 'moderator', a mechanism which inserts small strips of cloth between the leather covered hammers and the strings. The ubiquitous sustaining mechanism to keep the dampers raised from the strings, operated by the right pedal of a modern piano, is another offspring of Hebenstreit. Indeed, so much did they in those days relish the cacophonous effect of notes colliding together, that some early continental pianos dispensed with damping altogether, and, like Hebenstreit's instrument and the keyboard version, employed totally undamped strings. However the halo of sound caused by very light dampers, which became a salient feature of English-type pianos, did not lend itself musically to the clear incisive voice of the Viennese instrument. As a result, instant cutting off of sound by the dampers soon became the norm with Viennese pianos, while undamped strings through the sustaining mechanism became more the reserve of special effects.

These various gadgets undoubtedly had their uses as musical adjuncts. The pianos, although louder than clavichords, were still very soft, and tended to be a little quieter perhaps than the average harpsichord. Undamping the strings increased the volume, and this could be resorted to occasionally, since the purity of tonal texture failed to obfuscate the clarity to an undesirable level. Mutation devices, such as the moderator, are more effective with clear sounding instruments, which is one reason why they were seldom found in the somewhat coarser toned English pianos at that period.

These then are the two great dynasties of classical pianos, known today, somewhat illogically, as the Viennese and English schools. Most pianos, made anywhere in the world, adhered to one or other of these types, or to an amalgamation of the two. The English piano became the one we all know today, whereas the Viennese died out, not because it was not good enough, but because it failed to become loud enough to cope with large modern concert halls. Yet paradoxically the Viennese piano was arguably the finer instrument. Its clarity and wonderful touch put it on a high pedestal. Cristofori's action is the prototype of the modern piano action, but the Viennese action was every bit as efficient and musical. However, as pianos became louder, hammers became bigger, and large heavy hammers mounted directly onto the keys rendered the touch both tiring and unwieldy. Bösendorfer, arguably the greatest of all modern piano firms, used the Viennese action throughout the nineteenth century, and indeed kept it as an alternative action for customers who owed loyalty to it until 1908.

NOTES

1. The Harmonicon 1829 part I, page 291, editor's footnote under a memoir of C. P. E. Bach, whose favourite instrument the clavichord was. It would seem that nothing goes from memory more quickly than that which has just gone out of fashion.

2. It would be a mistake to infer from this reference to puppet shows that they were of no consequence, and that the dulcimer had no useful function. Puppet theatres in London, which drew fashionable crowds, had considerable social and political import, for they were, in a sense, physical and active versions of the caricatures that existed in prints and drawings.

The Viennese pianos at Finchcocks

I. The eighteenth century instruments

At Finchcocks we have Viennese pianos ranging in date from 1793 to 1867. The earliest is the 1793 grand piano by Sebastian Lengerer. The instrument was built in the town of Kufstein in the Tyrol before Lengerer moved to Vienna. Little is known about this maker, other than that he worked in Vienna until 1809, in which year both he and his forty-eight year old wife died. The piano has many of the attributes of Stein's pianos, and it is thought that Lengerer may himself have been a pupil of Stein. The frame of the instrument with its double bentside is typical, and the action is remarkably similar. The Lengerer is the nearest the collection has to an early 'Mozart' piano. The touch of the Viennese action is excellent, and the timbre is quite sparkling, which is characteristic of pianos of an early date. The case is decorated with beautiful cherry wood parquetry in a herring-bone pattern. The inside of the lid however is a bit of a disappointment, since it is covered with what at first sight appears to be rather dirty featureless wallpaper. Since a veneer exerts a certain stress on wood such as the lid of this instrument, it is usually advisable to veneer both inside and outside to prevent any cracks appearing. But the underside of the lid of the Lengerer has never been veneered, and the paper was therefore probably put on to hide fissures in the wood. This sort of treatment was certainly not uncommon at the time. While it is true that beautiful lid paintings are found on many antique keyboard instruments, particularly harpsichords, some of the most exquisitely decorated have totally plain lid interiors. It would seem therefore that the innards of an instrument were not considered to be of visual importance, and this implies that it was customary to play with the lid of the instrument closed. This appears to be borne out by the many depictions in contemporary art of musicians seated at the keyboard. But why this should have been so is not at all obvious, since these pianos speak less clearly when muffled in this way. Possibly it was considered inelegant to observe the nuts and bolts of an instrument while being used for musical entertainment, and this too would at least explain one purpose of the mysterious so called 'dust cover' – the wooden board resting over a large area of the strings on some pianos, and which is singularly ineffective at keeping dust away.[1]

Pedals are not exactly objects of beauty either. Knee levers on the other hand tuck away and do not detract from the outline of a piano. The Lengerer, like most similar pianos of its period, has just two knee levers, one for the sustaining mechanism and one for the moderator. The strange predeliction for the left rather than the right which we have noted before concerning English squares is also very common with this type of instrument, so instead of pressing down with your right foot, as you would do at a modern piano, you have to press up with your left knee. Some writers have averred that this shows that the sustaining device on Viennese pianos was seldom used since it is so cumbersome to operate. But I can find no evidence for this, and most players in my experience find not the slightest difficulty in managing knee levers, so long as the legs are long enough, and even then a footstool can overcome the problem. But it does require a little more muscular effort, whereas to operate a pedal with the heel resting on the ground is undoubtedly more relaxing. Viennese-type pianos eventually followed the fashion of English instruments therefore, and by the second decade of the nineteenth century knee levers had become fairly uncommon.

Elegance was very much a desideratum for builders of pianos of the Viennese type, and the Lengerer is a fine example of this. The key naturals are of ebony and the accidentals bone. This was the norm at the time in Vienna, though not in England, and people then, as now, found it attractive. After about 1810 however, most Viennese pianos had changed to white naturals of ivory or bone with black accidentals of ebony or of fruitwoods stained black. Various reasons have been given for this. Christo Lelie[2] suggests that, because there were in

Grand piano by Sebastian Lengerer, Kufstein in Tyrol, 1793

classical Vienna so many undated pianos, the makers, by changing the colour of the keys, demonstrated that they were building the latest models. He also mentions that most Viennese pianos had cases decorated in vivid cherry, whereas English instruments, which were becoming increasingly influential on the continent, and which invariably had white naturals, normally posessed cases of a more gentle mahogany. While this is certainly true, it hardly explains the reason for the change. As the nineteenth century wore on, the cases of English pianos were often decorated with an astonishing array of garish veneers, but the modern colour arrangement of the keys still obtained. The most likely explanation is the simplest. It is only the accidentals that define the layout of the keyboard. The naturals count for nothing in this respect. But black overpowers white, and a sea of black naturals deflects the eye from the accidentals, and makes it difficult to take in the whole layout of the keyboard at a glance. While this is of little importance for the experienced keyboard player, it seems to be a definite disadvantage for beginners and the less advanced. An

Grand piano by Michael Rosenberger, Vienna, circa 1800

analogy can be made with signposts. White writing on a black background is often considered attractive, but is not so clear to read as black writing on a white blackground.

Roughly contemporary with the Lengerer is the beautiful grand by Michael Rosenberger (1766-1832). The instrument is undated but was probably made between five and ten years later. Rosenberger was the most distinguished of a family of piano builders. Although he had no direct descendants, one of his brothers (Johann Baptist) and two nephews (Peter and Balthasar) worked independently in the trade. As well as making pianos, Rosenberger enjoyed a considerable reputation as an experimental organ builder, and four years before his death commenced a new line in combination piano-organs. His innovative approach to instrument building is evident in the Finchcocks piano. Although superficially fairly similar to the Lengerer, being veneered in cherrywood, though plain this time, and with the standard two knee levers for, on the left, sustaining, and, on the right, moderator mechanisms, it is actually technically more advanced. The instrument is much more sturdily built and there are improvements in the mechanism, including dampers which land on the strings noiselessly, unlike those of the Lengerer, which make a perceptible plonking sound. Also the mechanism now has a back check to stop the hammers bouncing excessively. This useful improvement to the Viennese action was first incorporated into pianos by Anton Walter, under whom Rosenberger is believed to have trained. The bridge is considerably thicker, thus tending to reduce the rapid decay of sound, which is such a feature of early Viennese pianos. Evenness of volume is an aid to legato playing, and although the difference in this respect between the Rosenberger and the Lengerer is marginal, it is nonetheless in line with developments in musical interpretation, when a somewhat choppy staccato type of playing was becoming gradually outmoded.

Michael Rosenberger was however just one of a great many piano builders trading in Vienna at this time. Most operated small family businesses, the husband and wife often joined by the children as unpaid semi-skilled assistants. They catered for the enormous demand for domestic instruments by the Viennese middle classes. Vienna at this time was an outstandingly beautiful city, full of gardens, parks, cobbled streets and magnificent buildings; a lovely place to live and work in – so long as you kept your head down. For Vienna was also venal and corrupt, and the centre of a police state. Subversion was highly dangerous, so if you were intelligent and sensible, you didn't dabble in political waters. The Biedermann, therefore – the honest citizen – kept himself to himself and made his own amusements, of which home musical entertainment was the most in evidence.

II. Some early nineteenth century instruments

By the early years of the nineteenth century domestic music-making had become such an essential ingredient of family life that piano building was becoming big business. In London, too, there were many piano firms, but in London anyone could set up shop as a maker if they set their mind to it. Not so in Vienna, where all public activity was highly regulated. Restrictive practices were oppressive and instrument building was the ultimate in closed shops. To obtain a licence to sell an instrument that you had made was no mean feat. To begin with you had to be articled to a builder for up to five years, after having first been approved as a suitable applicant by the guild. Further years had then to elapse before you were entitled to apply to become a fully fledged builder. For this a large fee was demanded, often far beyond the means of the applicant, together with a sample of craft work for assessment. If successful you then had to purchase a licence to run a workshop. These licences were inordinately expensive, sometimes as much as thirty times the annual salary of the builder. Licences though were fixed in number, and you might have to wait years before one became available. But even when all hurdles had been cleared, your troubles were not necessarily over. Innovation was frowned upon, and experimental work was considered tantamount to unfair competition. This produced of course a tendency towards uniformity of design and detail, itself exacerbated by the fact that materials had to be bought from sources licensed by the guild. If you acquired ivory, say, from an unlicensed trader, you could be prosecuted.

While it is true there were certain ways you could operate legally outside the guild system, such as by paying an annual state tax, it would seem however that many builders made pianos surreptitiously, often passing them off as secondhand instruments in which they were dealing. Quite the most successful builder to operate outside the guild system was Anton Walter (1752-1826). During a wait of ten years to obtain a workshop licence, he claimed to have produced no less than 350 instruments with the help of fourteen employee assistants. Walter eventually joined the guild and exerted great influence on many contemporary builders including Michael Rosenberger. The years of freedom outside the guild apparently allowed Walter to experiment uninhibitedly, and this led to the technical improvements, some of which are to be found in the Rosenberger grand.

The upsurge in demand for pianos during the first few decades of the nineteenth century was such that between 1815 and 1833 no less than 387 keyboard instrument builders have been found to have carried on their trade in Vienna. Pianos were now being produced in all shapes and sizes and for many different purposes, and their influence spread far beyond the confines of Vienna and Austria. There were uprights – not as common as half a century later, but often magnificently ornate and of strange proportions. An interesting example at Finchcocks is the Viennese-type upright from the first decade of the nineteenth century by Leopold Sauer of Prague. The instrument is in pyramid shape, a very popular design for uprights in the German speaking countries, and one in which some Viennese builders, (Martin Seuffert, for example, who in 1816 advertised his Pyramidenklaviere) specialised. Sauer's instruments frequently feature a clock, which is perhaps a little surprising, as it makes one wonder whether one would have to play in time with the ticking. At the time of writing, the Sauer piano's clock does not work, so this is a supposition sadly waiting to be verified.

Another unusual upright of the collection is the 'Lyraflügel' or 'lyre piano', attributed to Johann Christian Schleip of Berlin. Schleip specialised in instruments of this nature, and although other builders made lyre pianos, ours follows very closely the design of the Lyraflügel by Schleip in the Museum of Fine Arts, Boston, which is thought to have been built around 1835. Instruments such as this are very rare in England, and display the German commitment to bold experimentation in piano case design. The imaginative use of the lyre and the lion's paw feet shows how serious was the interest in neo-classicism at this time, especially in Berlin, where the great urban building projects of Schinkel were in progress. It is an upright grand in a mahogany case, with a hopper action which could be regarded as a variant of the English system. The compass from DD in the bass finishes in the treble most surprisingly on an accidental – $f^{\#4}$. There are strings for g^4, however, so it seems that some embarrassing error occurred during construction. Although interesting from a decorative aspect, the instrument is unpleasant to tune because of the position of the wrestplank. This, instead of being directly above the keyboard, is placed to the right side of the lyre, so that the tuner must stand in an uncomfortable position for the lower notes.

While uprights were often clearly intended to be valued as objects of beauty, some pianos were actually built as integral parts of fine pieces of furniture, the keyboards appearing as drawers in

TOP **Pyramid piano by Leopold Sauer, Prague, circa 1805**
BOTTOM **Lyre piano attributed to J. C. Schleip, Berlin, circa 1835**

German or Austrian portable square piano, circa 1815

tables or in bureau bookcases. The very smallest instruments were the 'dressing table' or 'sewing table' pianos, often very pretty with a mirror and toiletry accessories attached. The anonymous Finchcocks example is not perhaps a typical dressing table piano, since it has no toiletry accessories, though it does possess a small mirror within the interior of the lid, which is surrounded by a maple veneer and decorated with penwork. It was probably made in Germany or Austria around 1815. It may well have been used for a lady's dressing table, but very small portable pianos such as this one very frequently had mirrors attached, and were used for many different purposes. The instrument is veneered in cherry and is only twenty-one inches wide. There are just three octaves, f^1-f^4, which implies that it was only expected to be used for very simple melodies without much accompaniment.

Bigger than the dressing table piano, but still remarkably small, is the delightful little square by Anton Walter. Squares, or Tafelklaviere (table pianos), to use the more appropriate German term for them, were far and away the most popular type of piano at the time, not just in Vienna, but all over the western world, and the sort of keyboard instrument for the home that the average family aspired to. They were not as cumbersome as grands and fitted neatly into the drawing room, while at the same time, as has already been noted, they were handy as articles of furniture. Grands in any case were not always regarded as superior instruments, as modern ones are today when compared with uprights. There are instances in classical times of composers and pianists actually preferring squares to grands, not for visual reasons but for their musical qualities. In the nineteenth century, square pianos had indeed become an honoured and cherished part of family life, and in the New World in particular they were generally very highly appreciated.

Anton Walter probably set up shop in Vienna around 1780, for it was in January 1780 that he married in Vienna. His bride was a widow (Elisabeth Reisinger) with three children. One of these children joined Walter's business and became a partner. The Walter square is undated but was probably built during the first decade of the nineteenth century. It could not be earlier than this, for on the name board is written 'Anton Walter und Sohn' and 'Sohn' refers to this stepson, who joined the firm shortly after 1800. For its type, the piano is quite outstanding and a joy to play. In spite of its diminutive soundboard, the definition is so true that it can be heard with great clarity at considerable distances. The tone colour is very beautiful, and the pure sound is aided by the fact that there are no unison problems in tuning, for there is only one string for each note, and a single string cannot go out of tune with itself. The action – Walter's advanced Prellmechanik in miniature – is every bit as good as that of a contemporary Viennese grand, and the touch is as sensitive as one could wish for. The compass of four and a half octaves (C-f^3) of course limits the number of works that can be played. This is unfortunate in the case of Mozart, for Mozart had a piano by

Square piano by Anton Walter and Son, Vienna, circa 1805

Walter (a grand, dating from around 1783 and now in the Mozart Geburtshaus in Salzburg), and one therefore naturally wishes to hear Mozart on the Finchcocks instrument. Mozart's piano music uses a compass of five octaves almost throughout, and after a page or so, one usually finds oneself running off the bottom of the keyboard. Even so, a surprising amount of classical music is playable, including in particular some of the early sonatas of Haydn, and even a little Beethoven. Also, when trying pieces out on the instrument it becomes clear that a lot of notes written for the missing bottom half octave are in fact the doubling up of notes an octave higher, and can therefore often be omitted without courting disaster.

The Walter square, although so small, is one of the loveliest pianos in the collection, and one tends to relish and treasure the notes as one plays them (particularly as there are so few of them). It is so light that it can be easily carried under one arm, and was probably designed to be used as a travelling piano. Pianos by this time had become such essential adjuncts of social life, that instruments were being built specifically for taking on journeys. A certain early nineteenth century Viennese builder of such instruments enjoyed the most apt name of Joseph Klein (Joseph Small) and his Kleinklaviere were sought after by customers, who even arranged for him to install them into their carriages.

Throughout the nineteenth century Viennese grand pianos remained remarkably consistent in design. In a sense they were so outstandingly musical that they did not need to change, whereas in contrast the rather coarser-toned English instruments somehow had the seeds of development within them. In addition, the negative influence of the Viennese guild of instrument makers, which had such a pervasively stultifying effect on entrepreneurial activity, meant that for a long time the only really obvious difference between them was the varying usage of strange ancillary tonal gadgets, such as 'janissary', or 'Turkish' music. 'Turkish Music' meant extraneous objects put into the piano, that you would not expect to find there: drums, bells, cymbals – almost anything went. Some pianos had as many as eight pedals, the better to exploit these devices.[3]

Turkish military bands had been known to the Viennese for many years and itinerant gypsy musicians from other parts of the Habsburg empire, who played entrancingly exotic folk music, were very much in evidence on the streets of Vienna in the early nineteenth century. Satirical pieces, making fun of this music, and for which these devices could add an enjoyable frisson, then started to appear in print.[4]

Unfortunately there is no hard and fast evidence that the great classical composers were either interested in or took these devices seriously. Hummel, a purist, indeed wrote dismissively in his huge didactic study of piano playing, published in 1828, 'Anweisung zum Piano-forte-spiel', page 437

> ...[apart from sustaining, and soft – i.e. keyboard shift or moderator mechanisms] all other
> pedals are superfluous and good neither for the instrument nor the player.[5]

However, a sense of humour was very much a characteristic of many of the greatest composers, and it seems unlikely that they would have ruled these effects out of court. Because they were peculiar to Viennese-type pianos and seldom found elsewhere, it is probably the case that publishers, who always hate to put into print that which may not be understood, simply ignored composers' intentions in this respect. Be that as it may, most of the signs denoting these devices are found only in the works of the minor composers, who, because they had themselves to pay for their music to be printed, were at liberty to put in what they wanted. As a result, a considerable quantity of fairly awful music, laden with careful instructions for the correct use of these gadgets, found its way into print.

The Viennese grand at Finchcocks by Johann Fritz is a typical example of an instrument equipped with janissary effects.[6] Its four pedals operate, from left to right, keyboard shift to due corde; moderator; sustaining; and Turkish Music mechanisms. The latter does three quite separate things simultaneously. First, three little bells, mounted at the left hand edge of the soundboard, are struck by three little

The Hungarian hussar dancing outside an inn to the accompaniment of violin, tambourine, triangle and a pretty young lady

hammers. A cluster of three bells seems to have been the standard arrangement with these mechanisms, and they look pretty enough, but on their own make rather a desolate feeble sound, (playing the very high pitched notes of $c^{\#3}$, a^3 and $c^{\#4}$ – a forlorn chord if ever there was one), and produce less volume than one larger bell would do. Secondly, a strip of brass on a batten descends onto the bass strings and makes a noise for all the world like the clashing of cymbals. Finally, a large round padded beater smacks a wooden plaque glued to the underside of the soundboard and makes it resonate like a drum. This, it should be said, does nothing for the stability of the piano. All of this certainly makes a surprising effect, but if you press down the sustaining pedal at the same time, the result can be quite startling, for sympathetic vibrations are set in motion in a great many of the undamped strings, thus vastly increasing the volume and adding cacophony for good measure.

Little is known about Johann Peter Fritz, apart from the fact that he had several children, all of whom died before reaching double figures (with one exception, a son, Joseph, born in 1808, who became a piano builder in his own right). His beautiful piano that we have is undated, but is unlikely to have been made before 1814, since a piece of parchment in a part of the action has this date written on it. The exterior is veneered in mahogany and much of the interior in alder, varnished yellow. The keywell has been painted black and has

Grand piano by Johann Fritz, Vienna, circa 1815

ormolu decorations, as have the bevelled corners at the front of the instrument. The four tapered legs are decorated with carved and gilded mouldings and acanthus leaves. The support for the pedal board is, typically, in the shape of a lyre, and this and the accompanying dolphins[7] are painted green with gold details. They rest upon a curved board which is hooked to the two foremost legs. For its period the piano is quietly spoken, with a delicate touch, and its voice, fresh and sweet toned, coupled with its pretty, innocent appearance, makes a quite comical contrast with the violence that it is capable of.

Besides the four pedals there is a knee lever operating a bassoon (Fagott) mechanism. This type of gadget is probably the most frequently encountered in Viennese pianos after the sustaining and moderator mechanisms have been taken into account. It is first mentioned in the 1790s but became commonplace in grands during the first two or three decades of the nineteenth century. It consists usually of a long strip of material, often parchment, pressed down on top of the strings in the bass register, to make a kind of growly bassoon-like noise. By the time the Finchcocks Fritz appeared, knee levers in Viennese pianos were becoming uncommon, so the bassoon mechanism here is perhaps a throwback to the eighteenth century. It would certainly have been safer were the device operated by a fifth pedal rather than a knee lever, for one tends to forget about it while playing. It fits comfortably above the left knee, and a careless movement of the leg can easily activate it. The instrument has been used regularly at Finchcocks over the past twenty years, and on a number of occasions recitals have been greatly enlivened by the unexpected employment of this device.

III. Conrad Graf and later Viennese pianos

Conrad Graf (1782-1851) can lay claim to being the wealthiest and most successful of all classical Viennese piano builders, and he illustrates well the maxim that ready money to hand was an essential requisite for aspiring technicians. For although in the early nineteenth century the guild system was beginning to break down, and indeed, in respect of keyboard instrument makers, had by 1820 been replaced by a somewhat less restrictive association, it clearly remained difficult to operate effectively without financial backing, and the lives of so many luckless craftsmen in those days makes for rather harrowing reading. A certain Maximilian Haidinger, for example, who was born in 1784, applied at the mature age of thirty-three for a permit to make and sell keyboard instruments in Vienna, which however was turned down. He tried again in 1824 and was once more refused. In 1826, at the age of forty-two he made a final unsuccessful attempt. By this time he had acquired a wife and three daughters, seven to thirteen years old. The following year he died without a will in dire poverty in the care of a monastic order.

Graf by contrast appears to have belonged to a family of some means. He was born and brought up in Riedlingen, South Germany, where his grandfather on his mother's side was mayor, and in his late teens moved to Vienna and became articled to Jakob Schelkle, a piano builder. Schelkle died a few years later in 1804, whereupon Graf, following what would appear to have been at that time almost a social convention in the piano trade,

Grand piano by Conrad Graf, Vienna, circa 1820 This piano, with its lively veneer scheme in vertically grained figured walnut, demonstrates the extremely high standards of craftsmanship found in the best Viennese workshops. There are gilt-brass enrichments on the legs and the lyre, and the original inner cover ('dust cover') has been retained. The natural keys are covered in bone rather than the more expensive ivory. The instrument is in outstandingly good condition. It has had very few string replacements and in most respects is in a condition similar to that in which it left Graf's showrooms in around 1820. When it was put into playing condition in the late 1970s all that proved necessary was to replace some of the more moth-eaten cloths and a few strings. The walnut veneer was originally stained or varnished a dark reddish colour. This has almost entirely faded and can now be seen only on the central part of the board which supports the pedals, where the base of the lyre has protected it from light.

Grand piano by Conrad Graf, Vienna, 1826 This is in most respects very similar to the Graf of circa 1820. The main differences are only superficial ones. The veneer is mahogany, the legs are plain, the keywell has ormolu decorations of superb quality, featuring anthemion (or honeysuckle) and other plant motifs, and the naturals are ivory plated. It lacks though the true una corda of the earlier instrument and in addition has lost its dust cover, of which only the metal mountings remain. It still retains however many of its original strings.

married the widow Katherina. Graf then found himself, at the age of twenty-three, the head of a keyboard instrument firm. The business though operated in the outer suburbs of Vienna, and to work in the more desirable inner suburbs, where most of the successful firms were located, Graf had to acquire the correct professional permit, which in 1811 he managed to obtain. The subsequent years saw rapidly increasing progress, so much so, in fact, that in 1824 Graf received the royal and coveted accolade of k. k. Hof-Fortepiano-und Claviermacher (royal and imperial court fortepiano and keyboard maker). The following year he purchased a very large property for his business, a defunct dancehall known as Mondscheinhaus (Moonlight House) in the well-known commercial district of the Wieden (no. 102 Auf der Wieden), which remained his headquarters until his retirement in 1841. The Mondscheinhaus was however more than just a business centre, for it became the home of Graf himself and a considerable number of his employees, who lived in the twelve apartments that he arranged to have built. The main part of the complex was the large workshop where some forty craftsmen were engaged in building pianos. This was a large concern by Viennese standards, and meant that Graf himself would probably have been unable to oversee every detail of the instruments' construction as would have been the case with very small businesses. It probably approached the factory methods of the large English piano firms, where specialized workers operated in different areas, and specialist firms supplied parts and materials. That Graf kept a beady eye on what went on, though, there can be little doubt, for the pianos show a remarkable consistency of excellence.

Graf was very conservative in his approach to the design of his instruments, which was based on the legacy of the eighteenth century master builders, and which remained little altered throughout the years. At Finchcocks there are two Graf pianos of the 1820s, the one dated 1826 and the other undated, but probably made around 1820. Each instrument is highly individual, yet each is recognisably a Graf. The 1826 piano has a mellow tone colour, and has proved itself to be a fine vehicle for the interpretation of early romantic music, such as Chopin and Schumann. The earlier Graf, perhaps surprisingly, is rather more powerful, and has an incisive attack. Both instruments exemplify the highest standards of Viennese piano building, without exhibiting any attempt to be innovative. They can truly be regarded as loud, powerful versions of earlier instruments, and they thus represent the full flowering of the classical Viennese piano. As is normal with Viennese pianos, however, the extreme treble is weak compared with contemporary pianos of English origin, and the contrast in volume between bass and treble is therefore very marked. Both instruments have the standard four pedals – from left to right, keyboard shift; bassoon; moderator; and sustaining. Slightly unusually, the keyboard shift of the earlier instrument moves to una corda, whereas the 1826 piano stops at due corde. Although una corda is sometimes found in Viennese pianos, it was never as common as in English-type instruments. The earlier instrument still retains its dust cover, the subsidiary soundboard that can be employed or removed in performance according to acoustical requirements.

These two grands are the most rewarding of all the Viennese pianos at Finchcocks, for there is little that cannot be played on them satisfactorily. They somehow stretch the music and the musician in a more exciting way than most other contemporary makes. Poised in time at the onset of the romantic age in music, they face both ways historically, and can be effectively employed for the interpretation of repertoire from Mozart to Liszt.[8]

Liszt himself, and many other distinguished musicians, played Graf pianos, and the Mondscheinhaus became something of a Mecca for visiting artists. Chopin, who played in Vienna in 1829 and 1830, recounts how he used to practise every day after lunch at the Mondscheinhaus 'to loosen up my fingers'. For his public appearances he played on Graf pianos on several occasions, and indeed chose them in preference to other makes that were offered to him. His first concert was on 11th August 1829, shortly after arriving in Vienna, and he describes the Graf that he played on as being probably the finest piano in Vienna. Another great artist to visit Vienna was the renowned pianist Clara Wieck. A glamorous nineteen year old, she dazzled the royal court in 1838, who promptly appointed her Kammer-virtuosin (lady virtuoso of the chamber). The following year Graf presented her with the gift of a grand piano, which joined the Schumann household on her marriage. After Robert Schumann's death the instrument was acquired by Brahms. It finally made a return journey to Vienna, where it was installed in the premises of the Gesellschaft der Musikfreunde (the Society of the Friends of Music), the organisation of which Clara had been made an honorary member during her triumphant tour as a teenager.

The most famous recipient of a Graf piano is Beethoven. His instrument, which unusually had four strings instead of three throughout the compass, apart from the extreme bass, was loaned to the composer in January 1826, and was intended as a temporary replacement for Beethoven's much treasured but sadly battered Broadwood grand, which Graf had in his care and on which he was working. Also, to help with Beethoven's appalling deafness, Graf had apparently rigged up some sort of amplifying gadget to be used in conjunction with the piano. Although there are contemporary references to this machine, the only actual description comes from Beethoven's friend, Stephan von Breuning, who describes it as being made of softwood and similar in appearance to a prompter's box (Souffleurkasten).

It had long been thought that this grand piano had been built specially for Beethoven, but this now seems most improbable. Quadruple stringing was one of the very few unsuccessful experiments that Graf indulged in during his long working life. He first started making these pianos around 1812 but production had ceased by 1820. They never took on. The tone colour was not admired, they would seem not to have been appreciably louder than the three stringed variety, and of course they took longer to tune and to maintain in tune. They were strongly criticised by both musicians and builders, including one of Graf's rivals for Beethoven's attentions, the builder Matthäus Andreas Stein, who incidentally also tried to prevent Beethoven from letting Graf take his Broadwood under his wing. So an obsolete unpopular piano of this type would not have helped Beethoven much. Why then did Graf bother about it?

Could it be that he happened to have one of these instruments in stock for which he could not find a use? If this were so, he may then have decided to lend it to Beethoven, not because it was louder, but because four strings per note did have the advantage of being more resistant to rough treatment than three. Beethoven by this time was severely deaf, so the quality of the instrument did not matter too much, while at the same time it stood a chance of withstanding the onslaught of his attempts to hear it. Then when Beethoven had finished with it, or after his death (which in fact took place the following year), Graf would have been able to take the instrument back, and, because of the kudos attached to the composer's name, easily sell it on secondhand (which he did – to a certain Franz Wimmer, a bookseller, a descendant of whom sold it in 1889 to the Beethoven House, Bonn).[9]

Graf however certainly stated that he had made the instrument for Beethoven, for in 1849, some twenty-four years later, on being asked to verify the piano, wrote

> *I made it some years before Beethoven's death, placed it at his disposal and took it back after his death*[10]

Here I think that Graf was either, near the end of his life, very forgetful, or, more likely, somewhat economical with the truth, for he would not have liked it to be known that he had palmed off an unwanted piano onto such an illustrious musician. Certainly he made the amplifying machine, but probably not the instrument itself expressly. It stretches belief that he would have taken the trouble to build a one-off of an outmoded model (for which possibly the design had been abandoned), merely to loan it to Beethoven rather than present it as a gift, as was the case with Clara Wieck. In any event, there would scarcely have been time to build it from scratch, particularly as he was no intimate of the composer, and had apparently been given little advance warning of his being entrusted with the Broadwood. A truer indication of what happened can perhaps be gleaned from a note written at the time by Beethoven's temporary secretary, the violinist Karl Holz:

> *Graf says that it (the Broadwood) is in a pretty bad state, but that he will return it as soon as possible, and in the meantime will send along on Tuesday, to help him out, a four stringed pianoforte*[11]

Conrad Graf lost his wife, Katherina, in 1814, when he was only thirty-three years old. He never remarried, but devoted the years to fostering his business interests, which besides piano building, from which he retired in 1840, took in real estate transactions. One has the impression that he was both patriarchal and avuncular. Proprietors tended to look after their own, and Graf was no exception to this. He appears to have been helpful and generous to his employees, even allowing some of them, while remaining his tenants, to leave his employ and set up their own businesses. He also looked after them when tragedy struck. One such occasion was in 1828:

Mathias Jakesch was an emigrant craftsman, who was born near Loschin, Moravia in 1783. Whether he was actually an employee of Graf is not certain, but he became a tenant in one of the apartments in Graf's home, no. 182 Auf der Wieden. This was in 1827, and it coincided with the moment that Graf was moving house to live in his converted dance hall. Here Jakesch ran a small piano building business, but only for a very short time, for he died a year later, leaving a widow, Walpurga, and five young children, three boys and two girls, between five and fifteen years old. Graf thereupon became the children's guardian, and Jakesch's business managed to continue for a little while under Walpurga's direction. It must have been a struggle, for Jakesch left nothing. The Jakesch grand piano at Finchcocks has a nameboard inscribed Mathias Jakesch, Bürger in Wien (citizen of

Vienna). Bürger in this context refers to the professional status of a craftsman, which had to be acquired by licence. However, inside on the bottom of the instrument in ink an inscription appears. This is now very faint and some of it has yet to be deciphered, but the date 1832 can be clearly seen, and also the words 'Frau Jakesch'. It would seem therefore that the piano was built under the control of the widow, probably with the help of her children, for the following year Frau Jakesch's business ceased, and this was the year of the death of her eldest son, Franz, aged twenty.

Grand piano by Mathias Jakesch, Vienna, 1832 This is the only example in the collection of a piano of the triple bentside type, which first appeared around 1820 and which was characteristic of the more imaginative designs of the central European makers. The exterior of the instrument is veneered in walnut, and the interior in maple.

The Jakesch is a fine example of a late classical Viennese grand, with the slightly extended compass of just over 6½ octaves, CC-g⁴. The most striking visual features are the six pedals, which operate sustaining mechanism, keyboard shift, bassoon, moderator and Turkish Music with cymbal, drum and bells. The moderator has two layers of cloth, one of which is longer and overlaps the other. Not one, but two pedals are employed to work the mechanism. The one moves the moderator bar a short distance so that a single layer is interposed between hammer and strings, while the second moves the bar fully so that a double layer can be struck, thus greatly increasing the level of muting. Indeed, with the two layers of cloth the volume is so quenched, that with a gentle touch the instrument scarcely speaks at all. Employment of the single moderator would probably have been used mainly for lyrical playing (see pages 193-195 for further discussion of this), while the double moderator would have been reserved for very quiet atmospheric passages. Two pedals for this device became quite common in Vienna during the first three decades of the nineteenth century. Graf, for example, fitted them to the 1839 grand that he gave to Clara Wieck.

How much the moderator was used in those days is not known, since there are so few clear indications in printed music of the classical period. But the fact that builders took the trouble to fit two pedals for this device is certainly circumstantial evidence for its popularity.

Yet the moderator, together with all other extraneous gadgets, apart from keyboard shift and sustaining mechanisms, suddenly, from the 1840s onwards, vanished from piano production, not just in Vienna but virtually everywhere. As far as the main commercial firms were concerned, it was as if they had never been. Just occasionally we find remnants of them here and there (cf. the square by Mathushek below), and a crude progeny of the moderator is the left pedal of some cheaper uprights, which, instead of employing the rather expensive keyboard shift, simply covers the whole compass with a large strip of fabric inserted between hammer and strings.[12] There seem to be several reasons for this sudden collapse. First of all, many of these now obsolete devices are more effective with soft spoken instruments, but seem superfluous and rather childish with loud ones. They were also attacked vehemently in the didactic writings of many of the leading musicians. Pianos were becoming ever more sought after, both for the home and for the concert hall, where the public paid to hear virtuosi performing on large powerful grands. Piano production, then, was becoming big business throughout the world, and intense cut-throat competition between manufacturers meant that they were most reluctant to increase costs unnecessarily. The sustaining mechanism of course remained, but of the other two important devices – keyboard shift and moderator – the keyboard shift won and the moderator dropped out. This happened, I think, partly because felt covered hammers, which gradually replaced leather ones over the years, slightly suggest the sound of the moderator anyway, and also because the influence of the English-type piano was so strong, and the keyboard shift was the device most closely associated with it.

The grand by the Viennese builder Carl Henschker, (of whom nothing appears to be known, though the name suggests a Prussian origin), is undated but was probably made around 1840. In appearance it is a bit heavy and lacks the elegance of earlier fortepianos. It is a useful concert instrument however, as it is considerably more powerful than most instruments of a decade or so earlier, yet retains the clarity of texture that is such a superb attribute of these instruments. For this reason it has been in demand for performances in large auditoriums and for recordings with orchestras.

The final instrument in the chronology of Viennese pianos at Finchcocks is the magnificent grand by Johann Baptist Streicher. Streicher was the son of Nanette Stein, history's most famous female builder of pianos. Nanette was the daughter of Johann Andreas Stein, and was brought up in the piano trade. She was apparently also a fine pianist and she married a pianist and composer, Johann Andreas Streicher, who joined her in the business. Streicher pianos soon commanded a leading position in Vienna, and Nanette Streicher's firm became the chief rival to Graf. Johann Baptist joined his parents as a partner in 1823 at the age of twenty-seven. Ten years later, though, both parents were dead, and Johann Baptist then continued to make instruments under his own name until his death in 1871. The present instrument is dated 1867, and is very much the end of the line as far as classical fortepianos are concerned. By this time Viennese makers were beginning to imitate the work of the London and Paris schools of building, and many of Streicher's instruments, as the century progressed, incorporated these features. The 1867 grand has certain concessions to modernity. Although the frame is basically wooden, there are two large iron bars. The keyboard is lower down in the instrument, which makes it look a bit more like an English piano, and there is no moderator mechanism, but the normal modern arrangement of two pedals, keyboard shift and sustaining.

In essentials however the instrument is very traditional, straight-strung instead of cross-strung as some more advanced pianos were by this time, and with a true Viennese action. The instrument is much louder than the earlier Viennese pianos of the collection, and surprisingly sonorous. It possesses a fruity, plummy tone colour, particularly in the middle of the compass, yet at the same time the sound seems somewhat veiled and ill-defined. In these respects it appears very different from similar pianos of an earlier vintage. The one characteristic it has in common with most Viennese pianos is the weak treble, the top notes

Grand piano by Carl Henschker, Vienna, circa 1840 This instrument shows the tendency of Viennese pianos of this period to be designed with a more massive and less elegant appearance than those of a few decades earlier, which still retained something of a neo-classical severity. It can be regarded as a sort of half-way house between the instruments in the collection by Conrad Graf and the late Viennese piano by Streicher. Its heavy framing dispenses partly with the bottom planks found on previous types. However it has still only the minimum of metal reinforcement, consisting of one iron brace between the wrestplank and the header. The unostentatious walnut veneer has maple stringing around the lower part of the case and the instrument stands on three bulbous faceted legs.

being quite puny compared with the middle register of the compass. English pianos have soundboards which are glued firmly down on to the rim, but later Viennese pianos have 'floating soundboards', that is to say, they are only partly glued to the rim in the middle and upper part of the compass. The floating soundboard of a large Viennese piano such

Grand piano by Johann Baptist Streicher, Vienna, 1867 The Streicher of 1867 represents the Viennese-type of piano design at almost the ultimate stage of development. Although it possesses two iron bars above the soundboard and a pressure bar in the treble, its massive wooden framing, especially along the bentside, shows its descent from its predecessors of nearly a century earlier. Its action is similar to the Grafs in design, but heavier, and because of its large hammers the touch is awkward and cumbersome in comparison with the earlier types, which combine delicacy with moderate power. The dampers are quite light and less effective than those found in earlier Viennese instruments, and they thus produce an aftersound which one associates more with pianos of the English school of building. Even at this late date the sharps are capped in ebony rather than made solid as was normal at the time in London and Paris. The case is veneered in walnut, with rosewood inside the front fall which also has some inlaid brass decoration.

as the 1867 Streicher, which has heavy hammers and high tension wire, exacerbates the rather unclear sonority in the lower part of the compass, while the increased compass in the treble makes the top notes seem even weaker by comparison. By this time, too, the Viennese action is clearly beginning to head for extinction, for the heavy hammers mounted on the keys make the touch disconcertingly unwieldy. In spite of all these apparent disadvantages, the Streicher remains a glorious sounding instrument, and an excellent vehicle for late romantic music. It is particularly interesting in this connection that the instrument appears to be virtually identical to Brahms' own Streicher, which was built just a year later in 1868, and which was presented by the firm to the composer in about 1873.

NOTES

1. The dust-cover is discussed fully on page 137-139.
2. 'Van Piano tot Forte' (Uitgeverij Kok Lyra, Kampen 1995, page 102)
3. The most bizarre example of this sort of thing was a combination piano-organ, the brainchild of a minor Czech pianist and composer, Thomas Anton Kunz (1756-1830). Several of these were built by the Prague piano firm of J. and T. Still. Known as 'orchestrions', they apparently were capable of producing no less than one hundred and five different tonal effects.
4. The most famous example of which is of course the 'rondo alla turca' from Mozart's sonata in A major K. 331, a splendid cartoon in sound, which however was written some time before many of these devices had become commonly available on pianos.
5. ....die übrigen Pedale sind überflüssig und haben weder für das Instrument noch für den Spieler Werth.
6. The word 'janissary' is derived from the Turkish 'yeni' (new) and çeri (soldier or military force). In the Ottoman empire, boys from Christian families in the Balkan peninsula or Anatolia, and between the ages of eight and sixteen, were liable, in tribute to the Turkish government, to be compulsorily removed from their homes, taken to Constantinople, brought up as Muslims and educated for a wide range of positions, from gardeners to high-ranking civil servants. Those who eventually entered military service were known as 'yeniçeri' and formed the élite corps of the Ottoman army, numbering from fifteen to twenty thousand. As well as performing military duties they also acted as a police force and formed a body of guards for the Sultan and the Greek Orthodox Patriarch. Their band consisted of shawms (oboes), trumpets, fifes, and a number of rhythmic instruments including cymbals, triangles, kettle drums, bass drums, and the çaĝana (known in English as 'Jingling Johnnie') – a stick furnished with small bells and jingles, surmounted by a crescent and decorated with horse-hair streamers. It was this exotic combination of percussion instruments which began to be included in some Western European military bands from the early eighteenth century, and which became known as 'Turkish Music'. Its ultimate fate was to be relegated to special effects on a number of early nineteenth century pianos, in particular those made in the German linguistic zone.
7. The association of dolphins with lyres derives from the Greek poet and musician, Arion, who lived in Corinth in the seventh century B.C. According to the myth, Arion had taken part in a music festival in Sicily, and had been showered with expensive gifts by his many admirers. However, on his return to Corinth by sea, his success had incited jealousy amongst the sailors, who demanded his death. Arion, therefore, after one last passionate song, jumped into the sea, only to be rescued by a musical dolphin, who carried him on its back to safety.
8. It is strange to imagine a keyboard titan, such as Liszt, coping with a relatively frail wooden-framed and lightly strung fortepiano. Liszt in fact did tend to play havoc at the outset of his career with early pianos, and for this reason sometimes not one but several instruments were provided for him on the platform, so that if one became ruined he could turn in mid stride to another one – which on occasion he did. However, a review of an 1838 recital in Vienna, in which he played on a grand by Graf,

comments first on the lovely sound of the instrument, but then expresses amazement that the instrument held up to the onslaught and that no strings were broken.

9. The episode throws an interesting light on Graf's business practices, which may possibly have been at times somewhat devious. The famous portrait of Liszt seated at a Graf piano in the Mondscheinhaus in front of a distinguished audience of admirers is clearly fictitious. It was commissioned for advertising purposes from Josef Danhauser, whose works, along with many contemporary artists, Graf avidly collected.

10. ...*ich einige Jahre vor dem Tode dem Beethovens Eigens verfertigt und Ihm zu seinem Vergnügen stelt, nach seinem Tode es wieder zurück nahm,....*

11. *Graf sagt, es sey schrecklich zugerichtet; er will es aber, so viel als möglich wieder herstellen, und schick ihn indessen zur Aushilfe ein viersaitiges Pianoforte, welches am Dienstag hierherkommen wird.*

12. French upright pianos, however, often employed the moderator in the nineteenth century, because the characteristic oblique stringing of many such instruments rendered keyboard shift mechanisms difficult to install.

CHAPTER ELEVEN

France

I n the late eighteenth and early nineteenth centuries the city that most rivalled London and Vienna in importance and influence was Paris. It can be said that the ingenuity and innovations of the French makers, more than anywhere else, opened the road towards the modern piano. The collection has several pianos by the three most famous builders of the time – Erard, Pleyel and Pape, all of whom were, as it happens, German speaking and came respectively from the Alsace, Austria and Germany.[1]

I. Erard

The most distinguished of the three is undoubtedly Sébastien Erard (1752-1831), whose importance for the development of the instrument in future years cannot be overstated.

Erard was born in Strasburg, where his father was a furniture maker. The original spelling of the name was Erhard, which Sébastien later frenchified by removing the 'h'. For a time Sébastien trained as a cabinet maker in his father's business, but on the latter's death in 1768 set off to Paris at the age of sixteen to seek his fortune, where he rapidly became apprenticed to a succession of harpsichord makers. There would seem to be a kind of spiritual osmosis between the two great continental artistic centres, and analogies between Paris and Vienna keep cropping up. Like Conrad Graf, who, some thirty years later, made his pilgrimage as a teenager to Vienna, Erard achieved astonishingly immediate success, so much so in fact that he was head-hunted by a great patroness of music, the Duchesse de Villeroy, who gave him a workshop to manufacture harpsichords in her private residence in Paris. As in Vienna, the Paris Guild was both very powerful and very restrictive, and thus opposed to innovation. But Erard, like the Viennese, Anton Walter, was an experimenter by temperament, and so insisted on remaining free from such shackles. This did not go down at all well with the Guild, who tried to force him to close his workshop in the Rue de Bourbon, which he had recently opened after leaving the duchesse's employ. This disaster was however narrowly averted by the intervention of King Louis XVI, no less, who issued a decree in 1785, which allowed him to continue trading outside the Guild. Erard's close connection with royalty and the aristocracy brought him fame, but also danger, and the following year, with considerable prescience, he betook himself to England shortly before the revolution commenced. This change of location turned out to have considerable long-term benefits, first, because it enabled him to foster a trading business in London, which he had previously set up, and which was soon to become immensely successful, and secondly, because it enabled him to acquaint himself more fully with the English technique of piano production, which by now had reached a

Square piano by Sébastien Erard, Paris, 1792

high degree of sophistication. English pianos were at this time greatly esteemed all over the continent, and were particularly fashionable in aristocratic circles in Paris. An inventory of contents, confiscated from aristocrats during the Terror, accounted for a great many pianos from England, far more in fact than for locally made ones, of which, interestingly, the largest number were by Erard. Erard returned to Paris in 1796, and put to good use what he had garnered from his enforced sojourn in London.

Up to now he had concentrated on squares, based on the popular designs of Zumpe, and the 1792 square of the collection is of this specification. The case and lid of this instrument are of mahogany, and the keywell is attractively veneered in fiddle-back maple with satinwood banding and dark stringing. The four tapered fluted legs, made of stained beech-wood, give a delicate feeling to the whole, and elegance is enhanced by the fact that the case is very narrow. The whole instrument is also short and compact, and it is because of this that the right hand end of the front board assumes a curved shape, in order to accommodate the bass strings. Buff and sustaining mechanisms, the normal effects found on early English squares, are present here, but for ease of operation are now controlled by knee levers instead of by hand. A strange feature of this little piano is the inscriptions on the name board of the titles of two operas by Cherubini: Médée and Les 2 Journées, produced in Paris in 1797 and 1800 respectively. What connection, if any, the instrument may have had with Cherubini himself, does not, however, seem possible to establish.

Back in Paris Erard for the first time turned his hands to grands, basing them, with but a few exceptions, on the instruments he had studied in England. None of these can be definitely dated to the eighteenth century, and there is only one known that may possibly be of this period. There are in fact surprisingly few even from the first two decades of the nineteenth century in existence today. The earliest to have survived that can be dated were built in 1801, of which the Finchcocks piano is one of two extant. This is the year that Erard provided grands for both Haydn and Napoleon Bonaparte, neither of which has come down to us. The present instrument is also remarkably similar to the 1803 grand that Beethoven acquired from Erard, and which is now in the Kunsthistorisches Museum in Vienna.[2]

The 1801 Erard is in essence an English grand, with the typical three strings per note throughout the compass, by which a rich tonal texture can be obtained. However, unlike Broadwood pianos, on which it is modelled, individual keys and hammers, for the purpose of adjustment or repairs, can be quickly and easily removed. This useful improvement foreshadows the important inventions of Erard's later years, that so influenced the whole future of piano technology.

A Germanic influence can also be observed. Indeed the 1801 Erard straddles both Vienna and London, so to speak, encompassing, quite successfully, salient characteristics from both these great centres. There are four pedals, reading from left to right, bassoon; sustaining (yet again, to be operated by the left foot rather than the right); moderator; and

Grand piano by Erard Frères, Paris, 1801

keyboard shift to due corde. As a supplement to this last gadget, a knee lever moves the keyboard fully over so that the hammers strike one string only per note (una corda). Here we have a real mishmash of English and Viennese. To begin with, bassoon and moderator mechanisms are never found in English instruments, except, on very rare occasions, by special demand of a customer. The keyboard shift, however, was specifically an English gadget, that was soon to become popular in Vienna, but which was rarely found in Viennese pianos at this date. Pedals were an English feature and knee levers Viennese, and both are present here. English pianos from this period normally had two pedals,

Watercolour of a girl at a French square piano

somewhat comically protruding inwards from the front legs of the case. Four pedals arranged in this way would certainly have posed a problem, so for the first time the pedals are located centrally – an idea that was subsequently exported to Vienna.

The instrument is beautiful to look at, with the neo-classical simplicity that is such a characteristic of French furniture of this period. In Paris alone there were said to be no less than ten thousand workers in the furniture trade, and during the Empire eighty-eight separate firms, many of them patronised by Napoleon himself. The rigorous architectural perfection of French furniture during the Napoleonic period led to rather more austere design, evident in the columnar legs of French pianos around 1810. The influence of the Napoleonic Empire soon spread to Vienna, where it surfaced in the pianos of the Biedermeier period. The two Graf pianos of the collection are good examples of this rather heavy sobriety.

The elegance of the 1801 Erard, like the 1792 square, is manifested most of all by the attractive tapered legs with stamped brass flutings, topped with brass capitals in classical leaf pattern. With very subtle effect two types of mahogany are used for the case: the lid and the longside are of a high quality plain variety, while the remaining sides are veneered in a very striking feathered mahogany. In contrast however to the overall delicate effect, the tail is squared off in the more robust Teutonic fashion. The lid is now faded, though the original colour can be seen on the inside. The lid flap above the keyboard has a double hinge, which is particularly interesting, since the rear part has its original colour, whereas the near part is faded. This implies either that they usually played then with the lid closed, which meant that there was no music stand that could be opened up, or else that the fall was constantly kept open, perhaps to keep the ivories from darkening. The keywell and the interior vertical surfaces, and also the wrestplank, are veneered in maple. This lightens the interior and conveys a delightful feeling of classical purity to the whole instrument.

II. Pleyel

The second great Parisian piano house was founded by the Austrian, Ignaz (Ignace) Joseph Pleyel (1757-1831). Like so many heads of piano firms, Pleyel saw himself first and foremost as a musician. A child prodigy, he had studied as a teenager with Haydn, with whom he retained throughout a lasting close relationship. Natural ability, and a quick instinct for popularity, served Pleyel well throughout his career. As a composer he wrote a vast amount of fairly anodyne music, which achieved quite astonishing success. Fortunately for later generations, the wealth thus created encouraged him to diversify into more

Upright piano by Pleyel, Paris, circa 1840
This pretty little instrument of the low vertical strung type is similar in appearance to the Pleyel preserved in the Convent of Valdemosa at Palma in Majorca, which belonged to Chopin and which he used during his sojourn there.

rewarding activities, including music publishing and piano building. Pleyel was a natural survivor. After some awkward brushes with the revolutionary authorities he succeeded in opening a publishing business in Paris, which was to achieve great importance, and twelve years later, in 1807, his own piano building firm.

The collection has two pianos by Pleyel: an upright and a grand. The upright is not dated but was probably made around 1840. The case is veneered in lovely rich Cuban mahogany, which is contrasted with a nameboard of rosewood. Surprisingly, parts of the interior of the instrument are also, quite unnecessarily, veneered with wood of the same high quality.

The grand dates from 1842 and is remarkable for its unusual partridge feather ('plum pudding') mahogany veneer. The deceptively straightforward appearance of the piano is belied by the subtle decorative details, such as the round wooden handles of the two lid fasteners, which reveal a glimpse of rosewood bursting out, sandwich fashion, between two layers of mahogany. There is also a third lid fastener, but this is merely a dummy, probably put there because English pianos of a similar type would have had a working handle in that position. The listing is of green cloth and both the tension bars and the iron hitchrail are painted green to match. The very short pedals, turned boldly outwards, give a curiously frisky slant to the whole.

An interesting feature of the Pleyel, and one often remarked on by visitors to Finchcocks, is its so-called dust cover, the wooden board housed above the strings and covering a large area of the inside of the instrument. Dust covers were frequently added to grands all over the continent in the late eighteenth and early nineteenth centuries, and to both continental and English square pianos. They are sometimes found in other types of instruments such as clavichords, but were not normally a feature of harpsichords, nor, perhaps rather surprisingly, English grands. Not much appears to have been written about these rather odd adjuncts, perhaps because their function is as yet little understood.

The Pleyel's dust cover is hinged to the spine, and when the lid is raised it too can be raised and fastened to the inside of the lid. Most covers however rest loosely on supports above the strings and are intended to be easily removable. For this reason many have disappeared over the years. This is true for example of the 1826 Graf at Finchcocks, which still retains supports for its cover.

Although there has been controversy over their purpose, the one thing we can all agree on, (as has been mentioned here previously), is that dust covers are pretty useless at keeping out dust, for they can never cover the whole of the innards of an instrument, and

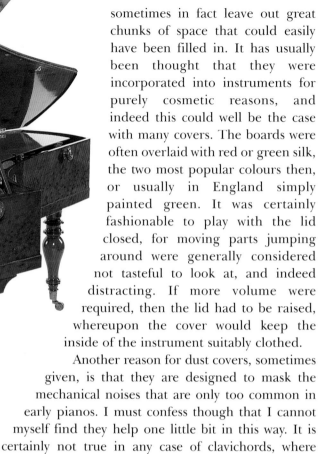

sometimes in fact leave out great chunks of space that could easily have been filled in. It has usually been thought that they were incorporated into instruments for purely cosmetic reasons, and indeed this could well be the case with many covers. The boards were often overlaid with red or green silk, the two most popular colours then, or usually in England simply painted green. It was certainly fashionable to play with the lid closed, for moving parts jumping around were generally considered not tasteful to look at, and indeed distracting. If more volume were required, then the lid had to be raised, whereupon the cover would keep the inside of the instrument suitably clothed.

Another reason for dust covers, sometimes given, is that they are designed to mask the mechanical noises that are only too common in early pianos. I must confess though that I cannot myself find they help one little bit in this way. It is certainly not true in any case of clavichords, where action noise is nil, and the big Swedish clavichord in the collection by Lindholm and Söderström once possessed a large cover.

For many instruments, though, the most likely purpose of dust covers is an acoustical one, and for this reason they are often referred to as subsidiary soundboards. However, if by 'soundboard' is meant a wooden board that augments the volume, then it is hard to see how this could be the case here. When the hammer strikes the strings of a piano, the vibrations set up are transferred via the bridge, over which they run, to the soundboard, which then amplifies the effect. The frames of early grands are quite vibrant, and if a dust cover were to be rigidly fixed to the frame, it is perhaps conceivable that volume could be increased, if only very slightly. But the usual result of having a dust cover inserted above the soundboard is not to amplify the volume, but very slightly to lessen it. If this is the sole intention, though, it seems singularly ill thought out, for one can easily play slightly less loud by finger touch, and if one wants to make a real difference one can simply shut the lid.

What then can be the point of it all?

The clue is to be found in those pianos in which the cover embraces only the upper register of the compass, leaving the bass strings exposed. The purpose here is to kill the upper partials, or overtones, of the instrument, thereby altering the tone colour and making it less resonant. The covers are normally made of softwood, or occasionally hardwood, such as that of the Pleyel, which is mahogany. Even when the cover reaches over the whole compass, the long waves of the lower partials can traverse the wood unrestricted, but the short waves of the upper partials tend to get lost. The result is increase in clarity, and this can be of benefit when an instrument is played in very resonant surroundings, while the removal of the cover can help greatly in dry acoustics. Dust covers are not normally found in English grands, but are very common in Viennese. But the Viennese set great store by clarity, whereas in England resonance had always been such a relished characteristic of pianos that it would never have occurred to the makers to consider trying to diminish it.

Whatever the purpose behind them, dust covers are a good instance of the pains piano firms took in those days over the refinements of their products.

Like so many contemporary French grand pianos, the Pleyel is essentially an English instrument, with four iron bars reinforcing the case to allow high tension wire to be safely used. The dampers, however, are longer than those found in pianos of similar date by Broadwood, and so there is less aftersound, which is more typical of pianos of Germanic origin. The instrument is of particular interest for pianists, since it is the same model as the Pleyel of 1839 owned by Chopin. Chopin had enjoyed a very close relationship with the Pleyel firm, the instruments of which possessed a specially beautiful and intimate tone colour, which clearly appealed to the composer. Whether the touch of Pleyel's grands were suited to him is another matter. Chopin's refined and delicate playing, so much admired but sometimes also criticised by contemporary writers, has often been supposed to have been aided by the light touch of his instrument. By putting two and two together, it has always been assumed that since Chopin was frail and loved his Pleyel pianos, therefore Pleyel pianos were gentle and light. Even the great Chopin scholar, Arthur Hedley, was able to write

[3] *He generally used Pleyel pianos, preferring their light touch and silvery tone.*[3]

[4] But Pleyel pianos do not have a light touch – quite the opposite in fact[4], and the tone colour is anything but silvery – rich dark golden, more like. The touch of the Finchcocks instrument, magnificently restored by the former Finchcocks craftsman, Christopher Clarke, is surprisingly heavy and quite awkward to handle. It is known that Liszt's bold and scintillating accounts of Chopin's music were admired and indeed envied by the composer, and one wonders whether his delicate playing was so, simply because, suffering as he did from consumption, he had not the strength to master fully his favourite instrument. Corroboration of this may be deduced from Chopin himself, when he wrote:

If I am not at my best, and my fingers feel rather stiff and slow, if I do not have the strength to mould the keyboard to my will, to make the keys and hammers behave in the way I want, then I prefer an Erard piano, for it produces its bright limpid tone colour effortlessly. But if I feel strong and ready to make my fingers work without fatigue and without worrying me, then I prefer a Pleyel. The expression of my inner thoughts, of my feelings, is more direct, more personal. My fingers feel in more immediate contact with the hammers, which then translate exactly and faithfully the feeling I want to produce,
[5] *the effect I want to obtain.*[5]

III. Pape

Between 1815 and 1818, and about a half century after Erard set off for France, a business was opened in Paris by the builder from Hanover, Henri Pape (1789-1875). Pape left his surname alone but transcribed his Christian names from Johann Heinrich to Jean-Henri. Like Erard, Pape had interests in London, where he spent many years. This was a period in England when a prodigious number of experiments were being made in piano

The page-turning device

production, most of which, it has to be said, died in their infancy. Nonetheless, their influence on the French builders was considerable, and it is not unreasonable to suggest that, in the case of Pape, they acted as a catalyst to his fertile imagination.

The ultimate in experimental abandonment is surely provided by the eccentric figure of John Joseph Merlin (1735-1803). Merlin was an excellent and ingenious builder, who made not only pianos, but also other instruments, including violins, harps and drums. But, apart from musical instruments, Merlin turned his hand to anything that took his fancy, and it was the astonishing variety of his inventions, coupled with his engaging personality, on which his fame depended. Merlin was born in Liège and came to London at the age of twenty-five. For a while he worked with the firm of James Cox, clockmaker, which gave rise to the invention of his mercury clock, a large and heavy time-keeper, permanently powered by the movement of mercury, an example of which is housed in the Victoria and Albert Museum, London. News of him spread rapidly, and he became the confidant of many in the arts, including Gainsborough, who painted his portrait. Merlin would seem to have traded on the atmosphere created by his name, for he delighted in producing bizarre and spooky effects, one of which was an apparently riderless carriage, or trap, in which the horse was controlled by mechanical devices operated by the hidden passenger. He also ran his own private mechanical museum, with amusing toys, including a clockwork flying bat and an automaton flute, with artificial fingers and air pumped over an orifice. He has been claimed as the inventor of the roller skate, and it was certainly roller skating which caused his undoing. Apparently he had been skating around at a masked ball, while at the same time playing the violin, when he suddenly skidded off into a standing mirror, or cheval glass, shattering it and badly injuring himself. It has been suggested that this disaster prompted his most famous invention, the self-propelled invalid chair, still in use two centuries later.

At that time pianos were made in all shapes and sizes, and there were frequent attempts to disguise them as articles of furniture. William Southwell produced pianos in the shape of semi-circular side tables, and a number of so-called 'sofa table pianos' were made by Broadwood. Some pianos were hidden in bookcases, tallboys or bureau-cabinets, where a keyboard appeared when a certain drawer was pulled open.

Great pains were taken to make things easier for the performer. For lefthanded players, mirror image pianos were made, the treble being on the left and the bass on the right – a good idea, maybe, but one that never took on. Many ancillary gadgets were patented: page turning devices (there is one in the collection, which no one has succeeded in getting to work properly), mirrors to enable hands and music to be seen at the same time, hearing aids; the Brighton builder, Isaac Mott (one of whose exceedingly beautiful grand pianos is in the Royal Pavilion, Brighton) devised a vibrating rod, attached to the soundboard, which had to be clasped between the teeth of the player. Elaborate methods were sometimes indulged in to amplify the rather short sustaining powers of these early pianos, and strange Heath Robinson-like devices started to appear. One such, subsequently taken up by Pape, enabled very rapid repetition of the hammer on the strings of any given note while the key was depressed, the purpose being to imitate the tremolo effect obtainable on a violin. Another odd device sent currents of air over the strings to keep them vibrating, and an even more bizarre invention aimed to stimulate the strings by having pieces of leather flapping against them. Most of these complicated inventions had to be operated mechanically by treadles.

Another fairly obvious way of dealing with the problem of the piano's lack of sustaining power soon occurred to builders. This was simply to join the piano to the organ as a single instrument. This expedient proved popular for a time, and many such combination instruments were built throughout Europe in the latter half of the eighteenth century. Sébastien Erard himself apparently made one for the Queen of France. Another combination instrument was the pianoforte/harpsichord. Since pianos and harpsichords ran neck and neck in popularity for many years, it seemed a good idea for the player to get the best of both worlds by this means. Several British builders, including Robert Stodart, attempted them, with varying success. Probably the cleverest were those of Merlin, two of which have survived. One of these is in the Deutsches Museum, Munich, and is most ingenious. The most important aspect of this instrument is that the hammers have their own eight foot strings, which are struck from above, thus enabling the piano action to be kept clear of the plucking mechanism. Although this may sound rather obvious, most similar instruments by other makers had actions, the freedom of which were to some extent vitiated by the linking process. The Munich instrument also has a piano-like sustaining mechanism for the harpsichord parts, whereby all the jacks are lifted up together from the strings. This is another example of the English relish for cloudy effects caused by sympathetic vibration. Quite the most remarkable thing about the instrument, however, and a typical Merlin tour-de-force, is a clockwork-operated recording device, consisting of a very long roll of paper running the length of the soundboard and connected via the jacks to pencils which marked in code the pitch and duration of each note. Improvisation was traditionally an admired art, and the purpose of the machine was of course to preserve the inspirations of the performer. Sadly, though, not one such flight of fancy has come down to us.

If Pape was not quite in the same class for inspired eccentricity as Merlin, he was nonetheless one of the most tirelessly inventive piano technicians who has ever lived. In the course of his career he took out no less than one hundred and thirty-seven patents, all in connection with pianos. He also outdid Merlin, who built some instruments with six octaves, by producing a piano with an astonishing eight octaves, something not seen again until the arrival of the great Bösendorfer Imperial Concert Grand of today. Pape's importance today, however, lies in the field of instruments of a more modest kind.

The upsurge in popularity of the piano had given rise in England to a steadily increasing number of builders, many of whom, as in Vienna, operated very small, in some cases one-man, businesses. Whereas squares had long been in vogue, and grands less so because larger and more expensive, the upright was a rarity at the beginning of the nineteenth century.

'Piano-console' by
Henri Pape, Paris, 1841

Upright piano by Sébastien Mercier, Paris, 1831

The first and most costly uprights at this time were grand pianos on end, such as the Clementi instrument discussed previously. While they were undoubtedly fine playing instruments and beautiful to look at, there was, to put it mildly, wasted space, both to the right of the instrument, with its hidden bookshelves, and underneath between the legs. Although upright grands continued to be made in small numbers until the late 1820s, the true upright, in the form seen today, with the strings reaching to the floor, began more frequently to appear. Some, such as the cabinet pianos, were still large, six feet or so in height, but there was a definite trend towards smaller instruments. One of the most successful and inventive makers of these was the Londoner, Robert Wornum, (1780-1852), who, around 1815, at the time of the death of his instrument building father, also called Robert, started making really diminutive uprights, somewhat like the mini pianos of today. And it was these instruments that so influenced Henri Pape.

Pape's importance is reflected in the intense interest in very small uprights that was soon to take hold in Paris, and many firms specialised in these instruments during the first half of the nineteenth century. The great advantage of such a piano is the fact that, instead of having one's back to the audience, the player can see over the instrument and can thus, like most performers on other instruments, face the right way – an extremely important factor when the piano is used for accompanying purposes. Another important reason for their popularity stems from the fact that they were often destined for small Parisian apartments. For this reason they were often provided with carrying handles, the better to be lifted up flights of stairs. From 1811 until he set up his own business, Pape had been engaged as foreman in Pleyel's factory, and it was under the aegis of Pleyel that he developed his mini uprights. These pianos, which Pape termed 'piano-consoles', and which were generally known throughout Europe in later years as 'pianinos', were highly

6 regarded.[6] The 1841 Finchcocks instrument is a fine example. Truly a masterpiece of compression, it is only 3¼ feet tall (98 cm) and less than 1¾ feet from front to back (52.2 cm), while the case itself is a mere five inches thick (12.7 cm). Economy of space is achieved by placing the bridge and bars on the front side (keyboard side) of the soundboard, thereby enabling the soundboard itself to form the rear of the piano. The back of the soundboard has been painted and grained in imitation of rosewood, so that the instrument could present a pleasant posterior if placed away from a wall. Pape was also one of the first to incorporate diagonal stringing, which enables a tiny instrument such as this to have reasonably long strings, essential for an acceptable tone quality. In addition he introduced hammers covered in felt rather than leather, to help make the sound less acerbic.

The little upright in the collection by Sébastien Mercier is a delightful example of what could sometimes be achieved by a minor French builder of the time. The instrument, less than 3½ feet in height, is dated 1831 and is both beautifully constructed and elegant, with its delicate stylised plant motifs on the case and the fall. Helpful details include a pencil rest on the right side of the keyboard and a holder for the tuning hammer. Also, most conveniently, the whole of the front of the instrument swings open like a door, to reveal the action – a not uncommon device for very small contemporary continental uprights. Nothing whatsoever, though, appears to be known about Mercier, as indeed is the case with several other Parisian builders of that period.

Pape's inventive genius soon achieved for him a commanding position as a builder, and at the zenith of his career he had about three hundred craftsmen working for him. He was too much of a boffin for his own good, however, for he could not resist indulging in extravagant and ultimately pointless ideas. It is said, for example, that in 1827 he exhibited at the Paris Exposition a piano veneered entirely in ivory, which, however eye-**7** catching, was regarded as being unworthy of a serious manufacturer.[7] Lack of business sense eventually undid him. The amount of bizarre and unpopular instruments put out by his factory led to its decline, and although the firm continued for a time after Pape's retirement, it closed for good in 1885, ten years after his death.

NOTES

1. Both France and England acted as a magnet for foreign piano builders. Apart from Erard, Pleyel and Pape, other notable names connected with Parisian firms include Herz, Kriegelstein, Kalkbrenner and Freudenthaler, all of whom were Germanic in origin. In England a majority of the most famous names came from abroad. Broadwood and Stodart, as we have seen, were Scottish, not English, and John Broadwood took care to recruit his most skilled craftsmen either from Scotland or from the Scottish community in London. These included his foreman, James Forsyth, and the action maker, Alexander Finlason (later spelt Finlayson), whose direct descendant, Dr. Alastair Laurence, a consultant to John Broadwood & Sons Ltd., and one the country's leading piano technicians, has been closely involved with the maintenance of the Finchcocks Collection.

2. Rather surprisingly, perhaps, Beethoven does not appear to have enjoyed his 1803 Erard very much. Possibly, though, this was due to his increasing deafness, which caused him to give the instrument more of a thrashing than it could take, for by 1810 it was thoroughly worn out. The piano was however the first that Beethoven had had with an extended compass of 5½ octaves (FF-c⁴), and this unleashed a great deal of piano music for this range, including two of the most famous piano sonatas, the Waldstein of 1804 and the Appassionata of 1805.

3. 'Chopin' (J. M. Dent and Sons Ltd. London 1947, page 129)

4. David Winston, the piano restorer, tells me that he has worked on fifteen Pleyel pianos, all of which, apart from some very early ones, have heavy actions. He has also found that restorers in the past have

sometimes attempted to lessen the weight of the hammer heads by drilling holes through them.

5. *Si je n'ai pas la libre disposition de mes moyens, si mes doigts sont moins souples, moins agiles, si je n'ai pas la force de pétrir le clavier à ma volonté, de conduire et modifier l'action des touches et des marteaux, comme je le comprends, je préfère un piano d'Érard, le son se produit tout à fait dans son éclat limpide; mais si je me sens vaillant, disposé à faire agir mes doigts sans fatigue, sans énervement, je préfère les pianos de Pleyel. La transmission intérieure de ma pensée, de mon sentiment, est plus directe, plus personnelle. Je sens mes doigts plus en communication immédiate avec les marteaux qui traduisent exactement et fidèlement la sensation que je désire produire, l'effet que je veux obtenir.* quoted from: A.Marmontel, 'Histoire du piano et de ses origines' (Paris, Heugel, 1885, page 256). Chopin's desire to feel in immediate contact with the hammers is revealing, in view of his experience in Vienna as a young man, when he played and practised on the pianos of Conrad Graf, the actions of which have hammers mounted directly on to the keys.

6. Pape's 'piano-consoles', when closed, were designed to resemble sideboards, or 'consoles'. But the term is a slight misnomer. The true (furniture) console is built without rear legs and is fixed to the wall, whereas Pape's pianos are free standing.

7. cf. 'The Harmonicon 1828' (Part I, page 6)

Mathushek and the American Square

Henri Pape's enormous reputation as an inventor attracted to him a great many able and ambitious young apprentices. Of these (who included for a time the distinguished piano manufacturer, Carl Bechstein) quite the most remarkable was yet another young German, Frederick Mathushek, born in 1814 in Mannheim. Mathushek's personality and ability appear to have been in many ways remarkably similar to Pape's, for he shared Pape's fertile imagination and also unfortunately Pape's lack of business sense. Apart from a few unusual instruments, inspired by Pape, which he produced after his apprenticeship (one such, an octagonal table piano, was acquired by the Ibach Museum, Barmen) Mathushek's output remained rather more conservative in its aims, though highly innovative and influential in its inventiveness. Mathushek eventually emigrated to New York and from 1849 worked for a time for several firms on piano design before in 1866 setting up his own firm, The Mathushek Piano Company in New Haven, Connecticut.

In 1998 a square piano by Mathushek, which was built at New Haven in 1873, was generously donated to Finchcocks by Mr. Gerry Higgins of Hove. This magnificent instrument incorporates many of the qualities that earned Mathushek such a high reputation in the piano industry in the late nineteenth century. Every detail of his instruments Mathushek finished with the utmost care, and this it would seem turned out to be eventually his undoing, for he kept experimenting and altering instruments in the course of manufacture – a dangerous course to adopt when trying to keep a business afloat at a time of cut-throat competition between manufacturers. Tone colour depends greatly on type and thickness of soundboard, and Mathushek, who by all accounts was a fine pianist, attempted to achieve through the design of the soundboard a combination of sweetness of timbre and power. In the Finchcocks instrument he has entirely succeeded in this purpose. The soundboard is slightly thicker in the treble (just over 9.5 mm) than in the bass (6.35 mm). Beautiful atmospheric effects can thus be achieved by gentle playing, whereas in powerful passages one can create an almost electric brilliance, particularly in the extreme treble. None of this would be possible, however, were it not for the complicated and elaborate double over-stringing, which Mathushek is reputed to have introduced into his square pianos in 1851, and which became a model for many rival firms; for the chosen thickness, length, and striking point of the strings are essential ingredients for the production of the correct sound vibrations, which are then augmented by the soundboard, and these are thus crucial for the success or otherwise of the tone colour.

Square piano by Frederick Mathushek, New Haven, 1873 Another rarity for a European collection, this instrument, an example of the American square piano in the last stages of its evolution, has almost the power of a modern grand. Typical of transatlantic pianos of this period are the cabriole legs with plant motifs carved in high relief, and grained to match the rosewood veneer of the case. The legs themselves are made from liliodendron – an inexpensive and plain grained whitewood which lends itself very well to this treatment.

An interesting account of Mathushek is given in Alfred Dolge's 'Pianos and their Makers', originally published in 1911 in California, and reprinted by Dover Publications Inc., New York. Dolge was an eminent piano technician, who had worked for a short while (1867-1869) in Mathushek's factory. He clearly admired Mathushek greatly, because of the enormous care he took over the tonal refinement of his instruments. He refers to the latter's wonderfully sensitive and trained ear, and writes that

> *it is no exaggeration to state that Mathushek could, as a voicer, produce a tone quality in his own pianos that no other man could imitate.*

The Finchcocks instrument is an example of Mathushek's so-called 'Orchestral' square, about which Dolge writes:

> *...his orchestral square piano has never been excelled, if it ever had its peer. In volume and musical quality of tone these orchestral square pianos were far superior to many of the short grand pianos of the present time, possessing, especially in the middle register, an almost bewitching sweet mellowness of tone, reminding vividly of the cello tones.*

Certainly 'orchestral' is an apt term for the Finchcocks instrument, since the astonishing contrast in timbre in the various parts of the keyboard remind one of certain instruments of the orchestra – a sparkling piccolo in the extreme treble compared with a lyrical viola in the tenor register and a rich mellifluous cello in the lower regions. This remarkable range of tone colour is caused very largely through the complicated lay-out of the strings – three layers of strings running on top of each other in different directions – thus in a sense making the instrument three pianos in one.

In 1871 Mathushek attempted to keep going by moving to New York, where he set up with his grandson the firm of Mathushek & Son, but it was eventually taken over, and sadly, in 1891, Mathushek, like his former master, Pape, died in reduced circumstances.

The first thing that strikes the visitor when confronted with the Finchcocks Mathushek square is its quite startling size. It is simply enormous, yet pianos like this one were very much the norm in the U.S.A. at this period. They were sometimes nicknamed 'Black Dragons', and ours, when it first arrived, had been at some time ebonised. Stripping it down revealed the high quality rosewood veneer, which somewhat softens the overpowering effect of the whole. The immense stress on the instrument caused by the cross-stringing is held at bay by the iron frame. One-piece cast-iron frames were introduced into pianos in America generally earlier than in Europe, the first patent for one having been taken out as far back as 1825 by Alphaeus Babcock of Boston. In 1853 Steinway set up shop in New York, and soon started to build square pianos. In 1855 they achieved a triumph at an exhibition in New York with an overstrung iron framed square. Both Babcock's and Steinway's iron frames were initially designed for squares, not grands. Many craftsmen from Europe settled in America in the late eighteenth century building typically English-type squares and the addition of the iron frame in the 1820s enabled them to become ever larger and more powerful. The iron frame in the States also had the added advantage, in a country where there were often extremes of humidity changes in the different seasons, of allowing greater stability to an instrument. By the 1840s the square piano had firmly established itself in the United States of America as the most desired instrument in the average respectable home. Indeed, the American love affair with the square piano hardly faltered throughout the entire nineteenth century, much to the exasperation of the major piano firms, who dearly wished to impose on the public uprights and grands, since they were both easier and cheaper to produce, for the awkward corners of the innards of large square pianos tended to prevent efficient streamlining of production. In addition, as American squares became ever larger and more cumbersome, they became more difficult than uprights for the manufacturers to store. These bulky instruments also became intensely unpopular with professional tuners, since it was only too easy to strain arms or back while reaching for the tuning pins. In Europe, by the 1870s, although some very large square pianos were still being built by a few firms, they had on the whole become quite outmoded, yet in the United States they obstinately refused to die away in popular esteem. After 1890 hardly any square pianos were being built, yet this still did not help much. The trouble was, the huge iron framed square was so stable, reliable and durable that the public could not easily be induced to trade them in for new instruments.

Such was the irritation and despair of the big firms that they decided on a grand gesture to wean the public from its infatuation. In 1904 they clubbed together to put on a huge display of square piano destruction to show their contempt for the instrument. This event apparently took place in May on the beaches of Atlantic City, New Jersey, not however without tremendous opposition from the public at large, as is made clear from a report by the Chicago Daily Tribune of 25th May 1904:

> *When the project was first broached* [Mayor Stoy of Atlantic City] *was deluged with letters not only from charitable organisations but individuals, begging him not to permit a waste of property that might give pleasure to so many.....*

Mayor Stoy did indeed do his best to prevent the vandalism, but to no avail, and a vast pile of square pianos was set to the torch on May 23rd. This was reported the next day by the New York Journal in a headline:

> *Square Pianos in Big Bonfire – Instruments Ushered Out of Life at Atlantic City to Tune of Bedelia.*

The enigmatic reference to Bedelia was made clear in the following vivid account from the same paper:

> *After a concert of 'Bedelia', 'Hiawatha', 'Hot Time in the Old Town Tonight', and other atrocities once as popular as the old squares, the discarded pianos were piled in a heap, the bonfire was kindled, and while the flames burned merrily the dealers grasped hands, and in a ring danced about the ruins.*

How many squares were incinerated is not known since accounts varied, though one paper, The Evening Star, stated that one thousand were burnt. But the New York Times rightly judged the long term importance of the event with its headline

> *Great Piano Bonfire. Death Knell of Squares Sounded at Atlantic City.*

A great outcry was to ensue, but in spite of acrimony amongst professional musicians as well as the general public, the piano trade remained obdurate, and the citizen was thenceforth compelled to accept the modern tenet of 'supply creating demand' rather than its reverse.

The Great Fire can be regarded as a memorable landmark in the history of the development of the piano, for all subsequent 'early' instruments were from that time onwards to be built solely for nostalgic reasons or for the purposes of 'authentic' performance.

Part 2 – Performance

Introduction

Apart from their inherent beauties, early pianos can provide a marvellous opportunity to re-evaluate one's interpretations of the classics. The printed score can be treacherous, for it is incapable of identifying the minutiae that make music an art, and needs the help of an instrument to clarify a composer's intentions. There is little doubt that most musicians of the period under discussion were fascinated by the actual sounds obtainable from the various types of instruments at their disposal, and it seems reasonable therefore to assume that they used with subtlety the many possibilities open to them. A study of the classics on these pianos can thus be a rewarding experience for every musician. Not only will it enhance one's appreciation of the great masters, but it can reveal the worth of some of the lesser-known composers, whose works can so often spring into life when performed on period instruments. One is then in a position, when reverting to the modern piano, to put into practice, if necessary by a certain amount of compromise, what one has discovered.

In this section, therefore, I shall attempt to put down my own thoughts on the matter, in the hope that they will provide players with something to think and argue about.

The salient characteristics of the two great schools of piano building – the Viennese and the English – were appreciated well before the end of the eighteenth century, for although English pianos were not common on the continent until the 1800s they were by no means unknown. Hummel, the great virtuoso pianist and composer, and pupil of Mozart, had played English pianos as a boy in Vienna as well as in England, and although he was undoubtedly more influenced by Viennese instruments he was still sympathetic to the English type. At the close of his enormous treatise on piano playing, 'Anweisung zum Piano-Forte-Spiel' (Vienna, 1828), he expounds on their characteristics. Viennese pianos, he writes, are known for their ease of execution, the touch being very light but also very direct and subtle, while the English piano, though harder to play, the touch being deeper and heavier, nonetheless possesses greater power and resonance. (It is twice the price, though, he adds.)

Whichever type of piano one plays, the cardinal rule is to realise fully the potentials of a particular instrument. An early piano needs exercising, it likes to be stretched, but one should never make it do what it doesn't want to do. At the same time one should allow oneself to be swayed by what it does want to do, and to let it direct one into the style of playing that best suits it.

The Viennese style

When confronted with an early piano, the first thing you should do is to assess its dynamic range. This is particularly important with Viennese-type instruments, where there is relatively little difference between loud and soft. The wonderful touch of the Viennese action allows the subtlest gradations of volume, but it does mean also that the instrument should be played out to the full when required. One needs therefore to find out the maximum volume the instrument is capable of without making an unpleasant noise (sometimes known as 'breaking the sound'). This is absolutely essential, and unfortunately frequently neglected, since one of the commonest faults with students is either to bang or to play too feebly. On a modern grand one can of course attempt to emulate the range of dynamics that Mozart, for example, would have known, but there is little point in this, and it would seem logical and more sensible to play the instrument out to the full, subject only to the limitations of the acoustical environment.

The first thing one notices when testing the level of volume is how weak the treble is in comparison with the bass. This is true of every Viennese piano that I have yet come across. And this makes the apparent difference between high and low so great. When touching the notes at the extreme treble one feels one is somehow teetering on the edge of a precipice, while at the bottom of the compass one is in a cavern. The weakness of the treble is the main reason why a number of concert pianists today have no time for these instruments. But Mozart, Haydn and Schubert succeeded in making a virtue out of an apparent defect, and often deployed the different registers of the keyboard in subtle and delightful ways. It is this very marked contrast between high and low which makes the Viennese piano such an exciting and rewarding instrument to play.

None of this would be so obvious, however, were it not for its idiosyncratic tonal quality. Compared to the classical English piano the Viennese instrument has a massive and rigid frame, the whole enclosed within a thinner outer case, which is only really needed for decorative reasons. At the same time the soundboard is quite thin, nearly half the thickness in fact of the English grand, (three millimetres, for example, as against five millimetres or more), with a light bridge and light and thin reinforcing bars. It is also fairly flat – a statement not as obvious as it seems – since nineteenth century English grands are usually fitted with a soundboard that is slightly domed (known as 'the crown') the better to withstand the downward pressure of the strings. In addition to this the dampers of the Viennese piano are both accurate and efficient, and cut off the sound immediately, unlike the very light damping of its English counterpart, which enhances the resonance of the instrument and allows considerable aftersound.

These then are the chief factors that give the Viennese piano its individual quality – a very gentle, pure and clearly defined tone. At the same time the action, in which the hammer is mounted directly onto the key (instead of being pivoted from a rail, as in English instruments), gives one the sensation of being in close contact with the production of sound, in the sort of way that is experienced for instance by a violinist. And this is augmented by the fact that the early Viennese piano is constructed of softwood of excellent quality – not just the soundboard, but the outer case and keyboard as well. As a result, both instrument and music become, as it were, alive under one's fingers. It is this combination of intimacy with delicacy of sound which induces such a personal relationship between player and instrument, in which each note is cosseted and relished in a very special way.

To make up for the relatively rapid tonal decay the Viennese action allows a sparklingly direct attack, which is ideal for the detailed but rapid passage work of composers such as Mozart and Haydn. The soul of the classical Viennese style is wit, amply exemplified by Haydn, and transmogrified in different ways through Mozart, Beethoven and Schubert, and it can be most convincingly conveyed through this characteristic immediacy of sound.

Haydn's piano sonatas are full of effects that benefit greatly from the character of the Viennese piano. The scintillating presto from Sonata no. 35 in A flat commences as follows:

Fig 13.1 Haydn: Sonata no. 35 in A flat Hob XVI/43 presto bars 1-8

and this theme is repeated in various ways. Towards the end of the movement, and after a lengthy transitional passage (bars 156-182) it is repeated an octave lower which, because of the richer sonority of the instrument, produces a comically grave effect. This is immediately followed by the same tune at the original pitch with the last note of the first full bar sounding cheekily an octave higher:

Fig 13.2 Haydn: Sonata no. 35 in A flat Hob XVI/43 presto bars 191-198

When playing the high E flat in this passage it is important not to attempt to force the sound, but rather to point or place the note by waiting a fraction of a second before playing it. This, a technique much used by harpsichordists, allows one to play it very quietly, which has the effect of emphasising the higher register of the compass. This manner of playing can be perfectly well reproduced on a modern piano.

The amount of music involving the piano that Mozart wrote in his thirty-five years demonstrates the delight he took in what was at that time a novel instrument. The purity and clarity of texture clearly captivated him, as shown by the studied simplicity of repeated notes, one of the hallmarks of his style.

Fig 13.3 Mozart: Sonata in G, K. 189h andante bars 1-4

Like Haydn, Mozart makes effective use of the different registers of the keyboard. A good example of this is the B flat section of the Fantasy in C minor K. 475, in which the melody is repeated twice, each time at an octave lower.

continued on page 154

Fig 13.4 Mozart: Fantasy in C minor, K. 475 bars 91-106

But the most telling example of Mozart's piano style, in which the points mentioned above are beautifully demonstrated, is the slow movement of Concerto no. 23 in A major K. 488, in which every note of the opening theme is individual and special. As early as bar two we have a characteristic huge leap from $g^{\#2}$ to E sharp in

Fig 13.5 Mozart: Piano Concerto in A, K. 488 adagio bars 1-12

the bass, while in bar 10 the melody climbs to higher reaches before collapsing back into the following bar nearly two octaves lower. When playing this sort of 'mountaineering' on the early Viennese piano it is often effective to reach the summit in a state of exhaustion, so to speak, after which one can, if the music permits, tumble down on the other side. An example of this is given later. This is a trick that can be easily imitated on a modern piano so long as one remembers to play the upper notes quietly so as to suggest distance.

The wonderful coda of this movement is a supreme example of the composer's delight in the sound of his instrument, in which the simple soft sustained notes in the different registers of the keyboard, highlighted by the chasm-like drop from $f^{\#3}$ to g in bars 89 and 90 (followed immediately by d^3, 2½ octaves higher), are supported by the delicate pizzicato of the strings (see fig. 13.6 on pages 155-156).

Unfortunately, this is one passage the effect of which is not immediately obvious on the modern piano. As a result the point of it all has been misunderstood and performances given which are marred by misguided ornamentation. Ornamentations on early pianos should always be exercised with discretion, and many a beautiful theme has been wrecked by reliance on 'authentic' embellishment. To fill in such a beckoning open

Fig 13.6 Mozart: Piano Concerto in A, K. 488 adagio, bars 84-92

expanse as the coda to the adagio of K. 488 is a temptation that has proved hard to resist. Certainly the lack of volume of the early piano would appear to give weight to the argument for interfering with it. The resonance of a modern grand allows it to cope with the long but quiet sustained notes, but this is out of the question with the weakness of the Mozart piano. But paradoxically the richness of the modern piano makes it all seem slightly bare, whereas the very limitations of the early piano provide a magic – the vulnerability of the notes lending a poignancy and pathos to the passage.

A good example of both 'mountaineering' and 'vulnerable notes' is provided by Beethoven in his Bagatelle in B flat, op. 119, no. 11:

Fig 13.7 Beethoven: Bagatelle in B flat op. 119 no. 11, bars 9-11

The diminuendo at the beginning of bar 9 presages the climb up to $e^{\flat 3}$ at bar 11. Played without any ritardando the semi-quaver passage makes no musical sense, whatever the piano used, but on an early Viennese piano the effect would be quite disastrous, since the placing of the pianissimo $e^{\flat 3}$ in bar 11 requires the gentlest and most studied approach. The only way the following bars can be played molto cantabile, as marked, as well as pianissimo, is for the accompaniment to be rendered as clearly as possible, hence the quaver figuration in the bass.

Schubert too has given us an astonishing amount of piano music – astonishing because he was not by all accounts a particularly good pianist. Yet he shows throughout an instinctive grasp of the nature of the instrument. His four hundred or so dances make lovely use of the different parts of the keyboard. In these the top octave is usually kept for echo effects or for imitation of yodelling. This example (fig. 13.8) is taken from a group of country dances or Ländler. In order to emphasise the height, the top B flat ($b^{\flat 3}$), four bars from the end, should be rhythmically delayed and then placed very lightly indeed. This delay is subtly encouraged by the time taken to play the turn on the preceding crochet.

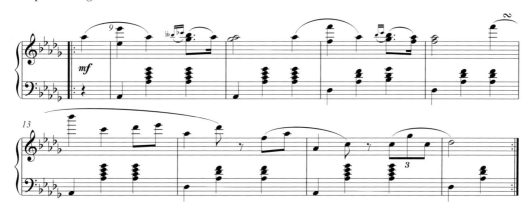

Fig 13.8 Schubert: Ländler D. 145 no. 4, bars 9-16

For sustained lyricism there is nothing to beat the tenor register of the classical Viennese piano. Schubert is the most lyrical of composers, and the deceptively innocent Impromptu in G flat (D. 899 no. 3) is a fine example of his ingenious and subtle handling of the instrument. The main melodic theme is centred throughout round the tonic $g^{\flat 1}$, the ideal place for making the piano sing.

Fig 13.9 Schubert: Impromptu in G flat D. 899 no. 3, bars 32 and 33

In the first of the dramatic E flat minor sections the harmony moves to a tender passage in C flat major (bar 32) with the melody attaining a high e^{b2} at the beginning of bar 33. When later on the same short passage is repeated (bars 48 to 51), the G natural in bar 49 (g^2), (not in itself specially high, yet the highest note in the whole piece,) played pianissimo as marked, takes the breath away. This moment is the emotional epicentre of the work and the composer here makes the most imaginative use of the higher register of the compass.

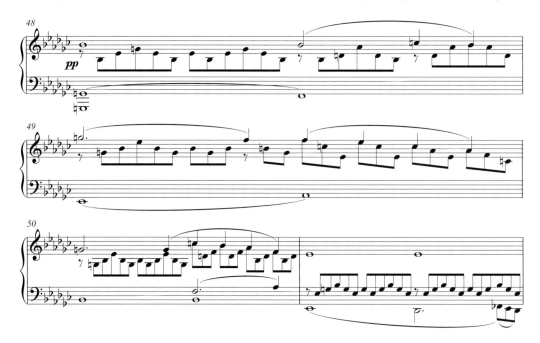

Fig 13.10 Schubert: Impromptu in G flat D. 899 no. 3, bars 48-51

Meanwhile the growly bass part plays a most significant role, providing a turbulence of unease throughout, sometimes pianissimo as in bars 35 to 39 (fig. 13.11), sometimes reinforcing a crescendo in a rising melody as in bars 19 and 20 (fig. 13.12). The element of danger thus evoked is a characteristic of Schubert, seldom recognised, often latent and hidden, but frequently there.

continued on page 159

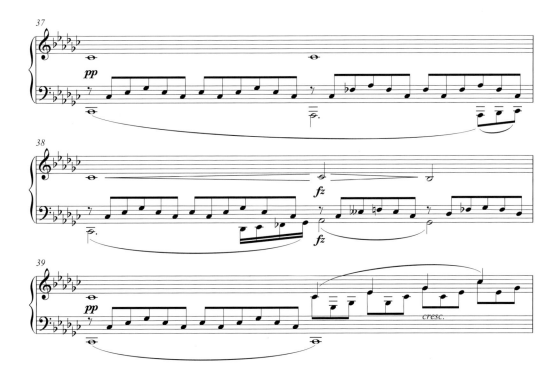

Fig 13.11 Schubert: Impromptu in G flat D. 899 no. 3, bars 35-39

Fig 13.12 Schubert: Impromptu in G flat D. 899 no. 3, bars 19-20

The writer, Bernard Levin, used to refer to Mozart as 'the music of God'. On this basis it can, I think, be argued that Schubert exemplifies the music of the gods, for a kind of pantheistic pagan power runs as an undercurrent through his output. With Beethoven for example, one knows when he intends to be angry, but with Schubert a sunny landscape can be lit up by bolt lightning.

So it is here, when, at the end of the recapitulation (fig. 13.13) the music suddenly and rapidly builds up from pp to ff, supported by a trill at the bottom of the compass, and is then repeated in the remote key of G minor, before subsiding back to pp in the home key (bars 82 onwards).

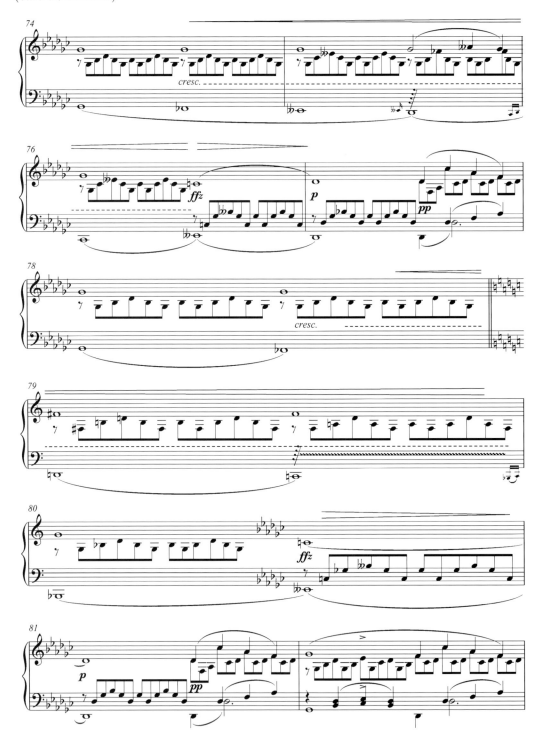

Fig 13.13 Schubert: Impromptu in G flat D. 899 no. 3, bars 74-82

A contemporary of Schubert, who exercised considerable influence on the latter's music, was the Bohemian composer, Jan Václav Voříšek. Unlike Schubert, Voříšek was a consummate virtuoso pianist, and the fact that the success or otherwise of his music depends so much on the correct use of the type of instrument he had in mind gives his output considerable importance in the stylistic use of the Viennese piano. Throughout Voříšek's piano compositions one senses a relish for the extremes of the keyboard compass. Typical examples are found in the powerful violin sonata op. 5, where the bass passages are reminiscent of Schubert's G flat impromptu:

Fig 13.14 Voříšek: Sonata for violin and piano op. 5 allegro moderato, bars 15-17 (violin tacet)

Frequently in this sonata the effect of the thin tones of the upper registers of the piano is emphasised by unusual climbing passages, such as the following example from the first movement (bars 74 to 76) which commences loud and reaches a high C sharp almost out of earshot.

Fig 13.15 Voříšek: Sonata for violin and piano op. 5 allegro moderato, bars 74-76 (violin tacet)

In this sort of piano writing amusing and memorable effects can often be obtained if one thinks in physical terms of ascending passages, as if one were to struggle up a steep slope. A good example is this fragment from Voříšek's exciting Fantasy op. 12 (fig. 13.16), where to get the right results one needs to indulge in a great deal of freedom of tempo. The first climb (bars 41 and 42) is clearly a laboured one, with the climber wondering whether he is going to make it. Eventually the slow ascent ends safely, if faintly, on the dominant (bar 42).

For the second attempt, though, the climber's blood is up, and after a sort of whistling-like pianissimo passage (bars 46 and 47) to pluck up courage, charges through bar 48 to land triumphantly on the high D, after which, exhausted, he tumbles gently down through the home tonic chord to finish softly and safely two and a half octaves lower. Whatever one may feel about this sort of whimsical approach to interpretation, treating the Viennese piano in this way does bring out well the tonal variety of the different registers of the keyboard, which is surely here one of the intentions of the composer in such a roller-coaster-like passage.

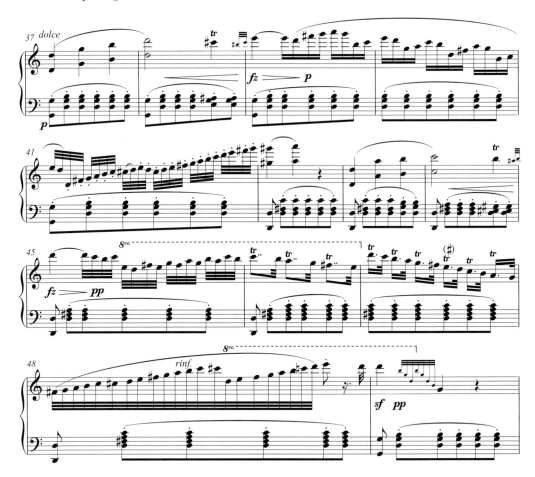

Fig 13.16 Voříšek: Fantasy op. 12, bars 37-49

Speed

In several of his works Voříšek applies metronome markings, based on Maelzel's successful invention, patented in 1815. On the whole these seem to work reasonably well, if a little on the fast side. However the last movement of the violin sonata op. 5 has a ludicrously fast tempo marking, which renders the whole movement both technically and musically well-nigh impossible. Ultra fast metronome tempi would seem to be an extraordinary and recurring feature of much classical and romantic music, and this puzzle has been discussed at length by many musicians without anyone coming up with a convincing solution to the problem. The light touch and in many cases very clear sounds of early pianos certainly lend themselves to fast playing. In the case of Viennese pianos, however, there is sometimes a way of discovering whether a given speed is possible or not. Because of the classical Viennese action, extremely rapid repetition of notes is often not possible, and this should therefore be a helpful guide line in ascertaining whether a metronome marking for music designed for these instruments is authentic or not. Unfortunately, this is not quite so simple as it sounds. In my experience, some very early Viennese-type pianos give very fast repetition, thanks to the extremely light action. It is therefore not unreasonable to assume that there was an inclination towards rapid playing on these instruments. With nineteenth century pianos of this type the situation is altered, albeit subtly. Fast repetition on the heavier Viennese action can indeed often be achieved, but only by playing with some force in order for the hammers to bounce back rapidly. To test the above theory, then, one needs to discover a passage in music written for the Viennese piano, where rapid repeated notes are required to be performed quietly. The quoted example (fig. 13.17) is taken from a set of variations on an Austrian waltz, op. 203, by Carl Czerny (1791-1857). The passages starting at bar 24 limit the speed at which clarity can be maintained, when played on a six octave Viennese piano for which this piece was written.

A detailed study of metronome markings by the musicologist Clemens von Gleich on a number of classical and early romantic composers such as Mozart, Clementi, Mendelssohn, Schumann and Rossini, has highlighted an astonishing emphasis on fast tempi. A common reason given for this is that composers were often slack in taking trouble over written speeds. It is certainly true that if one tries to establish a speed in one's imagination, rather than by taking the trouble to verify it by working with a metronome in a live performance, one tends to exaggeration. Carelessness in this respect may well have been true with some composers, though it stretches belief that this could have been so in most cases. Von Gleich's contention is that composers sometimes took the left-right movement of the metronome as one beat rather than two, thus halving what appears to be the intended speed. In some instances this appears to work well enough, but in a large number of cases the results seem far too slow and boring. Von Gleich's somewhat lame explanation for this is that the dynamic limitations of early pianos required slower tempi in order to express clearly the intentions of the composer. In the case of the Voříšek violin sonata, quoted above, the metronome marking indicates a speed approximately halfway between too fast and too slow – a kind of frustratingly unmusical golden mean. The Czerny example is similar. A satisfactory speed for this excerpt on a Viennese instrument of Czerny's time would be perhaps crotchet = 112. Czerny's own marking of 88 per minim is impossibly fast on any instrument, and ludicrously slow if one takes this reading to refer to a crotchet.

A reason advanced to explain Beethoven's often extreme tempi for fast movements is that the composer was aiming at an idealized speed, whether or not these were possible in practice.[1] It has also been claimed that false readings have been given by inaccurate metronomes of the past. None of the above reasons given to explain this strange mystery appears plausible on its own. Perhaps the truth lies in a complicated and unverifiable combination of factors. However, for the practical musician, should metronome markings not correspond with musical judgment, the only sensible solution to the problem is simply to ignore them. In any case, no speed set by the metronome should prohibit considerable latitude on the part of the performer. That liberties of tempo were customarily taken is very clear from the many examples in printed music where markings such as 'sostenuto', 'espressivo', 'con espressione' are followed by 'a tempo'. The distinguished concert pianist, Adelina de Lara (1872-1961), who had been a pupil of the great Clara Schumann, once memorably described in a BBC broadcast how the latter's style of playing consisted of an almost constant rhythmic ebb and flow. From the enormous influence that Clara Schumann exerted throughout the major part of the nineteenth century, one can reasonably accept that tempi directions should therefore be regarded as essentially advisory rather than mandatory.

Fig 13.17 Czerny: Austrian Waltz

Fig 13.17 Czerny: Austrian Waltz *continued*

Fig 13.17 Czerny: Austrian Waltz *continued*

NOTES

1. In slow movements, on the other hand, it seems that Beethoven sometimes aimed at ultra-slow tempi. A sketch of a movement from an unfinished piano concerto in the British Museum, for example, contains the following instructions by the composer:

   > '*In diesem adagio muss alles durchaus piano gespielt werden nur ein einziges forte darf vorkommen.*
   > *Die Klavier Solos so kurtz und ausdrucksvoll als möglich. Das tempo muss so langsam als möglich sein.*'
   > 'Beethoven and England. An account of sources in the British Museum' (page 7).

   (In this adagio everything must be played softly throughout – only one forte should occur. The piano solos as short and expressive as possible. The tempo must be as slow as possible.)

The English style

It has to be admitted that, after one has experienced the joys of the classical Viennese piano, the English instrument, until one has had time to appreciate its considerable merits, can seem by comparison a somewhat cruder beast. Unlike the former, the construction is of hardwood rather than softwood. The strong influence of the subtle clavichord on the design of early Viennese pianos meant that sensitivity was the goal to be sought for. And it is certainly true that early English square pianos, the ubiquitous instrument for the home, had a touch that could hardly be considered refined. The 1769 Zumpe and Buntebart square of the collection, for example, has a delightful and piquant tone colour, but it is very difficult to play delicately on it without losing the sound altogether. It has been suggested that early English grand pianos were primarily designed for wealthy families who simply wanted more noise, and were concerned more with efficiency than musical taste. This is certainly not true of early English square pianos, which tend to be quiet-spoken, and probably only partly true of early grands, for there were many professional musicians in those days (and, it would seem, quite a number today), who preferred the English instrument to the Viennese, because of its greater resonance, deeper touch and richer tone colour. There were, indeed, excellent features of the early English grand that differed from its Viennese rival. The arching of the English soundboard helped stability enormously, allowing the strings to remain longer in tune than those of its Austrian cousin. This design also prevented the soundboards from cracking. Although the heavy down-bearing of the strings made for a rather brittle sound, at the same time the thicker soundboard increased the brilliance in the treble. Also, the rim of the English soundboard is glued down rigidly, which adds to the brittle quality of the extreme treble, in contrast to the Viennese piano where the soundboard is 'floated' in the treble, (that is to say, unattached to the rim), thereby resulting in a weaker, gentler, but nevertheless pleasant amorphous glow to the tone quality. The early English grand has a soundboard which is thicker in the treble than in the bass, while contemporary Viennese grands have soundboards which, besides being fairly flat rather than domed, are thicker in the bass than the treble.[1] It is these factors which go far to explain the astonishing difference in sound and musical qualities of these two schools of piano building. These differences were much discussed and commented on in those days without any obvious adverse criticism. I think therefore that invidious comparisons are a mistake. English pianos were much admired on the continent, and owners of these instruments often enjoyed considerable cachet. By the 1790s the touch had been much improved, and greater brilliance, combined with the richness and resonance of timbre, made an exciting contrast to the more restricted purity of the Viennese.

A curious feature of the soundboards of English pianos (and also many French pianos) is the fact that they are invariably varnished. This is true of the very earliest ones right up to the present day. In contrast to this Viennese pianos have soundboards which are left unvarnished. This at any rate is true of the Viennese pianos of the collection, from the tiny travelling piano by Walter to the 1867 grand by Streicher. The Viennese makers considered soundboard varnishing to be detrimental to the tone quality, whereas the builders in London were less concerned by this, but varnished the soundboards as protection against the rigours of a damp island climate.

The touch of an early English (or English-type) piano is much more like that of the modern instrument, and as a result most people feel at first quite at home with it. Also the different registers meld together more evenly. The treble is usually more powerful than that of Viennese instruments (or at any rate, if not actually much louder, possessing a kind of 'sting' to the tone colour) and one can thus bring out melodies in a more straightforward and 'modern' manner. As iron reinforcement of the casework became ever more prevalent (in England from the 1820s onwards), so higher tension wire could be employed, and by the 1860s the difference between an English piano of that period and a twentieth century one, insofar as it affected the performer, was only marginal. Before the introduction of ironwork, however, English pianos still retained elements of the harpsichord. This is particularly evident in the timbre of these instruments.

Resonance

The most remarkable difference between the earlier and the later types of instrument is the greater resonance. This is something that the early performers and builders clearly relished. Until the 1830s the dampers on most English pianos, whether square, upright or grand, are very light, indeed unnecessarily so. It is thus simply impossible to quench the sound at birth. To play staccato is frankly not on under these conditions, and the most one can hope for is a kind of portamento. But this is something they loved in those days, and they often amplified the wash of sound by constant, and many musicians would say, excessive use of the sustaining mechanism. So at any rate thought Charles Burney, who in Paris in June 1770 called on Madame Brillon, well known in the city as a pianist and composer, and who, as has been previously mentioned, had apparently been presented with a piano by J. C. Bach (probably a Zumpe square, with hand levers to operate the sustaining mechanism). In his diaries he describes her playing:

> She played a great deal and I found she had not acquired her reputation in music without meriting it. She plays with great ease, taste and feeling...

But then,

> I could not persuade Madame B. to play the piano forte with the stops on' (i.e. with the dampers in contact with the strings) – "c'est sec" she said – but with them off unless in arpeggios, nothing is distinct – 'tis like the sound of bells, continual and confluent[2]

In the hands of a major composer, however, this characteristic resonance could be employed to considerable advantage.

By far the most significant composer associated with the early English grand piano is Muzio Clementi. Because Clementi grands are not quite so resonant as most other English makes[3], Clementi was able, by his patent harmonic swell mechanism, to have the best of both worlds. His harmonic swell is a superb means of employing controlled resonance as an aid to interpretation, for with this mechanism the player is given a choice between a relatively clean and dry sound and a gentle wash, which can be increased by the simultaneous employment of the sustaining pedal.

Of all the gadgets found in early pianos the harmonic swell is the one, the passing of which seems the most regrettable. The problem with playing melodically on a modern piano is that you cannot fully use the sustaining pedal to add richness without risking an obfuscating cloud of harmonics. And so-called half-pedalling is only a half solution. The harmonic swell works beautifully because you can veil the music yet retain transparency of texture. The device was not cheap, though. The whole chassis of a grand had to be enlarged to accommodate a wider soundboard over which a second bridge could be placed, and a separate pedal and attendant trapwork were required to operate the system. It is for this reason, coupled with the fact that its benefits are not perhaps immediately obvious, that the idea was discontinued after the composer's death in 1832.

Almost every pianist has at some time or other studied the 'Six Progressive Sonatinas' op. 36. Clementi himself was proud of these pieces, and justly so, for they are very models of controlled and lucid pianism. They were first published in 1797, but Clementi kept putting out further editions through his own publishing company, making emendations as he went along. Since these pieces were clearly of great importance for teaching purposes, so Clementi added helpful details such as fingering. He still however made no mention of pedalling although almost all pianos of the time had some method of sustaining the sound by mechanical means. It is only when the sixth and final edition appeared in 1820 that we find any mention of this. This last edition is especially interesting, since by this time English pianos had grown considerably. They were more powerful and had a compass of at least six octaves, and more commonly six and a half octaves. Clementi thus partially rewrote the sonatinas for the extra compass, and in doing so made them a great deal more vivid and exuberant. For the first time in this sixth edition we find pedal markings, but they appear only very occasionally. Once again, the assumption is that one will use the sustaining mechanism freely but in a sensible way, adding richness and colour in legato passages, but avoiding its usage in staccato passages or whenever it is liable wrongly to obscure detail. When Clementi does indicate use of the pedal, it is almost invariably in passages where its usage might be considered unexpected or undesirable. Thus at the end of the middle section (before the recapitulation) of the rondo from Sonatina no. 5 in G he places a pedal marking which continues right through the last four bars (fig. 14.1) Played pianissimo, as marked, one achieves the desired atmospheric effect.

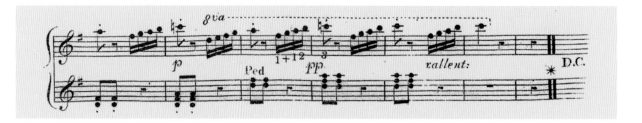

Fig. 14.1 Clementi: Sonatina no. 5 rondo (end of middle section)

Another even more surprising pedal marking in this edition is found at a linking passage into the A major section of the rondo from Sonatina no. 6 in D, in which the dampers should apparently be kept raised right into the middle of bar 40, after the harmony has changed into the new tonic A, thus obscuring the clarity of the new melodic subject. Several commentators today have assumed that the end of this pedal marking had been falsely positioned and that it should have come off just before bar 40. This however is scarcely credible. Clementi, who both edited and published the first and subsequent editions himself, always took great care over details, and the fact that there are so few pedal marks at all makes it almost inconceivable that a mistake could have been made. In any case, overlapping of harmonies through use of the pedal is by no means uncommon in Clementi's later compositions. The whole point of this surprising instruction is that it is indeed surprising. What Clementi is aiming for at this point is for the new melody to arise out of a wash of sound, like the sun coming out from behind the clouds. (This analogy is not quite so far-fetched as it sounds, since the heading at the top of the movement has been changed from its original 'allegretto spiritoso' to the more elegiac 'allegretto pastorale'.)

Fig. 14.2 Clementi: Sonatina no. 6 rondo, bars 37-41

The sixth edition of the sonatinas appeared in 1820, and a year later Clementi published his delightful monferrinas, the Italian dance that, as previously mentioned, became fashionable for a time in Regency London. In the twelve Monferrinas, op. 49, pedal markings occur throughout, but often scantily and in unexpected places, while at other times they continue through extensive passages, containing shifting harmonies. They appear however to have been carefully positioned by the composer, so a study of these ought to reveal many of the purposes of the sustaining mechanism, even if at times Clementi's reasoning would seem to be somewhat perplexing. The first monferrina in G (fig. 14.3) has a middle section in the minor mode, marked dolce. Here pedal markings continue throughout in four groups of mainly eight bar phrases, the intention clearly being to convey a gentle wash of sound, (something which could be beautifully conveyed by the harmonic swell as an alternative to the sustaining pedal). What are we to make, though, of the final twenty-four bars of this dance, being the recapitulation of the main theme in G major? Either the pedal markings have been placed carelessly or the composer has intended the dampers to play a subtle role in the execution. If we assume the latter to be the case, then a possible interpretation might be as follows: pedal markings in tonic bars 49, 56, 61, 64 and 69, are clearly designed for emphasis. In bar 50, the dampers are lowered to allow the frisson of the high B natural to sing out against the cleanly spread A minor chord in the left hand. When the same bar reappears towards the end of the piece the effect of the discord is no longer novel, so it is no longer necessary to dispense with the use of the damper pedal. In the preceding half bar the melodic G's of the opening bar are now raised to $g^{\#2}$ above the dominant seventh of the A minor harmony in the following bar. This emphasises the commencement of bar 70, and the pedal marking here also aids a crescendo through the semiquavers into the penultimate bar, after which a decrescendo

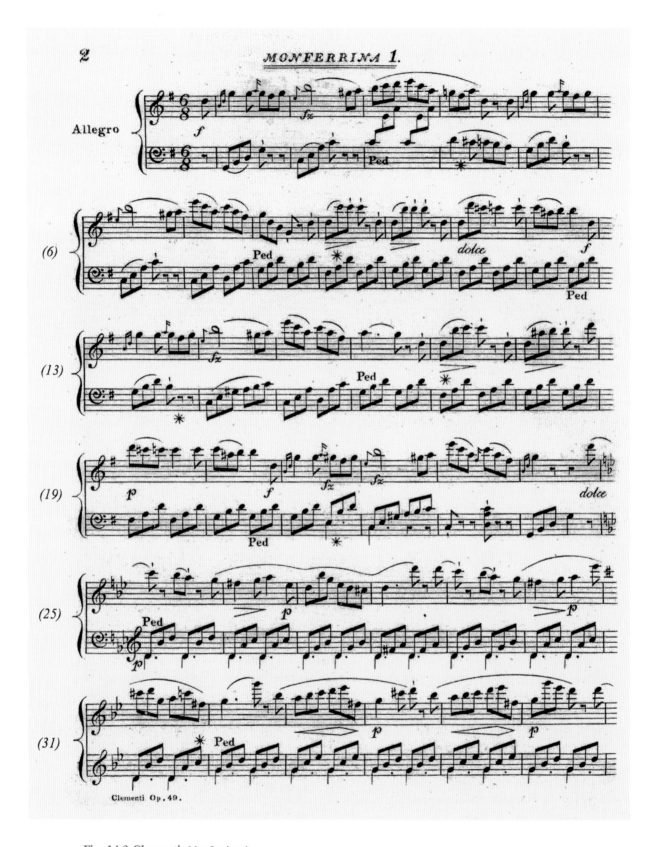

Fig. 14.3 Clementi: Monferrina 1

Fig. 14.3 Clementi: Monferrina 1 *continued*

Fig. 14.4 Clementi: Monferrina 12

Fig. 14.4 Clementi: Monferrina 12 *continued*

leads into the final bar, played only mezzo forte and cleanly, without the use of raised dampers. The high note E appears at the climactic first half of bar 71, after which the pedal marking ceases. In bar 51, by contrast, e^3 appears half way through the bar. For this reason the pedal marking is carried through this bar to the commencement of bar 52, as an aid to crescendo, after which a diminuendo leads to bar 53, played, as in bar 72, without the help of the raised dampers.

All this seems very complicated and rather fussy. It is certainly a far cry from the way most pianists, if it were left to them, would employ the sustaining pedal on today's instrument, but it is indeed indicative of the considerable importance attached in the past by composers such as Clementi to the subtle use of this device. It has to be said, however, that Clementi only occasionally goes in for such detailed pedal markings as are found in this particular miniature. Over larger canvasses he usually leaves discretion to the performer, often only insisting on the use of the sustaining pedal for special effects.

In the other monferrinas pedal markings occur spasmodically, or, in the case of numbers three and eleven, not at all. The main theme of number twelve (fig. 14.4) has pedal markings similar to the middle section of number one, i.e. eight bar phrases with dampers raised through shifting harmonies. The discordant effect of the change of harmony at the forte chord at the start of bar 11 is alleviated by the fact that several notes are shared with the end of the preceding bar. A far more shocking jolt to one's ears however is provided by the harmonic change in the very next bar, and the instinctive reaction of any pianist today would be to lift the foot off the pedal. But Clementi is quite adamant in what he wants; hence the direction 'Continua il Ped'. No pedal markings however are given in the C minor middle section of this dance since of course the melodic bass line needs to be heard cleanly (see fig. 14.4, pages 174-175).

In 1821, the same year in which the monferrinas appeared, Clementi published his final three piano sonatas, op. 50, the last of which is the magnificent 'Didone Abbandonata'. This sonata represents the apex of Clementi's compositional style and brings together a fulfillment of two important facets of his makeup – his asceticism and his love of the classics. The spare writing, with its predilection for open fifths, has no immediate appeal for many listeners, who often require sugar with their meal, but the tenderness with which Clementi here invests the story of Dido's fate is very evident. Throughout the work there are copious pedal markings, but once again they appear mainly at places where it would not otherwise be clear to the player that the pedal should be used.

The opening of the slow movement is a case in point (see fig. 14.5, page 177).

Here the pedal marking starts right at the commencement of the movement and is not removed until well into bar 10. In case, because of the changing harmonies, there should be any doubt in the matter, 'Continua il Ped.' has again been written. The operatic nature of this great sonata is beautifully conveyed by this treatment of the dampers. For the first ten bars Dido is sunk in a slough of despond, out of which she manages to pull herself together a little in the following section. Such at any rate is the sort of conclusion one is entitled, if one so wishes, to draw from all this. The point though is that impressionistic effects are the bedrock of so much of Clementi's piano style. Throughout the third and final movement (allegro agitato, e con disperazione), the sustaining mechanism can be used to increase the volume and to accentuate Dido's despair. As usual, there are very few pedal markings, since this is left to the discretion of the performer. When played on a Clementi piano with harmonic swell, this device can be effectively employed to add to the feeling of overwhelming stress without at the same time clouding the texture and the

Fig. 14.5 Clementi: 'Didone Abbandonata' adagio dolente, bars 1-17

change of harmonies. During the whole 127 bars of the exposition there is just one pedal marking covering a mere 2½ bars.

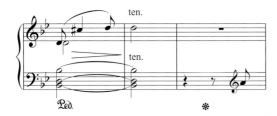

Fig. 14.6 Clementi: 'Didone Abbandonata' allegro agitato e con disperazione, bars 70-72

At first sight it seems inexplicable why such an apparently innocuous passage should be singled out in this way. A moment's thought, however makes it quite clear. Clementi requires the player to make sure that the C sharp continues through the tenuto bar into the held third bar so as to invest an otherwise bland B flat chord with a gentle yet disruptive dissonance. A similar effect is asked for in bars 201 to 207 of the development section, where the player would otherwise instinctively lower the dampers at bar 205 for the change of harmony.

Fig. 14.7 Clementi: 'Didone Abbandonata' allegro agitato e con disperazione, bars 201-208

Most remarkable of all, however, is the following passage:

Fig. 14.8 Clementi: 'Didone Abbandonata' allegro agitato e con disperazione, bars 265-280

Here the dampers must be kept raised right through this long dominant passage sinking down in volume to pianissimo, after which two bars of crescendo lead back to the first subject of the recapitulation, for which, during the first three bars, the dampers must be kept raised. This treatment of the sustaining pedal is identical to that of the passage in sonatina no. 6, discussed above, though here the purpose has a different function – not "sun coming out from behind the clouds" but a continuance of despair.

Although he spent his formative years as a harpsichordist, Clementi was throughout his long career far and away the most influential musician connected with the early development of the English piano, and it is not for nothing that his memorial at Westminster Abbey refers to him as 'The Father of the Pianoforte.' His subtle treatment of the instrument was not however by any means unique, and the English piano had a great influence on many other musicians who visited, or worked, in England. Haydn, for instance, came over twice in the 1790s and was clearly captivated by a type of instrument so very different from the Viennese piano. According to his friend and confidant, the diplomat G. A. Griesinger, Haydn always composed at a keyboard instrument[4], and right at the outset of his first visit in 1791 he called on Broadwood's in Great Pulteney Street where the firm lent him a room in which to work. During these visits he made acquaintance with many makes of pianos, and eventually returned to Vienna with a Longman and Broderip grand which he had acquired. It is natural therefore that the last three great piano sonatas, the 'London Sonatas', should have reflected this influence. The very beginning of the first of these, the C major sonata, Hob. XVI/50, makes most subtle use of the natural resonance of the instrument.

Haydn writing at the keyboard of an English-type square piano

Fig. 14.9 Haydn: Sonata in C allegro, bars 1-6

Played staccato as marked, the bottom C becomes a faint pedal note under the opening six bars, thereby providing a beautiful and gentle shimmer of harmonics through the passage. Later on, in the development section of this movement, bars 73 and 74 produce a very gentle shimmering effect as the harmonic sequence moves down to the A flats.

A slightly similar though longer passage occurs in the recapitulation – bars 120 to 125.

In both these passages, the composer has stipulated the employment of the sustaining mechanism throughout ('open pedal' being in England a normal expression for this at the time). This has caused considerable perturbation amongst some musicians, who have

Fig. 14.10 Haydn: Sonata in C allegro, bars 73-74

Fig. 14.11 Haydn: Sonata in C allegro, bars 120-125

been unable to bring themselves to believe the evidence in front of them, and who have concluded that Haydn must have meant by these markings the keyboard shift to una corda. The distinguished musicologist, H. C. Robbins Landon, for example, falls into this trap, when he writes, referring to the sustaining pedal being held down throughout the passage, that

> *such a use of the sustaining pedal would be wrong, blurring the music in a quite absurd way.*[5]

Haydn, though, who knew Clementi well, dedicated this work to one of the latter's pupils, and the passages are very reminiscent of the sort of effects that Clementi enjoyed. Again, as Clementi would have done, Haydn has required the sustaining pedal for passages where one would not naturally have used them. If played as soft as possible (and perhaps at a slightly slower tempo), on an early English instrument, bars 120 to 123 can sound truly ethereal, and will contrast effectively with the subsequent running figurations in semiquavers. There seems no reason, mind you, to refrain from employing keyboard shift at the same time, and this will certainly add to the beauty of the passages. Since the majority of the public who might have bought this sonata when it first appeared in London in 1800 would not have had the keyboard shift mechanism on their instruments, there would have been no special advantage in stipulating its use. The oblique layout of the strings of a square piano posed great problems as far as incorporating keyboard shift was concerned, and although not entirely impossible (Adam Beyer for example, was one of the few craftsmen successfully to attempt it) the device was only normally to be found in grands, and later on in uprights.

Beethoven didn't seem to care for any type of piano much. This was not due to a lack of interest – quite the reverse in fact. And because of his great prestige he had no difficulty in getting instruments given or lent to him. So he became acquainted with many different makes and models. Yet he found them all to some extent unsatisfactory. This was to a large extent exacerbated by his appalling affliction of deafness, which was becoming acute in his thirties. Even so it seems that he was forever seeking an instrument that could fully express his creative ideas. The type of grand sent out to him by Broadwood in January 1818 would, one might have thought, have answered his needs perfectly, for, apart from the low compass CC-c^4, it had some of the qualities that Beethoven most wanted in his instrument – power, resonance and a keyboard shift to una corda. Beethoven was indeed highly proud of his Broadwood and treasured it till the end of his life. Yet paradoxically he apparently preferred Viennese instruments for his own playing.

How much one should use the sustaining mechanism in classical music has long been a bone of contention amongst leading players. In the case of Viennese-type pianos it is now generally accepted that the clarity of such instruments, coupled with the very definite, detailed and often minuscule phrasing of piano music by Mozart and others, demands great caution in its application. Some pianists, indeed, seem to be afflicted by a kind of moral aversion to it, and dispense with it altogether. It is certainly true that in much of Mozart's piano music, particularly fast movements, the sustaining mechanism can be dispensed with almost entirely. It is generally accepted in the world of early music that Mozart's phrases should be taken literally, and not joined together by legato playing. Indeed, to join two phrases together without a break is considered a most serious offence, rather like, for example, driving over double white lines on a main road. It must be admitted too that strict adherence to Mozart's phrases makes real sense when playing a Mozart-type piano, for the rhythmic buoyancy thus achieved suits the clear, sparkling quality of such an instrument. Even here, though, a certain amount of common sense is called for, because sometimes the gap needs to be almost imperceptible. Overdoing the gaps will make everything sound too choppy, and each pair of phrases should be judged carefully on their own merits to pinpoint the exact amount of 'air' needed. In slow movements, however, or when special effects are required, such as to enrich arpeggiated chords or to heighten the excitement of scale passages, raising the dampers can be very effective. It is difficult indeed to believe that sustaining mechanisms were not commonly in use in the past, since virtually every Viennese piano from the earliest onwards is equipped with this device. If this is true of Viennese pianos, it is even more so in the case of English-type instruments, where resonance had always been a desideratum.[6]

Beethoven, anyway, would appear to have thrown caution to the winds, and to have used the sustaining mechanism freely all the time. No leading composer of the day employed pedal markings in his music more copiously than he, yet, according to Czerny, Beethoven used the sustaining mechanism even more than is indicated in the printed score. Czerny goes on to say that the weak pianos of the time could not stand up to his powerful playing, from which one concludes that Beethoven often employed the damper pedal to increase the volume. But Czerny also writes that Beethoven's playing of adagio and of legato in sustained style had an almost bewitching effect on everyone who heard it[7], from which one can reasonably assume that Beethoven in these cases raised the dampers to achieve a gentle wash of sound. This is borne out by the instructions found at the start of the first movement of the 'Moonlight' Sonata (op. 27 no. 2) – instructions which have caused much soul-searching amongst musicians. They seem clear enough: *Si deve suonare tutto questo delicatissimamente e senza sordino* above the text and in the middle of the first bar *sempre pianissimo e senza sordino*. In other words you keep the sustaining pedal down throughout. This however is an instance where a blind adherence to apparent authenticity should be tempered with common sense. Because of the manifold gadgets in use in pianos in Beethoven's time it is reasonable to regard the instructions as a generalised indication rather than a strict imperative.

The sonata was written in Vienna in 1801. In the late eighteenth century domestic pianos throughout Europe were not in the least standardised. The great majority of piano-owning citizens would have had squares, many of them fitted with hand levers. Even when knee levers and pedals had become commonplace, instruments of an older type would have remained in use in households. To play this adagio sostenuto movement with sustaining mechanism operated by a hand lever, you would be bound to keep the dampers off the strings throughout, but a gentle square piano might well produce thereby a coherent and pleasing effect. There were in any case in the German-speaking countries a number of square pianos that had never been fitted with dampers at all, so this would have been the only possible way of playing. With the far more powerful grand, though, a very different situation arises, for if one performs the movement at a reasonable speed without once allowing the dampers to fall, the result can be muddy in the extreme. So-called half pedalling can help, but there are times when it seems essential to change the harmony cleanly. Worst of all is this interpretation on present-day instruments, and those who give 'authentic' performances on the ultra resonant modern grand usually find themselves obliged to play at a snail-like pace in order to lessen the cacophony, thereby unfortunately producing a gentle drizzle of sound, and, for the listener, a fairly dismal musical experience.

If the directions for the use of the damping mechanism in the first movement of the moonlight sonata can be regarded as ambiguous, no such doubt exists in the first movement of the sonata in D minor, op. 31 no. 2. The wonderful 'largo' passages towards the end of the development section must surely stand as one of the most perfect and thrilling examples of the use of the sustaining pedal in the whole of classical piano literature. The false sense of repose in bars 148 and 158, where the melodic line comes to rest on mere suggestions of tonic chords, is emphasized by the clouding of the dominant harmony of the preceding bars. Here Beethoven is employing the same tactics as the examples of Clementi, quoted above.

Czerny, in his 'Reminiscences from my Life,' recounts how Beethoven's style of playing, with its addiction to extremes of resonance, horrified the followers of Hummel – the

continued

Fig. 14.12 Beethoven: Sonata op. 31 no. 2 ('Tempest') first movement, bars 143-159

musical puritan and guru of Viennese pianism, who, in his 1828 treatise on piano playing wrote contemptuously of what had by then become common practice:

> *Performing with almost perpetually raised dampers, in order to cover up untidy playing, has now become so common, that one would hardly recognise the pianist if one were to hear him play without recourse to the pedals.*[8]

In this matter Beethoven was certainly, in Vienna at any rate, ahead of his time, and one would have thought that the Broadwood grand would have perfectly fulfilled his expectations. Possibly, though, extreme deafness, coupled with a long experience of playing Viennese pianos, meant that he was not able to take fully to such an instrument. Possibly, too, the ideal instrument for him would have been one that did not then exist – a piano with ultra clarity and delicacy of touch, but which could at will be instantly transformed into an agency of great resonance and power.

Lessons from the past take time to die, and throughout much of the nineteenth century musicians would seem to have taken far more trouble in the careful placing of pedal markings than has been the norm in more modern times. A typical example of this is provided by no. 6 of Grieg's 'Poetical Tone Pictures' op. 3[9], which were published by Wilhelm Hansen in Copenhagen in 1864 when the composer was only twenty-one years old (fig. 14.13).

In this piece the sustaining mechanism is used both sparingly and subtly. Pedal markings, missing in the first four bars marked pianissimo, first appear in bar 5 and continue throughout bar 6, (where the harmony is the same), and treated similarly in bars 7 and 8. In the following 'con fuoco' bars, where clarity is clearly all important, there are no pedal markings. Pedal markings appear again in bar 11, (where the initial e[1] is marked fp), and again in bar 12. From then on, however, there is the firm instruction 'senza pedale' throughout the rest of the piece until the final two bars, in which the three separated quaver chords are deliberately (and probably unexpectedly) clouded with the pedal sign. All this at first glance seems quite surprising, since, for example, bar 24 is more or less the same as bar 5, where the sustaining mechanism is required, and one's probable first reaction therefore is that pedal markings have been mistakenly overlooked. These bars, though, are not quite the same. To begin with, bar 5 is marked mf and has therefore to be played relatively gently, whereas bar 24 is marked fortissimo. Secondly, apart from the first bass notes, there are no staccato markings in bars 5 and 7. Staccato markings, however, are present in every half bar phrase through the stringendo and crescendo passages from bars 24 to 26, and these emphasize the change of harmony and chromatic descent of the bass line, which of course need to be executed cleanly.

Very seldom is thought given to anything of this nature in most early twentieth century editions. Indeed by the end of the nineteenth century the rot had firmly set in, and damper pedal markings, strewn like confetti, became the hallmark of editors' 'improvements'. An example of this, as good as any, is the version of this early Grieg piece

Fig. 14.13 Grieg: Poetical Tone Picture no. 6

published by Alfred Lengnick in London in 1899, with its ubiquitous pedal markings, including the ludicrous one for the staccato upbeat in the very first bar (fig. 14.14). Today, fortunately, proliferation of editions, wedded to a more scrupulous attention to the text, affords little excuse to overlook and fail to appreciate the niceties of composers' intentions.

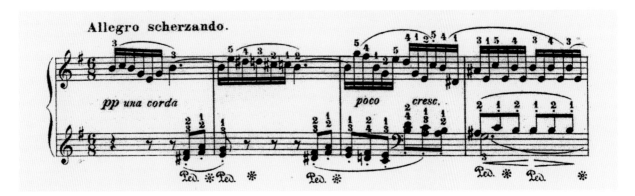

Fig. 14.14 Grieg: Poetical Tone Picture no. 6 bars 1-4 (ed. Lengnick)

NOTES

1. The difference in thickness can be quite surprising. An 1802 Broadwood grand, for instance, which had had its soundboard measured, revealed that the extreme treble was almost twice as thick as the tail end of the bass – 8 mm as against 4.4 mm. At the same time, a Viennese type instrument of the 1780s by Wirth had a soundboard in which the bass was just over twice the thickness of the treble – 3.5 mm as against 1.7 mm.

2. Burney, 'Music, Men & Manners' (pages 19-20)

3. A comparison between the 1846 Broadwood grand and the collection's 'cottage' grand by Collard and Collard of circa 1840 is revealing. The Broadwood, (described on pages 53-54) has by far the most ineffective dampers of any piano in the collection. Although a large and powerful Victorian concert instrument, it possesses dampers which are not much heavier in the extreme bass than they are in the treble compass. If one plays a fortissimo chord staccato in the bass, the sound can be heard distinctly for up to ten seconds. The sound of a chord played in similar fashion on the Collard and Collard will vanish rapidly. For this reason, of course, Clementi's music, with its spare texture, is ideally suited to the instruments of his firm.

4. Haydn, 'Two Contemporary Portraits' (University of Wisconsin Press, 1968, page 61)

5. Haydn: Chronicle and Works: vol 3 'Haydn in England' (Thames and Hudson, page 445).

6. How one should actually use the sustaining mechanism in classical times has also been a basis for argument amongst purists. Early, so-called rhythmic pedalling consists of raising the dampers in time with the placing of note or chord, in contrast with present-day syncopated damping, where the dampers are raised a tiny fraction of a second after the notes are sounded. This latter method is infinitely to be preferred, since the rhythmic method is cumbersome and essentially primitive, and was gradually discarded in the early nineteenth century. Sandra Rosenblum, in her very comprehensive treatise 'Performance Practices in Classic Piano Music' (Indiana University Press, page 105) cites the type of mechanisms in eighteenth century pianos as a reason for rhythmic pedalling, on the basis that knee levers and pedals were slower to respond than more modern pedals, and so were unable to cope with the split second timing that syncopated pedalling requires. This however is not the experience of

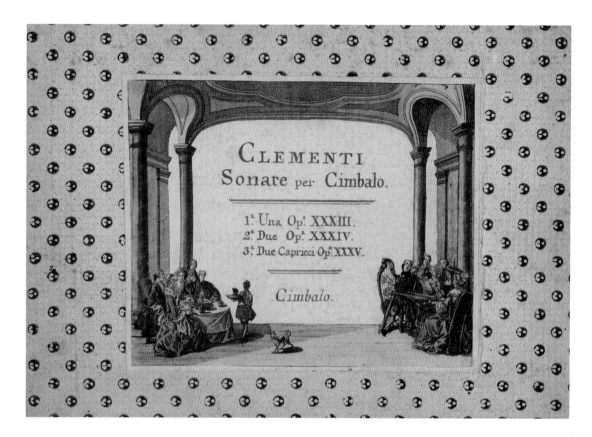

Paperboard cover, circa 1790, of a compilation of Viennese editions of Clementi's works.

anyone who plays the eighteenth century pianos at Finchcocks, where the mechanisms respond every bit as fast as the sustaining pedal of today's instrument. I think the most likely reason for the prevalence of rhythmic pedalling at the outset was simply that the sustaining device was a novelty, and musicians had yet to grasp its full implications and possibilities.

7. Carl Czerny: 'Anecdotes and Notes about Beethoven' (1852)

8. *Der Vortrag mit beinahe immer aufgehobener Dämpfung ist, als Deckmantel eines unreinen und notenverschluckenden Spiels, so sehr Mode geworden, daß man oft einen Spieler nicht wieder erkennen würde, wenn man ihn ohne Anwendung der Pedale hörte.* Anweisung zum Piano-forte-spiel (page 437)

9. Although Grove (2002) lists this as op. 2, it is described as op. 3 on the title page of the first edition (see bibliography).

Tone colour mutations

Early keyboard instruments are remarkable for the great variety of gadgets introduced to produce different tonal effects. In the case of early pianos, the three that survived the longest were the moderator, the bassoon and the keyboard shift. The first two are to be found mainly in Viennese-type instruments. The third is fairly common in Viennese pianos, and almost ubiquitous in classical English grands. The tonal effects of bassoon and moderator can not properly be emulated on modern instruments. However, together with the sustaining mechanism, the keyboard shift has survived to the present day, and is therefore of the greatest importance for the study of interpretation of classical piano music.

I. The keyboard shift

Beethoven's Broadwood, like most contemporary English grands, had a pedal that operated keyboard shift either to two strings (due corde) or single string (una corda). At the end of the eighteenth century, however, very few Viennese pianos, if any, had such a device. There were nonetheless a small number of much prized English grands to be found in Vienna at the time. There was the Longman and Broderip which Haydn had brought back with him from England in 1795, and both he and Beethoven subsequently acquired English-type grands from Sébastien Erard in 1801 and 1803 respectively, and both fitted with due corde and una corda mechanisms. Although, as mentioned earlier, Beethoven apparently never took to his Erard much, he was clearly enamoured of its potential for change of tone colour through this device, for in a letter of 1802 he wrote that he would buy a piano made by Walter so long as it was equipped with the means of playing on the single string.[1] The Moonlight Sonata made its appearance in print in this year, and one wonders whether Beethoven would have specified its use in the first movement had the keyboard shift been generally available at that time.

Although an extreme pianissimo can be easily obtained with una corda, and although this has always been one purpose for which it has been employed during its lifetime, it has never been its main function or its most musical one. Particularly is this true of early Viennese pianos, where their astonishingly subtle actions allow one to play almost inaudibly without extra assistance. The true aim of the una corda is to produce a very special rarified, ethereal sound. Although many Viennese pianos in the first few decades of the nineteenth century were equipped with una corda, it has to be said that it does work especially well with English grands of this period. The characteristic tone colour of early English instruments lends itself to changing into the clear thin sound of a lute or harp, whereas with the Viennese piano, although the device certainly has its uses, the fluty kind of 'oooh' sound of such an instrument does not permit much alteration of timbre. With English instruments the una corda was doubly important, for it was the only tonal device (apart of course from sustaining mechanisms) common to most grand pianos in the classical and romantic periods. Beethoven, however, residing in Vienna, certainly made extensive use of the keyboard shift, as is evident in the many markings in his music from 1806 onwards. He was also one of the few composers to distinguish between due corde and una corda. The difference between tre corde and due corde is not nearly so marked in most classical pianos as between due corde and una corda, and this is clearly the reason most composers ignored due corde in their writings. Possibly Beethoven's deafness was a factor in this. It is a great pity, though, that piano manufacturers today no longer incorporate una corda in their output, since due corde in powerful grands make so little difference to the timbre that many pianists cannot be bothered to use the keyboard shift at all, except as an aid to diminuendo. It is true that there are technical obstacles to overcome if una corda were to be introduced in modern instruments because of the diagonal layout of the covered strings in the bass, the direction of which the hammers have to follow. But the overriding reason for the makers' reluctance over this is the fear of damage to the single string through carelessly loud playing, when the heavy hammers might send it out of tune or indeed break it. There was a period towards the middle of the nineteenth century in England when quite powerful bichord grands were being produced, such as the two instruments by Collard and Collard at Finchcocks. Production of bichord grands in England appears to have commenced in about 1834 by Broadwoods and many other firms simultaneously, and continued to about 1850.[2]

With only two strings to each note, the keyboard shift has to move to the single string, and a very beautiful effect is indeed the result. But this didn't last long because of the danger to the strings. Also, at a time when makers were trying to attain as much brilliance as possible, bichord stringing in the extreme treble was not so effective as trichord. Czerny, in his 'Pianoforte-School' op. 500, published in 1839, warned about mistreating the single string by playing too hard, and stressed that the device should always be reserved for change of tone colour. While Czerny's advice was no doubt sensible, it does seem unnecessary to dispense with such a lovely effect because of the possibility of occasional misuse. So long as one is careful, however, there is no reason to eschew crescendos with the keyboard shift in the una corda position, and this can sometimes be very effective in a transition to tre corde.

Clementi once again provides an excellent example, and one that is in some ways analogous to the use of the sustaining pedal in his sonatina no. 6, quoted above. The following is a passage from the end of the development section of the first movement of the vivid and lively little sonata in D op. 16 (or in some editions 17) entitled 'La Chasse'.

The piano marking in bar 83 has a subtle bearing on the cumulative build-up towards the recapitulation which commences in bar 88 in a powerful linking passage leading to the second subject in the tonic key in bar 98, and the emotional point of this can be made very clear by judicious employment of the keyboard shift. Bars 73 to 80 are the more tense by the very fact that there is no crescendo marking, which first appears in the short phrases of bars 81 and 82. If one chooses una corda from bar 73 right through bar 82 but then reverts to tre corde in bar 83, this produces a highly dramatic result, which is heightened if one makes sure that bar 83 with three strings sounds quieter than bar 82 with one. It is the calm before the storm, or the sizzling of a kettle which appears to cease just before it starts to boil. Use of the keyboard shift in this way can work wonders with what at first sight would seem to be a simple straightforward passage, and many such opportunities for imaginative treatment of una corda can be found in classical piano music if one looks for them.

Fig. 15.1 Clementi: 'La Chasse', bars 73-99

Apart from Clementi himself, in the last decade of the eighteenth century Dussek is the musician one most associates with the burgeoning success of the English grand. Dussek arrived in England in 1790, and like Haydn, who came a year later, made early acquaintance with Broadwood pianos. In chapter five we have seen how it was apparently on Dussek's recommendation that John Broadwood started to produce pianos with an extra half octave compass in the treble – 5½ octaves, FF to c⁴ in order to allow greater brilliance in performance, and how mention of the extended compass – "for the grand and small pianoforte with additional keys" – is found on the title page of the composer's happy and exuberant sonata in B flat, op. 23, the first of these written in England. Already in this early work, however, one feels that Dussek could have done with even more notes in the treble. The first movement (allegro con spirito) for example, abounds in brilliant runs from bass to treble. One such run in the recapitulation ends on f³ (fig. 15.2). It is hard to believe that he would not have made use of f⁴, when writing this passage, had that note been available.

Fig. 15.2 Dussek: Sonata in B flat op. 23 first movement, bars 115-118

There appeared to be a definite proclivity among pianists/composers writing for the English piano in classical times to maximize the treble of their instruments. The exciting runs that one finds in Dussek's works often move from bass to treble with the intimation, whether written or not, that they should end with a sparkling flourish. Quite the opposite is the case with many composers writing for the Viennese piano, where, because of the characteristic weak treble and powerful bass of these instruments, dramatic runs often commence pianissimo in the extreme treble and end fortissimo in the bass. Czerny's vast corpus of virtuoso pieces is full of such examples (fig. 15.3).

There is no mention here of a crescendo down to the bottom note, but this would be the natural way of playing this passage on a Viennese piano since the sonority of such an instrument in the bass would totally overpower the high treble, particularly when, as here, pianissimo is called for in the two bars preceeding the run. The sf on the b♭³ minim is there to suggest a frisson at the start of the trill.

'Small pianoforte' refers of course to the popular square piano, which was not equipped with keyboard shift, so the lack of these markings in the music does not for one moment imply that Dussek would not have countenanced their use. An excellent way to add colour to the different registers of the keyboard is by employing the keyboard shift both to due corde and una corda through the development of the lively first movement of this work. The motif in semi-quavers of the first four bars becomes the mainspring of the whole of this section between the end of the exposition and the commencement of the recapitulation. To overdo any mutation stop in classical piano music is very often dangerous, since constant repetition can so easily become irritating. In this case, though, the music is purely jocose, and since the whole point of these figurations is to highlight the exciting sounds of the English piano, this is one time when it seems unnecessary to hold back.

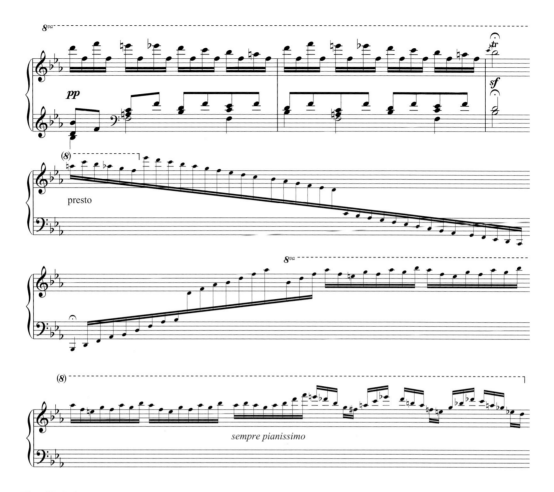

Fig. 15.3 Czerny: 'La Ricordanza', penultimate variation

Few pianos by the middle of the nineteenth century were being built with keyboard shift mechanisms to single string. Most people, however, just as they do today, were accustomed to play on instruments of an earlier period, and it may be because of this that we still find composers of this later period specifying its use. At the same time, though, we cannot be sure that the term 'una corda' did not signify simply keyboard shift, whether or not to two strings or one. The later romantic composers certainly used the term loosely in this way. Some composers, however, who spanned the classical and early romantic periods, almost certainly meant the single string when referring to una corda. For example the term crops up frequently in Mendelssohn's scores right until the 1840's. Mendelssohn made no less than ten visits to England and was very well versed in English pianos. Much of his music seems ideally suited to these instruments, and indeed he himself owned a fine Broadwood grand of 1820, now in a museum in Germany.[3] One of the loveliest examples of una corda that I know of occurs in the third movement (adagio) of the cello sonata in D op. 58, written in 1843, where the rich arpeggiated chords with which the movement commences beautifully complement the sprightliness of the preceding scherzando movement (see fig. 15.4, page 192).

The sign 'una corda' first appears halfway through the movement in three pianissimo chords that herald the reprise of the opening theme (see fig. 15.5, page 192).

Fig. 15.4 Mendelssohn: Cello Sonata op. 58 adagio, bars 1-3

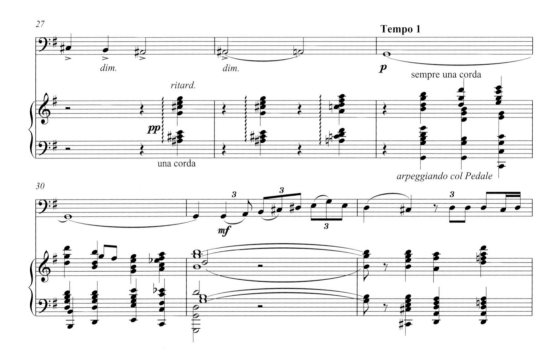

Fig. 15.5 Mendelssohn: Cello Sonata op. 58 adagio, bars 27-32

After a short return to tre corde in a crescendo passage una corda reappears for a couple of solo bars. An unusual feature here, and one that I have never before come across, is that the first chord is marked with a 'sforzando'. It is particularly subtle that this chord is preceded by a quaver rest to allow the previous held chord to clear, thereby investing the C major chord, when played with emphasis, with an effective kind of frisson.

II. The bassoon

The bassoon mechanism, as explained in chapter ten, page 122, is frequently encountered in Viennese-type grand pianos. It would seem somehow to fulfil the role of the poor man's Turkish Music, providing exciting rasping noises, but lacking the complete range of shocking effects found in more expensive instruments. Since the bassoon is such a feature of many classical instruments, it would be satisfactory if one could find a serious musical

Fig. 15.6 Mendelssohn: Cello Sonata op. 58 adagio bars 39-41

use for it, instead of merely deploying it for dance music and the like. The search, it has to be said, is not an easy one. Schubert's songs, however, offer possibilities. The wonderful accompaniments, which are so integral with the vocal line, often have a strong suggestion of something physical that is alluded to in the text. The early 'Gretchen am Spinnrade' is a good example of this. Throughout this whole song the spinning wheel, so simply yet effectively conveyed, blends with the changing mood of the singer. If a mutation stop, such as the bassoon, can enhance the pictorial element of a song such as this, without being unduly obtrusive, then there seems no good reason not to use it. An obvious opportunity for this is provided by 'Der Leiermann', the final song of 'Die Winterreise'. If played very quietly, as marked, the opening bass chords in the introduction will strongly suggest the sound of a hurdy-gurdy.

When combined with the moderator mechanism, the bassoon can be effective by providing a gently sinister accompaniment, as, for example, in 'Im Dorfe', no. 17 from the same song cycle, in which the short one-bar phrases in the accompaniment prelude the words 'Es bellen die Hunde' (the dogs are barking). Another excellent place for the bassoon to be linked with the moderator is in the middle of the seventeenth song from 'Die schöne Müllerin' – 'Die böse Farbe', where, to the words 'Horch, wenn in Wald ein Jagdhorn schallt' (Hark, when a hunting horn sounds in the forest) Schubert evokes the distant sound of the horn in the quiet piano accompaniment (see fig. 15.7, page 194). The use of the moderator at this point is well-nigh essential if a Viennese piano of the 1820s, contemporary with the work, is employed, for the slower repetition of an instrument of this period makes it very difficult to play repeated notes softly and fast at the same time. Here, though, the use of the bassoon when muted by the moderator will produce a wonderful effect – a sort of tonal version of colour stippling!

III. The moderator

The last great tonal device in classical pianos that needs to be considered is the moderator, fairly ubiquitous on the continent in the later eighteenth century and through the first three decades of the nineteenth, but hardly to be found at all in England. The neglect of this important mutation stop, very well known by builders such as Erard, who had set up shop in England, can best be explained by the fact that it simply does not easily meld with the astringency of the English piano's tone colour but blends remarkably well with the mellifluous sound of the Viennese.[4] Even with Viennese pianos, though, the difference the employment of the moderator makes in a piece of music is very striking, and far more so than when one uses the keyboard shift either in

Fig. 15.7 Schubert: 'Die böse Farbe' ('Die schöne Müllerin'), bars 41-48

continental or English instruments. So one has to be very careful how one uses it. With the keyboard shift, for example, you can get away with using it simply to help you play softly, but not with the moderator, for leather hammer coverings, overlaid with cloth, will make the contrast in tone colour jar. This is not to say however that one should never use it for muting purposes. Particularly in the lower registers of the keyboard the moderator can be wonderfully effective when played quietly. The opening of Weber's flute trio of 1819 for example, if played with the moderator on, will produce a most exciting feeling of suspense.

On the whole, though, the moderator is quite an awkward device and one must always be wary of it. In the normal sonata form (usually the first movement) of a typical classical sonata it is very difficult to find a suitable place for its deployment. However, for the trio section of a minuet or scherzo it can provide a useful tonal contrast. Another amusing way is to use it in repeated passages as if different instruments were speaking. A good example of this is provided by the section from Mozart's Fantasy K. 475, quoted on pages 153-154.

If one commences the theme with the moderator on, and then takes it off for the repeat an octave lower, an attractive and justifiable contrast is achieved. But if one then puts it back on for the final phrase another octave below, it can sound remarkably like the entrance of a bassoon into the ring. Another effective use of the moderator is to

Fig. 15.8 Weber: Flute Trio op. 63 allegro moderato, bars 1-5

accentuate a sudden change of mood. Excellent examples of this can be found in Schubert, when he moves from the minor mode to the major mode, frequently at the end of a piece, to convey a feeling of tenderness. By and large, however, the moderator comes into its own best when used for cantabile playing. It can thus be used throughout entire movements when lyrical playing is called for, and very often with Viennese pianos you can actually play louder with the moderator on than without it, since the addition of layers of cloth over the leather hammer heads tends to obviate the unpleasant 'breaking the sound', mentioned above. The sign 'p' so often appears in classical music when lyricism is required, so paradoxically one can sometimes find oneself playing fortissimo with the moderator on to get the right effect.

An excellent example of a sequence where the use of the moderator can accentuate a sudden change of mood is provided by the sudden and dramatic adagio passages of the last movement of Mozart's piano concerto in C, K. 415. If one holds back throughout this movement, and only employs the moderator at these passages, the effect is devastating. The composer in these sequences is clearly relishing the sound of his instrument. And the use of pizzicato strings (which need to be played pianissimo) in the accompaniment is indicative of this. In this respect these adagio episodes are similar to the end of the slow movement of the piano concerto in A, K. 488, though in the latter instance Mozart is savouring the sound of the individual notes rather than the filigree ornamentation of the former examples. This particular concerto is also remarkable for the many delicate cadenza passages throughout. On a modern piano these passages can sound somewhat empty and pointless, and indeed Mozart has often been criticised by scholars for his lengthy and apparently uninteresting cadenzas. It is for this reason of course that pianists so often play their own cadenzas. Mozart's cadenzas make a far greater impact on the pianos of his time, and again, he is usually employing them to show off the tonal possibilities of these, at that time, fairly novel instruments. The use of the moderator in K. 415, as suggested here, cannot of course be emulated on a modern piano, and these cadenzas on today's instruments can sound disturbingly superficial. Since Mozart's cadenzas in this and many other concertos are only partially concerned with the logic of the movement in question but equally desirous of showing off the beauties of the piano, then I think performers on modern pianos are justified in employing cadenzas which are more attuned to today's instruments.

NOTES

1. Letter to Nikolaus Zmeskall von Domanovecz (now in the Beethovenhaus, Bonn)
2. The 1846 trichord Broadwood concert grand of the collection is of the same specification as the Broadwood grand used by Chopin for performances in England. The 'Chopin' Broadwood, however, was not Chopin's favourite instrument. He much preferred the Broadwood bichord cottage grands, because of the lovely una corda, and the delicate and intimate tone colour of the instruments.
3. Manskopf'sches Museum für Musik – und Theatergeschichte, Frankfurt a. M.
4. That it was known in England, however, and possibly sometimes, if reluctantly, added to grand pianos, is evident from the following interesting letter from Broadwoods to a customer, from which one can deduce that the firm considered such foreign sounds to be ill suited to their instruments:

   Feb 6th 1804

   Miss Lee Place, Lewisham

   Madam, We have no doubt but that we shall be able to make the tone of your Grand Pianoforte both softer and as clear as you would wish – at the same time must remark that all soft tones on the piano forte must be accompanied with a noise which you describe as woody. –In respect to putting a soft pedal other than what it at present possesses no mode has as yet been discovered. –Indeed it has never been thought necessary, as the beauty of the instrument and which has caused it to supercede both the organ and the Harpsichord, has been thought to consist in the means it affords the player of modulating its tones from piano to forte by the delicacy of touch which is to be acquired by a little practice – we can put a soft stop, as used in Germany – the tones like a flute or rather sticcado* at we dare say about three guineas should you desire it

   Your much obliged servant J B & Son

   *a sticcado or sticcado-pastorale, a late eighteenth century English instrument, was a very gentle and soft spoken kind of glass xylophone.

Coda

Apart from their intrinsic beauties and their interest from a historical perspective, early pianos provide an excellent discipline for players. The tremendous variety of texture, timbre and touch of the various types makes it essential to gauge carefully the possibilities of every instrument. The tonal clarity, which they share with harpsichords and clavichords, enables the player to be fully aware of every detail of a piece of music and thus to be alert to the finer points of phrasing.

For the study of musical interpretation early pianos are indeed invaluable. This is not to say however that they should invariably be used for performance just because they are available. Music should be clearly heard, and if the acoustics are unhelpful, or the setting too large, then it is surely better to use a powerful modern instrument.

A truly vexatious word though in the lexicon of the early music movement, and one that has been much maligned, and unfortunately often rightly so, is 'authenticity.' Many are the sad and uninspiring performances that have taken place under the influence of this dread label. Authenticity, as a concept, hardly existed in classical times, and the contemporary accounts of recitals given by the great pianists from the late eighteenth to the late nineteenth centuries show clearly the enormous differences in their handling of their instruments. Yet these pianists all had their admirers as well as their detractors. The truth is that all interpretation is controversial. The best one can hope for when performing is to get away with it, for you are completely on your own and exposed to the snipings of anyone who cares to go for you. One of the wisest remarks said to me about interpretation (and I wish I had thought of it, but it was by the clarinettist, Alan Hacker) was: 'Never underestimate the subtleties of which a great composer is capable.' The subtleties of musical notation are easy, because they are there, in front of your eyes. All you have to do is to spend some time working to understand them. But the subtleties of sound are elusive and less easy to comprehend. Live music, though, is all about sound, yet performers, and perhaps pianists more than others (because the instrument makes the sound for them), still tend to base their interpretation on the printed score, and fail to qualify this by considering the evidence of their ears. None of the above however is intended to imply that one should ignore the didactic theories of writers of the past, whose opinions largely influence present day interpretations of the classics.[1]

These certainly have their value, but one does need to be wary. For pedagogues have bees in their bonnets and chips on their shoulders and they invariably detest their fellows. Sometimes hidden pitfalls have tripped up writers of today. Indeed some latter-day pundits have succeeded in grasping unhesitatingly quite the wrong end of the stick in their advice to performers. In the last analysis the instrument has to be the deciding factor, and one must yield to its dictates. Schumann wrote: 'Start early to observe the tone and character of the different instruments; try to impress the tone colour peculiar to each upon your ear.' Here Schumann is referring to the various instruments of the orchestra. But the principle applies equally to the great families of pianos. When writing for the piano the classical masters were much influenced, though perhaps sometimes unwittingly, by the instruments at their disposal. That is why it is so vitally important to marry up each composer with the correct type to find out what was intended. Fortunately there are so many excellent early pianos extant and increasing numbers of reliable copies being made today, that there is no insuperable problem. And, unlike people, the instruments cannot lie. They can be studied, they can be handled, and they relate directly to the music of the past.

NOTES

1. Of all the late eighteenth century theoreticians of performance practice, the German musician, Daniel Gottlob Türk (1750-1813) is surely the most thorough and painstaking. Towards the end of his lengthy study of keyboard playing, 'Clavierschule oder Anweisung zum Clavierspielen für Lehrer und Lernende', (Keyboard School, or Advice on Keyboard Playing for Teachers and Pupils), in a revealing passage concerning general style of performance, he makes three main distinctions:

   1. Church style. In this, all the rules relating to correct performance should be faithfully followed.
   2. Theatre style. Here, it is permissible to break the rules to convey the character of the performance. Dramatic performances – serious opera, comic opera – come into this category, as well as sensuous or descriptive music such as pastorales and serenades. Interestingly, he regards the theatrical approach to performance as being akin to the freedom enjoyed by an artist working on canvas (*oft gränzt dieser Ausdruck sogar an das Malerische*).
   3. Chamber music style. The aim of the performer here should be to achieve a synthesis of both the first two styles, by trying to observe rules of performance practice while at the same time allowing as much freedom of expression as possible – arresting turns of phrase, boldness, fire, emotion, splendour, tonal beauty – in short, anything which does not contravene the rules is in order (*auffallende Wendungen, Kühnheit, Feuer, Ausdruck der Empfindungen, Pracht, Wohlklang – kurz alles, was nicht wider die Regeln der Komposition und des reinen Satzes läuft, steht hier am rechten Orte*).
   Türk's final sentence in the paragraph on chamber music style is the most revealing in the context of the present study of the importance of historical pianos on the correct interpretation of the classical repertoire. He writes 'Above all, concerning this style of performance composers must bear in mind the skill of the player or singer, and seek to maximise the possibility of the instrument in question.' (*Vorzüglich nehmen die Tonsetzer in dieser Schreibart auf die Fertigkeit der Spieler oder Sänger Rücksicht, und suchen jedes Instrument nach Möglichkeit zu benutzen*.

Glossary

Keyboard chronology

Notes to accompany CD

Bibliography

Pictorial illustrations index

Music illustrations index

General index

Glossary

Action

The mechanical part of a keyboard instrument which enables the movement of the fingers to produce sound, varying from the simplicity of the clavichord to the complicated and elaborate modern double-repetition piano action.

Anglo-German or Anglo-Viennese action

An uncommon form of hopper action in which the hammers are positioned so that their heads lie to the player's side of the beam upon which they pivot.

Baroque

Derived from the Portuguese word for a misshapen pearl, and originally, like 'Gothic', a term implying disapproval. It is now a neutral term conveniently and somewhat loosely used to describe the visual arts and architecture of Europe in the 17th and early 18th centuries, characterised by a sense of movement and restlessness as seen in, for example, the painting of Rubens, the sculpture of Bernini, and the architecture of Borromini. It is also used, with less justification, to cover the music of the period from Monteverdi to J. S. Bach.

Barrel instruments

Various types of instruments which are made to sound by means of a rotating barrel or cylinder, powered manually or by clockwork. The notes of the music are represented usually by pins or staples fixed in the barrel. These operate the mechanism by means of levers when the barrel rotates. This can be provided with organ, harpsichord, piano, or free-reed actions.

Baseboard

The wooden bottom of the instrument to which the case sides and other members are attached and which forms an important part of the structure. In harpsichords and early clavichords this is relatively thin. In the Italian tradition the sides are assembled around the baseboard whereas in Northern Europe generally the sides and frame members are assembled first and the baseboard attached last. The early English grand piano is of this construction.

The baseboards of square pianos, clavichords after circa 1650, and grand pianos in the 'German' style are relatively thick, usually from one to two inches (2.6-5.2 cm) and provide a major structural component. After the 1820s the sides and internal members of the case of the grand piano were modified and thickened so that a baseboard was no longer essential, but square pianos retained this feature until the end of their period of manufacture.

Bassoon stop

A wooden batten with usually a half-cylinder of parchment or paper glued to its underside, positioned near the strings of the bass and tenor part of the piano. This is placed in contact with the strings by means of a pedal, knee lever, or hand stop, and gives a buzzing tone-quality. It is most commonly found on instruments of the Viennese type, from circa 1790-1835.

Beam

The transverse wooden member, fastened to vertical extensions on the sides of the key-frame, upon which the hammers are mounted. This is a feature found not only in the English grand action and its Italian and German forerunners but also in some types of square piano, especially the English and their imitators.

In the English grand action, the beam also houses the set-offs, which control the escapement. These are threaded iron pins, passing right through the beam, with at one end small wooden cylinders faced with leather pads, placed very close to the hoppers, and at the other end flattened heads, which can be turned by a socketed key to regulate the escapement.

In English-style square pianos provided with escapement action, the beam is of more slender dimensions, as it does not have to accommodate the set-offs, which are mounted on the key levers.

Belly rail

In harpsichords, spinets, and grand pianos, a transverse frame member, parallel to the wrestplank. In the northern European tradition, there is usually an upper, which supports the front edge of the soundboard, and a lower, placed slightly further back, which acts as a baseboard bracing.

As is usually the case, the Italian system differs. The belly rail extends almost as far as the soundboard, which is supported by a liner glued to the front edge of the rail. This results in an enclosed air-space under the soundboard, something which is also found in early English grands.

In clavichords and square pianos, the belly rail supports the left-hand edge of the soundboard.

Bentside

The curved part of the case of the harpsichord, spinet, or grand piano. In Northern European instruments, which had usually fairly thick cases, the bentside would be made by soaking the prepared board then clamping it to a former while it dried. Italian bentsides, which are considerably thinner, can be bent 'dry', possibly with the assistance of heat. Bentsides can also be laminated from more than one piece; Cristofori seems to have been the first maker to do this and the Viennese pianos in our collection show this form of construction.

Bridge

A wooden structure, curved or straight, the position and shape of which are determined by the desired vibrating lengths of the strings, which is fastened to the soundboard, and upon which the strings rest. Its purpose is to transmit the vibrations of the strings to the soundboard which acts as an amplifier. It is usually made from a deciduous hardwood such as beech, maple, walnut, or fruitwood, but in Italy cypress was also used. It is provided with metal guide pins to hold the strings and determine a clear speaking length. Early clavichords, with their straight bridges, did not need guide pins, and had instead a piece of wire on top of the bridge on which the strings rested. Bridges may be made by bending, sawing from a plank, or bending and laminating more than one piece.

Early grand pianos and northern harpsichords have normally a double-curved or S-shaped bridge, made in one piece, but Italian harpsichords usually have a short mitred bass section which is parallel to the tail.

Buff stop

A tone-modifier used not only on some harpsichords from the end of the 16th century, but also on many early square pianos. In harpsichords it is a batten placed against the nut with small blocks of buffalo leather glued to it. This can be slid sideways so that the block touches the string, partially damping it so that it gives a dry, harp-like timbre when plucked. Square pianos, and also the Finchcocks Antunes harpsichord, have a leathered batten which moves diagonally to touch the strings from below. The piano buff stop may be operated either by a hand lever, or more rarely, by a pedal.

Cabriole

In furniture, a leg of double-curved form, convex at the top and concave below, which came into use towards the end of the 17th century and generally disappeared with the advent of Neo-classicism towards the end of the 18th. It returned with the 19th century Rococo revival.

Cast-iron frame

From the earliest days it was realised that a grand piano required a more rigid case design than a harpsichord, and the gap between wrestplank and belly rail was provided with light bracing, usually of iron, although wood is also found. By the second decade of the 19th century more reinforcement was provided by wrought-iron bars in the treble. Soon more bars were added to the rest of the instrument in conjunction with an iron string-plate. The 1820s saw the first cast-iron square piano frame, but the first successful attempt with a grand was by Chickering, patented in 1843. A cast-iron frame supports all the string tension and there are no iron bars fixed to the wrestplank (as seen on our 1866 Erard or the two later Broadwoods), so that there is no compression of the wood. The casework of the piano is now a support for the frame rather than a tension-bearing structure.

Check

This arrests the fall of the hammer after the note has been played but while the finger remains on the key. It assists quick repetition of a note by ensuring that the hammer does not fall to rest until the finger is lifted from the key. In instruments of the English type until the modifications of Erard, the check is a leather pad mounted on a long wire set in the key lever. In German or Viennese instruments it takes the form either of a leathered bar or separate pads mounted on short wires, which are set into a wooden bar.

Cheekpiece

The short side of a harpsichord or grand piano, parallel to the spine.

Clavichord

The simplest and quietest of all stringed keyboard instruments, known definitely from written and iconographical sources from the early 15th century and made until well into the 19th. Almost all surviving examples have the same basic layout, an oblong case with soundboard to the right and fully exposed keyboard to the left.

The strings are either parallel to the spine, as in the earliest examples, or more commonly at an angle of about 10 degrees to it. The action consists solely of a piece of sheet metal, or in the 15th century a staple, usually brass, known as a tangent. This is driven into the upper edge of the key lever at the point where the strings cross it. When the key is pressed the tangent touches the strings (usually paired) and causes them to sound. The action of the tangent divides the string into two vibrating sections, of which that to the left of the tangent is silenced by cloth strips, known as listing, woven between the strings.

The sound from the right-hand part of the strings is amplified by means of the soundboard and bridge with which the strings are in contact. Releasing the key damps the vibrations immediately. Because the tangent remains in contact with the string for the duration of the note, it is possible to raise the pitch slightly by increasing finger pressure so that an effect of vibrato can be produced.

Until circa 1700, clavichords were 'fretted'. As a result of the way in which the strings are sounded by the tangents, it is possible to obtain more than one note from a pair of strings (see diagram). On the earliest instruments, as many as four notes could be sounded from one pair, for example f, f♯, g, g♯. As may be imagined, this system places certain restrictions on the player, as regards the use of certain tonalities, and demands non-legato fingering.

By the later 17th century this must have seemed a real disadvantage and a modified form appeared first on German instruments, which had no more than two notes to a pair of strings, as well as some notes with their own pairs. This type was so successful that clavichords using this system continued to be made until the early 19th century, and the Finchcocks 1807 Schmahl is a good example.

The normal layout of this type is c/c♯, d, e♭/e, f/f♯, g/g♯, a, b♭/b.

'Fretted' is a translation of the German word 'gebunden' (bound), describing the gut frets which were tied around the necks of lutes, viols, and early guitars, and the name is applied to the clavichord in order to characterise the way in which one string serves several notes.

Many 18th and 19th century clavichords were made with one pair of strings to each note (the earliest known at present dated 1716). These are referred to as 'unfretted' and impose no restrictions on the player as regards tonality, although a slightly different playing technique is required as the the keys have longer levers as a result of the greater width of the instrument caused by the larger number of strings and the frequent use of a compass of five octaves or more.

Clavichord action, plan and section • Schmahl 1807 When the key **A** is depressed, the tangent **B** is brought into contact with the string **C**. When the key is released, the string is damped by the woven listing **D** (section).

The plan view shows how the keys are splayed, so that two adjacent notes can be obtained from one pair of strings. The notes c¹ and c♯¹, e¹ and e♭¹ are 'fretted', whilst d¹ has its own pair.

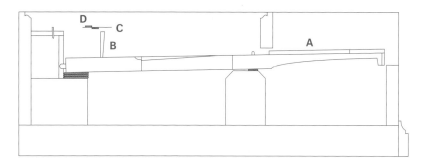

Clavicytherium

The term generally used for an upright harpsichord, with an action modified so that the jacks move horizontally rather than vertically. Various systems have been used, the simplest being that seen in the late 15th century instrument belonging to the Royal College of Music in London, in which the jack is fastened to a vertical extension of the key lever. Clavicytheria are not common, and those that have survived are usually noteworthy on account of their mechanical excellence and decoration.

Cross-stringing or overstringing

A concept of piano design in which usually the overspun bass strings cross over the lowest plain strings, permitting the bass bridge to be placed on the soundboard to the best tonal advantage.

Sometimes three rather than two levels are found – examples of this being our Mathushek and the square pianos of the Swedish maker Granholm. The earliest dated appearance of this type was in 1835, when Theobald Böhm, better known for his pioneering work on the flute, designed overstrung square and upright pianos which he had built by the London maker Gerock.

Damper

The means by which a string is silenced after the key has returned. The material is woven cloth, leather, or felt, and functions efficiently by being attached to a weight of some kind, whether this is the jack, as in the harpsichord family, or the independent system used in the piano. Early pianos had handstops, knee levers or pedals to control the dampers so that the sounds could be sustained or increased in volume. Only the pedal has survived in the modern piano. In the clavichord the damping system, whether woven listing or a cloth-covered board firmly held down onto the strings, cannot be lifted at will.

Double bentside

One in which the bentside and tail are made in one piece rather than two. It has the usual concave shape in the treble, but the angle formed by the bentside and tail joint is replaced by a convex bend. This is a feature usually associated with German harpsichords and grand pianos, but is also found in early English and French harpsichords and spinets.

Dulcimer

A stringed instrument sounded by hand-held beaters. It is in the form of a closed box, sometimes oblong, but more usually in the shape of a symmetrical trapezium. The strings, usually three or more for each note, pass either over two or more straight bridges or over a series of smaller bridges which serve only one course of strings each. Although in late mediaeval and renaissance European iconography the dulcimer is sometimes played by angels, it is usually thought of as a folk instrument, of which the Hungarian cimbalom is probably the most familiar type. In Iran, China, and the Indian subcontinent, however, it is employed in 'classical' music. The piano is a mechanised dulcimer.

English action

This was perfected in the 1770s, the product of the collaboration of Backers, Stodart, and Broadwood.

The hammers are pivoted in a separate assembly which is jointed into the sides of the keyframe. A hopper or jack engages a leathered notch in the hammer butt (the part through which the pivot wire passes) when the key is depressed and propels the hammer toward the string. When the hopper touches the set-off button, the hammer 'escapes' from the hopper and travels the remaining distance under its own impetus, thus ensuring that the hammer spends the briefest possible time in contact with the string. This distance in a well set-up early English piano should be approximately one eighth of an inch, or slightly more than 3 mm. A check is always present.

This type of action, unlike the Viennese, was capable of radical modification and improvement, and was eventually transformed by Erard into the double repetition action which is still in use. The hammer heads lie on the soundboard side of the beam upon which they are pivoted.

Escapement

1. The means by which the piano hammer is allowed to travel under its own impetus after having been released from propulsion.
2. The hinged, notched, and sprung wooden part fastened to the rear of the keyframe on a Viennese piano, responsible for the ascent of the hammer and its eventual escape from propulsion.

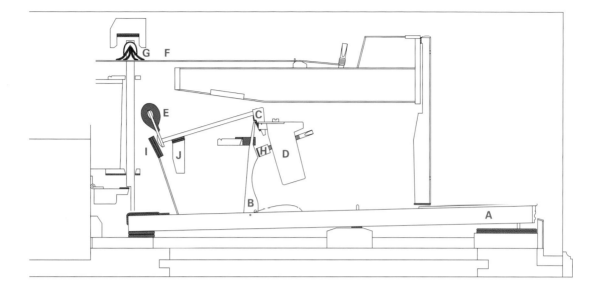

English piano action • Broadwood 1823 When the key **A** is depressed, the hopper or jack **B** engages a leathered notch in the hammer butt **C**, which pivots on the hammer-beam **D**. The hammer **E** is propelled towards the string **F** and the damper **G** is lifted from the string. The hopper comes into contact with the set-off **H**, escapes, and then travels the remaining distance (about 4 mm) under its own impetus. Having hit the string, the hammer is caught by the check **I** and returns to its rest **J** when the key is released. The damper also returns to its rest position on the string.

Fortepiano

This term was commonly, but not exclusively, employed in German-speaking areas in the 18th and early 19th centuries. Since the early music revival this term has often been used to refer to any early piano, especially the Viennese type, made before the introduction of the iron frame.

Free reed

The tonal component of the harmonium and related instruments. A very thin piece of brass or steel sheet is fastened at one end in a slotted metal frame. It is free to vibrate in this slot which is only fractionally larger than the reed itself. The free reed is believed to have appeared in south-east Asia, possibly in what is now Laos. The first instrument of this type to reach Europe in the late 18th century was the Chinese 'mouth-organ' or sheng. The possibilities of the free reed were quickly realised, and from the 1790s many makers experimented with it. The great advantage is its compactness, enabling an instrument such as the harmonium to have many registers, including low-pitched ones, in a case no larger than an upright piano.

Gadrooning

A type of carved, applied, or cast ornament using curved elements, fluted, reeded, or lobed, and first used towards the end of the 16th century.

German

Loosely used here to describe the areas in which the German language was predominant or widely spoken. This includes the territories of the Austrian Empire as well as the area covered by modern Germany. No national boundary is implied.

German action

Some prefer to use this adjective, rather than 'Viennese'. It is in theory possibly more correct, as this type of escapement action may have been perfected by the Augsburg maker Andreas Stein, whose instruments were praised by Mozart in 1777.

Hammer

The means by which the strings of a piano are made to vibrate. A hammer in its simplest form, as seen for example in the Viennese type, consists of only two wooden parts, the head and the shank, but those found on English grand pianos and their derivatives are more elaborate.

It is usual for the heads to be covered with a soft material, such as leather, felt, or woven cloth, but plain uncovered wooden heads are also found on some early Germanic instruments.

Hand stop

The mechanical means by which the registers of many harpsichords and early pianos are moved on or off, usually taking the form of a pivoted iron lever with a metal knob which forms the handle.

Harmonium

The name given by the Paris maker Debain to a type of free-reed organ patented by him in 1840, but now generally applied to any instrument of this type. It is now obsolete almost everywhere except in the Indian sub-continent and in Indian expatriate communities.

Harpsichord family

The name given to the genre of plucked keyboard instruments of whatever type or shape.

Harpsichord

Normally the largest members of the group of keyboard instruments whose strings are plucked by quills. These are normally wing-shaped, but some unusual rectangular examples exist also. Most surviving harpsichords have two or three sets or choirs of strings but single, quadruple and even quintuple-strung instruments are known. Their length can vary from three to eleven feet. Many have two keyboards or manuals.

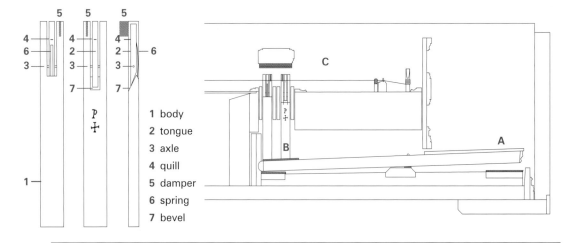

1 body
2 tongue
3 axle
4 quill
5 damper
6 spring
7 bevel

Harpsichord action • Gregori 18th century When key **A** is depressed, the jack **B** rises to pluck the string **C** by means of the quill which is housed in the tongue. When the key is released, the pivoted tongue allows the quill to slide over the string. The spring returns the tongue to the upright position.

Harp stop

This is the same as the buff stop, q.v.

Hitchpin

The metal pin, either brass, iron, or steel, on which the looped end of the string is fastened, at the opposite end to the wrestpin.

Hitchpin rail

A wooden strip which holds the hitchpins, around which the string eyelets are looped. In harpsichords, spinets (with the exception of most of those made in Italy), and grand pianos, this is glued to the bentside and tail area of the soundboard and sides. In most virginals this rail is placed to the left and rear of the case, and to the left in early clavichords. Square pianos and later clavichords have a thick trapezium-shaped rail which is fastened to the rear of the case, often incorporating a slotted rack in which the guide-blades of the key levers move.

Hitchplate

An important part of the structure of the transitional piano. This is an iron plate, usually about 7 mm thick, into which the hitchpins are inserted. First appearing in 1821, it eventually replaced the wooden hitchpin rail, giving a more secure fitting for the increasingly high-tensioned strings of the constantly evolving piano. It was itself displaced by the cast-iron frame, which incorporated hitchplate and bars in a single casting, after the middle of the century. Also called string plate.

Hopper

Also known as 'jack'. Found in the English grand action and its derivatives, and in a slightly different design, its Italian and German precursors. It is an upright wooden part, which in its English form pivots on a wire axle in a mortise in the key lever. It transmits the motion of the key to the hammer butt, and being movable, is able to escape when the hammer has travelled the required distance when the hopper touches the set-off. After escaping, it is returned to its rest position by a wire spring.

Jack

1. The plucking agent of the harpsichord family, consisting of a hardwood strip with a wooden tongue pivoted in a slot at the upper end. A plectrum, usually of quill, but sometimes leather, plastic, or even brass, is held firmly in a tiny mortise near the upper end of the tongue. The sloping lower end of the tongue rests against a corresponding slope at the bottom of the slot, and is maintained in this position by a spring, which may be of bristle, quill, wire, or sheet metal. When the key is depressed, the jack, which rests on the rear of the key, rises and plucks the string. When the key is released the jack returns by gravity. The pivoted tongue allows the plectrum to slide over the string, which is then damped by one or two pieces of cloth fixed in narrow saw-cuts or slots at the top of the jack. The first illustrations of harpsichord actions appear circa 1450, but in a much more complicated form than that described here. The standard and simpler type was probably perfected around 1500. This is still in use, in spite of the often misguided efforts of ingenious 20th century improvers, and is unlikely to be superseded.

2. Known also as hopper. See above.

Keyboard

See Keyboard chronology, pages 214-219.

Keyboard shift

The mechanism that moves a grand piano keyboard laterally, so that the hammer does not hit all the strings of a choir at once. It is returned to its original position by a heavy leaf spring screwed to the inside of the cheekpiece. It is normally operated by the left pedal, but in the pianos of Cristofori and Silbermann the keyboard is shifted manually. On early English and many continental instruments until approximately the third decade of the 19th century it is possible to obtain an *una corda*. English pianos have a wooden slider let into the treble keyblock which can be positioned to allow one or two strings to be played when the pedal is fully depressed. What may have been originally envisaged as a tuning aid became an expressive device in the hands of such composers as Beethoven and Mendelssohn.

Keyframe

The movable wooden assembly upon which the keys and action rest. In its basic form it consists of a back-rail, a balance-rail and often a front-rail, jointed onto two shorter side pieces.

Key lever

A wooden lever which connects the player's finger to the action. In keyboard stringed instruments it is pivoted on a guide pin on the balance rail, and guided at the rear end (in most harpsichords and clavichords) either by a metal pin or a wooden blade housed in a slot. The keys of many 18th century English harpsichords and most pianos from the early 19th century onwards are fitted with front guide pins working in mortises in the underside of the key head. The playing surfaces are covered with durable materials such as ivory, bone, or hardwood, and the levers themselves are usually made from lightweight woods such as lime, poplar, spruce or pine. In the Italian peninsula, however, hardwoods such as beech, walnut, and chestnut were usually preferred.

Keywell

The vertical surroundings of the keyboard.

Knee lever

A method employed in keyboard instruments other than those normally made in England, for changing registers, as in late French harpsichords, or operating the sustaining mechanism and moderator in pianos. The wooden lever is housed underneath the keyboard. The increasing use of tone-modifying devices in the early 19th century piano made this system impractical and it was supplanted by the pedal.

Lute stop

A harpsichord register which is placed very close to the nut. The close plucking-point results in a tone which is very rich in overtones, giving a reedy and nasal sound. This is found mostly in English and German instruments.

Moderator

A batten situated closely below the strings of a piano and furnished with a cloth strip, although soft leather is also found. This can be advanced by means of a pedal or knee lever so that the material lies between the hammer and the strings, softening the quality of sound made by the leather-covered hammers. It is found most often in Germanic pianos from the middle of the 18th century until about 1840, but also on some French instruments.

Nut

The smaller bridge placed on the wrestplank of the harpsichord, spinet, some virginals and the grand and upright piano, and on the hitchpin rail of the square piano. It is furnished with pins which keep the strings in position and mark off a clear speaking length. The wood is usually the same as that of the bridge.

Overspinning

A technique apparently discovered in the late 17th century, in which a string, either gut, metal, or nylon, is wound with a soft metal such as copper or silver. This allows a relatively short string to be tuned to a low note by increasing its diameter and mass without making it too stiff. Overspun strings were first made for the bass viola da gamba, and were later used for the lower notes of square pianos and fretted clavichords. After 1820 the downward extension of the compass made their use necessary on grand pianos.

Pallet

The hinged wooden valve that admits air to an organ pipe.

Pianoforte

The generic term for all keyboard instruments with a hammer action, irrespective of date, shape, or type.

Pitch

This is a large and possibly contentious subject, too great in its scope to be discussed here in detail. The present standard pitch, in which the note a¹ is at 440 cycles per second, was only internationally agreed in 1939. The keyboard instruments in our collection were made between 1668 and the 1870s, and during that period pitch was subject to local or regional custom or preference. Anyone wishing to find more information should begin by consulting the article 'pitch' in the New Grove Dictionary of Music.

Register

1. On harpsichords and organs, a complete set of strings or pipes at a certain pitch or of a particular tone-colour.
2. The slotted wooden part which guides the jacks of the members of the harpsichord family. If it is movable, as in the harpsichord proper, it can also be referred to as a slide. In spinets and virginals it is fixed to the wrestplank or the soundboard.

Rococo

A style in the fine and applied arts which was both a continuation of and a reaction against that of the so-called baroque era which preceded it. It originated in the early decades of the 18th century and displays typically a delight in sinuous lines, C-shaped scrolls, shell motifs and plant forms of a playful and capricious nature. The rococo style never became as well-liked in Britain as it was in France, Italy, or Germany and Austria. The word derives from the French 'rocaille', literally 'rock-work', used to describe the artificial grottoes at Versailles.

Scale

1. This refers to the string-lengths of the harpsichord and piano families and the clavichord, and is determined by the desired pitch and string material, whether iron, steel, or copper alloy.
2. In organ terms, the scale is the diameter of the pipe, and is one of the factors which affects the tone-colour.

Single action

The type used in the earliest English pianos, the squares made in London. A thick brass wire capped with a leather pad is screwed into the upper surface of the key lever. When the key is depressed the leather pad hits the underside of the hammer shank and propels it towards the strings. There is no escapement and only a limited amount of control over the hammer velocity, but a well set-up example (such as our own Zumpe) can produce satisfying results.

Soundbars

Wooden bars which are glued to the underside of the soundboard in order to reinforce it and to assist the propagation of sound, or to affect or limit the vibrations in certain areas. Soundbars may be absent in instruments with very small soundboards, such as are found in some clavichords, where the bridge alone is sufficient to provide the necessary strengthening.

Soundboard

The means by which the vibrations of the strings are amplified. This consists of a board varying in thickness, according to the type and date of the instrument, from approximately two to seven millimetres. In almost all surviving examples, the wood used is spruce, fir, pine or cypress. It is usually quartersawn (growth-rings approximately at right angles to the surface). This is considered to produce the best tonal results, although the cypress or fir soundboards of Italian harpsichords and clavichords often have slabsawn sections (growth-rings approximately parallel to the surface).

Spine

Normally the left or longest side of a harpsichord or grand piano. It is the rear side in the spinet, rectangular virginal, clavichord, and square piano.

Spinet

This now usually refers to the small diagonally-strung instruments, which are basically space-saving single-strung harpsichords, compressed in plan. The spine, instead of being at a right angle to the keyboard, is at an angle of approximately twenty-five degrees. There is usually a bentside, but smaller instruments, whose pitch is an octave higher than normal, lack this feature and have a straight right side. Their plan is that of a trapezium, unlike the harp-shape of the larger spinets.

Sticker

A batten or rod which is found both in earlier types of upright pianos, connecting the hopper to the hammer, and in many organs, where it forms part of the linkage between the key lever and the pallet.

Sustaining pedal

The purpose of this is to lift the dampers from the strings of the piano in order to sustain the sound and to increase the volume. Found in the earliest English grands, and in squares in the 1790s, but not used in Germanic instruments until the first years of the 19th century: before this time, knee levers were used.

Swell

Invented by the London organ builder Jordan in 1712, the swell is a device for mechanically modifying the volume of keyboard instruments. There are two types used in the harpsichord and piano families, the 'nag's head', in which either a part of, or the whole lid, is lifted by a pedal or knee lever, and the 'Venetian swell'. Patented by Shudi, this has a frame, fitted with a number of louvres (resembling a Venetian blind), which rests inside the case of the harpsichord or piano, and which can be operated by a pedal.

Tail

The narrowest side of a harpsichord, spinet or early grand piano. It may form either an acute or a right angle with the spine, or may be a curved continuation of the bentside. In order to simplify the laminated construction of the one-piece case or rim, the tail of the modern grand piano is curved.

Trapwork

The mechanical system which connects pedals or knee levers to the devices which they control.

Triple bentside

A design characteristic of some Germanic pianos around the 1820s, in which the three separate parts, cheekpiece, bentside, and tail, are replaced by a single continuous laminated curved piece.

Viennese action

Although sometimes known as 'German' it is now usual to refer to this as 'Viennese' in view of the importance of that city as a centre for the production of pianos using this action. It should be remembered, however, that instruments of this kind were made in many other places in the 'German' or Austrian areas of influence, in such places as Wrocław (Breslau), Brno, or Trieste.

The Viennese type is the simplest piano action that is capable of working really well. The hammer shank, with its head at the wrestplank side of the pivot, is held in a carrier, known as the 'kapsel' which is fixed into the upper surface of the rear of the key lever. In older examples, the kapsel is made of wood and is mounted on a thick piece of iron wire driven into the key. The hammer shank has a fixed brass wire axle which moves in a bushing of hard felt.

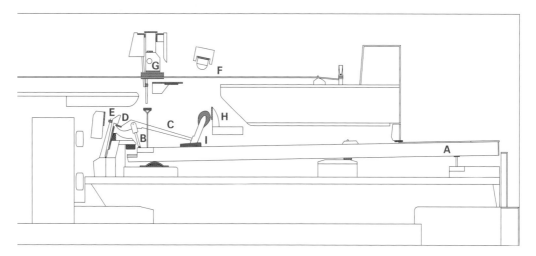

Graf circa 1820 • Viennese piano action The key **A** is fitted with a kapsel **B** in which the hammer **C** is pivoted. When the key is depressed, the beak-leather **D** engages the escapement **E**, pulling down the end of the hammer shark and propelling the hammer towards the string **F**. The damper **G** is raised. The hammer quits the escapement and travels about 2 mm under its own impetus. After hitting the string, the hammer is caught by the check **H**. When the key is released the hammer returns to its rest **I** and the damper descends.

This has the disadvantage of being difficult to adjust, and it was eventually superseded by a version in metal, in which the wire mounting is replaced by a threaded brass rod about 2.5 mm thick, and the wooden forked part is substituted by a piece of sheet brass, bent to a U-shape and riveted to the rod, with dimples to act as bearings for the steel axle of the hammer shank. This is a better system, in which the height of the kapsel and the tightness of the bearings are easily adjustable. In addition the rod can be bent to make minor alterations to the position of the hammer shank.

A piece of leather glued to the beaked end of the shank engages with the notch in the hinged and sprung escapement when the key is depressed. The end of the shank is pulled down and the hammer rises. When it is approximately 2 mm from the strings, the hammer escapes and travels the remaining distance under its own momentum. This allows it to spend as little time as possible in contact with the strings, thus producing the best tone quality. Once the hammer has hit the strings, the escapement moves backward to let the hammer fall back onto the key, and is itself returned to its rest position by the spring.

The check was applied to this action in the 1780s, but many early instruments lack this feature. An action without a check can work surprisingly well, with fast repetition. With a check the finger must leave the key momentarily in order to repeat a note, but without one this can be done without removing the finger. The rapidly repeated notes in, for example, the first movement of Beethoven's 'Sonata Appassionata' are well within its range.

Virginal (also known as 'Virginals')

A type of instrument belonging to the harpsichord family in which the long axis of the case is at a right angle to the keyboard, with the strings usually at an angle of from four to seven degrees to that axis. In most examples both bridges are on the soundboard, and that, and the points at which the strings are plucked, result in a tone-colour which is quite different from that of the harpsichord proper. In plan, virginals are usually rectangular or polygonal. The Italian pentagonal virginal is one of the classics of musical instrument design, on the same artistic level as the violin. The derivation of the name, which first appears in the 1460s, is unclear, but seems to be based on a confused etymological association, possibly biblical, with female performers.

In English-language sources, until well into the 17th century, the term refers to any member of the harpsichord family. This has led to the mistaken idea that the music of the Tudor and Jacobean composers was intended exclusively for the small rectangular instrument.

Wrestpin

Also known as 'tuning pin'. A pin of iron, or, later, steel, very infrequently brass, of diameter varying from approximately 2-7 mm, fitted into the wrestplank, and around which the string is wound. The top is flattened or squared, fitting a socketed tuning key which turns the pin to alter the tension and change the pitch.

Wrestplank

The piece of hardwood into which the wrestpins are fitted. It is positioned above the key levers in harpsichords, spinets, and grand pianos, and to the right side of the case in clavichords, earlier square pianos, and most virginals. In some virginals and later square pianos it is placed to the left. It forms the top frame member of an upright piano. The woods preferred are usually beech, oak, maple, and walnut, according to the place and date of manufacture.

In harpsichords and in grand pianos made before the era of the metal frame, there is a nut on the wrestplank, which in most examples extends as far as the gap. There is, however, a number of harpsichords, mostly from the 16th century, with wrestplanks wide enough only to accommodate the pins safely. A second soundboard, upon which the nut rests, extends from the edge of wrestplank to the gap. As a result of this the tone-colour is different from that of a harpsichord which has only one bridge on an area of soundboard.

Yoke
A wooden reinforcement glued to the front upper edge of the wrestplank of a grand piano. Its grain runs in the same direction as that of the wrestplank and it assists in resisting the distortion caused by string tension.

Keyboard chronology

The development of the keyboard is one of the major contributions made by Europe to the whole corpus of music. The organ and the system of keys which operated it seem to have been invented by the Greek engineer Ktesibios, who lived in Alexandria in the third century B.C. His instrument, a design of great ingenuity, was known as a hydraulos, and can be simply described as a small pipe-organ in which the wind-pressure was kept constant by being fed into a water-filled reservoir. The key took the form of a pivoted crank which pushed in a perforated slider which admitted air to the pipe. When the key was released a leaf spring returned the slider. This differs from the system developed in the 13th century and used until now, where the key operates a small hinged valve, known as a pallet, which lets air into the pipes.

The modern key-layout, with the accidental notes placed to the rear of, and higher than, the natural notes, can be seen in 14th century paintings, and more especially in the Ghent Altarpiece by van Eyck, as well as in the careful technical drawings in the treatise of Arnaut of Zwolle, which was written circa 1450. However, there are actual remains of four Swedish organs from about 1370-1400, which have keyboards with B flat as a diatonic note – so that there are eight natural and four accidental notes in each octave. The widths of the natural keys on these varies between approximately 3-6 cm on the different instruments. Those shown in Arnaut's drawings have been interpreted as either slightly larger or smaller than would be found on a modern keyboard. They are also very short – the length of the keys is twice their width, and the accidentals are only as long as the natural key-heads. This implies that the length of the naturals would have been approximately 5.5 cm. In the modern piano this dimension is roughly 13.5 cm.

The earliest written keyboard music to survive is in the Robertsbridge Codex, which is thought to date from the middle of the 14th century, and which was presumably intended for the organ. This consists of four complete pieces, two settings of vocal originals by Philippe de Vitry (1291-1361), and two anonymous dances, as well as two anonymous fragments, a dance and an arrangement of a song. The music is technically demanding, requiring a chromatic compass, with highly decorated top lines, and indicates that the keyboard had by then reached a stage of total efficiency. The actual range of the music is from c to e^2. The lowest note, c, is also the lowest found on the Swedish organs.

In all the keyboard instruments illustrated by Arnaut, the lowest note is B, but the top notes vary according to the type of instrument – on the organ f^2 is found, on the harpsichord and dulce melos it is a^2 (the dulce melos is a very distant ancestor of the piano). The highest note of his clavichord is b^2. A clavichord with the large compass F-f^3 is shown in the well-known marquetry decorations carried out in the late 1470s in the study of Federigo da Montefeltro in the ducal palace at Urbino .

The oldest known and authenticated domestic stringed keyboard instrument is the little clavicytherium, now in the Royal College of Music in London, dating from the 1480s, which had originally a compass unlike anything known subsequently.

The lowest note is an apparent E. The next note is an E♯, then F, G, G♯. How these lowest few notes were tuned has not yet been established.

This instrument provides an introduction to the 'short octave' which was to survive in some areas even as late as the beginning of the 19th century. This term refers to the lowest octave of notes on all types of keyboard instruments, in which unwanted notes were omitted and replaced by more useful alternatives. This makes very good sense with regard to large organs, where costs could be reduced by the omission of dozens of unwanted large and expensive pipes. This economy was not as important with harpsichords and clavichords as only a few extra strings and keys were involved, but nevertheless the stringed keyboard makers followed suit. When, in the second half of the 15th century, the compass was extended downwards to F, the notes F♯ and G♯ were omitted, because they would not be expected to be used in the music of that period. B♭ is the first accidental (fig. 1).

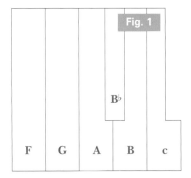

In the early 16th century an extra diatonic key and two accidental keys were added in the lowest octave, resulting in an arrangement usually referred to as the 'C/E short octave'. The apparent E is tuned to C, the F♯ to D, and the G♯ to E. As with the older system, the first accidental is still B♭ (fig. 2).

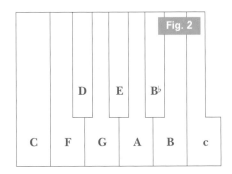

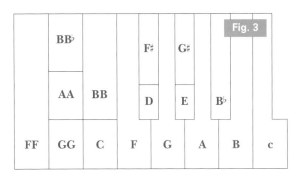

This configuration was standard throughout the 16th and much of the 17th centuries, judging by surviving instruments, mostly from Italy and the Low Countries. It was still in use in the 18th century, sometimes being incorporated into extended systems, such as that now known as the 'Viennese' short octave, in which a largely diatonic extension to FF was made by adding a further two natural keys, a plain one for FF and a laterally divided one which gave GG, AA, and BB♭. The C/E key was also divided, giving C at the front and BB at the back. This system lasted until at least the 1780s (fig. 3).

The keyboard compasses of surviving 16th century instruments tend usually to be either C/E – c³ or f³, with the larger range found on many Italian instruments. These upper notes hardly ever appear in written or printed music, and until the mid 17th century the usual written upper limit was a². There are exceptions however – in the 'Recercare Primo' in Marcantonio Cavazzoni's printed collection of 1523, the note e³ appears, and in the 'Iste confessor with a meane' by John Redford (d. 1545), f³. Some of the keyboard pieces of Redford and his contemporaries as preserved in the Mulliner Book, an anthology compiled circa 1560, also require the low F♯, the earliest evidence of the English practice of writing music which could not be fully realised with a short octave. It is unfortunate that there is apparently only one stringed keyboard instrument of English manufacture surviving from the 16th century. This is the harpsichord-organ (a combination usually known as claviorganum), made in London in 1579 by Lodewijk Theeuwes, an emigrant from Antwerp, which had an apparent chromatic four octave compass from C. The only surviving English harpsichord from the early 17th century is the 1622 Hazard at Knole, a tantalising relic without soundboard or action. After this there is nothing else until the Thomas White virginal of 1638 which marks the first appearance of the characteristically English school of virginal makers.

This is a matter for regret in view of the comparatively large surviving quantity of fine keyboard music, much of it by the leading composers of the time, men such as Tallis, Byrd, Gibbons, and Tomkins.

There are many pieces in the Fitzwilliam Virginal Book, which is the best known and biggest collection of this period, requiring notes not available with the C/E short octave. Those which appear most often are F♯ and G♯, but AA also occurs. The most extreme requirements are those of Bull, who uses AA and C♯, Giles Farnaby, who employs AA and E♭, and Tomkins, in whose compositions AA and BB appear. It is of course possible that players tuned unwanted notes to give a more useful alternative; for example C♯ could be retuned to AA.

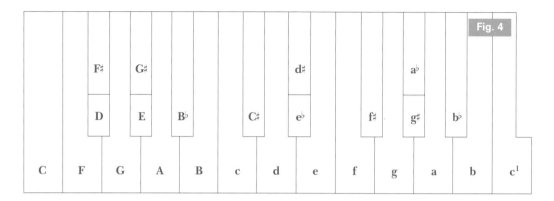

Towards the end of the 16th century there appeared a modification of the short octave, in which the F♯ and G♯ keys were laterally divided, the front giving the customary D and E and the back F♯ and G♯. This was presumably available to Peter Philips, who, in the 'Pavana Dolorosa' not only takes advantage of the idiosyncratic key layout in a remarkable passage in alternating octaves and tenths, but also uses G♯. It could be argued that this could be played on a 'normal' i.e. fully chromatic bass octave by a player with large hands, but more evidence for the use of the short octave is provided in the final bar of Philips's 'Cosi Moriro' – a seven-note E major chord which can be played as written only by a C/E short octave.

Surviving instruments of this period with such an arrangement, usually referred to as a 'broken octave' are mostly of Italian manufacture, although the German writer Michael Praetorius, in his 'Theatrum instrumentorum', published in 1621, provides an illustration of a rectangular virginal, possibly of German origin, which has this feature. Its virtue is that it retains the convenience of the short octave whilst adding two useful accidentals.

Quite a number of surviving Italian harpsichords and virginals have divided accidentals which give the notes D sharp and A flat as well as the more usually encountered E flat and G sharp. This enables the use of a wider range of tonalities than would have been possible with the then prevalent 'meantone' tuning, which favoured keys with two accidentals in the key-signature at the expense of the remoter keys (fig. 4). 16th century Italian theoreticians devoted much time to discussions of subdivisions of the octave and some experimental instruments were constructed. The only survivor of these seems to be the 'Clavemusicum Omnitonium', a harpsichord with 32 notes to the octave, made in 1606 in Venice by Vito Trasuntino, which must have been extremely difficult to play and keep in tune. The much simpler type with two or perhaps three divided accidentals per octave was a much more practical solution to the desire for better possibilities of modulation. Instruments with this type of keyboard, however useful, were not common and do not seem to have been made much after circa 1710.

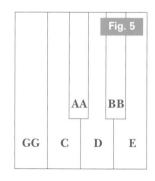

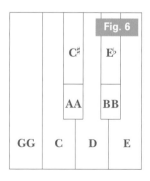

The late 16th century also saw the first appearance of harpsichords with two keyboards. The purpose of this was not to give, as in later 17th century examples, dynamic contrast or a change of tone-colour, but to provide means by which a transposition of pitch could be more easily effected. These instruments, which were first made by the Ruckers family in Antwerp, had non-aligned keyboards, in which the lower manual was a fourth lower than the upper. The top note of the upper manual was c^3, that of the lower, f^3. These transposing harpsichords were made until the middle of the 17th century, but in almost all surviving cases were later modified by the provision of new keyboards, both at the same pitch.

The gradual expansion of the keyboard compass of the harpsichord continued through the 17th century. France became the centre of an important and influential style of keyboard composition from about 1640, and about twenty-five instruments have survived. The compass is $GG-c^3$, usually with a short octave. This compass is also found in instruments of Italian, English, and German manufacture, sometimes in the 'broken' form with accidental keys divided to obtain the chromatic notes from the rear portions (figs. 5 and 6).

The clavichord did not immediately follow the harpsichord's expansion in range, but remained a small fretted instrument with a four octave keyboard, usually with a short octave. It took on a new lease of life in Germany during the first half of the 18th century, when it began to be made in an unfretted form, and by 1750 some much larger instruments were being made, with a completely chromatic five octave compass from FF. This is the type for which idiomatic compositions were written by such composers as C. P. E. Bach. Smaller fretted instruments continued to be made and appreciated, and both these and the larger varieties remained in use until well into the 19th century. The large clavichords made in Germany and Scandinavia from circa 1790-1820 often have a compass of $FF-c^4$, and at least one descends to the benthic zone of CC; this was made by Söderström of Stockholm in 1814.

In the 18th century there was still a certain amount of local variation in keyboard range, but by 1750 the five octave FF compass was well established in England, France and Germany. Early pianos tended to have the same compass, although many German squares kept the $C-f^3$ range found also in the small fretted clavichords. Towards the end of the century some German or Viennese pianos had g^3 or a^3 as the top note. The next significant upward extension was to c^4 – apparently first appearing in a six octave piano made in 1777 by Merlin for Dr. Burney. At the suggestion of the virtuoso pianist-composer Dussek, Broadwood further increased the range of his pianos to c^3 around 1790. In 1794, with the addition of notes down to CC, Broadwood's first 'production' six octave grand appeared.

For some time, various piano compasses overlapped – in the early 19th century grands, squares, and uprights could have been made with compasses from five to six and a half octaves. It was not until roughly after the mid-century that the seven octave $AA-a^4$ keyboard became standard. This was later extended to c^5, and this is now the compass of most pianos currently manufactured. Makers have occasionally attempted something even larger – the tirelessly inventive Pape made a downstriking square with eight octaves. Bösendorfer's 'Imperial' grands also have this range, the downward extension having been requested by Busoni in 1892. The notes CCC-GGG are either covered by a hinged lid, or have the natural keys coloured black, so as not to give the player a feeling of disorientation. The lid is lifted only when the extra notes are needed.

Materials and decoration

The materials used to provide durable playing surfaces for the keys have been few in number – wood, bone, ivory, celluloid and more modern thermoplastics, although sometimes freaks appear. Two examples are to be found in the Victoria and Albert Museum: the Rossi virginal of 1577, whose natural keys are of ivory with inlays of figured semi-precious stones,the accidentals of ebony inlaid with lapis lazuli, and an anonymous early 17th century virginal with natural keys covered with embossed copper plates, enamelled blue. Mother-of-pearl and tortoiseshell are found on some German and Austrian instruments from the 17th to the 19th centuries, especially in harpsichords and clavichords from the 18th century Hass workshop.

The natural keys of most surviving instruments, until the beginning of the 19th century, have a simple decoration consisting of scored lines, from two to four in number, where the key-heads join the tails, sometimes with a filed notch at the edge, between two lines. From the end of the key to the first score line, the edges are usually rounded or bevelled.

Italian harpsichords and clavichords normally have boxwood natural keys. Ivory is much less common, found more often in the small luxury polygonal virginals rather than in harpsichords. The use of ebony is even rarer. The key fronts – that is to say the vertical end surfaces of the key levers – are decorated with arcades which have a semicircular moulding. These are usually made from one piece of wood but many 16th and early 17th century examples have a more elaborate design in two layers, in the form of a tiny Gothic arch. The end-grain of the key lever is visible and may be painted or covered with silk, and sometimes an ivory stud is placed in the centre.

As a result of the rarity and subsequent high cost of ebony, the accidentals are normally made of a stained local hardwood such as service, beech, or walnut, with a capping veneer of ebony, but in luxury instruments solid ebony is sometimes found. A number have survived with gilt decorations, either lines or floral patterns, but these are usually worn away by playing. One of the most exquisitely-made instruments to be found in Britain, the 1540 Marcus Siculus virginal in Fenton House, still has remains of gilt fleur-de-lys patterns on the sloping fronts of the accidentals. The rear upper surfaces are decorated with ivory studs, a feature which it shares with some other elaborately decorated Italian keyboard instruments of this period.

The Antwerp harpsichords and virginals of this period have natural keys covered in bone, decorated with four scored lines with a notch filed at either edge of the key between the two inner lines. The accidentals are of bog oak, notched and chamfered to match the decoration of the natural keys. The arcades are made not of wood but rather of stamped and cut paper, behind which the painted end of the key lever can be seen.

French keyboards of the 17th century have usually ebony or black-stained naturals and solid ivory or bone-capped accidentals, sloping downwards from front to back. The ends of the key levers have Gothic arcading cut directly into the wood, rather than being applied: this eventually disappeared in favour of turned arcades.

Pre-Restoration English keyboards have a superficially Italian appearance, with boxwood naturals and dark accidentals, but with arcades of stamped and gilt paper. The reverse-colour arrangement began to be used after about 1660 and persisted until almost the middle of the 18th century. The woods used were ebony and sometimes partridgewood or snakewood, with ivory accidentals, often solid. During the first decades of the 18th century a change of taste led to the increasing use of ivory for the natural keys and solid ebony for the accidentals. The use of arcaded decoration for the keys was eventually discontinued in favour of an applied moulding, possibly to reduce time and costs. An arcade begins as thin rectangular piece of wood or ivory with a circular pattern cut into the centre. This piece is then cut in half to provide two semi-circular pieces which are then glued individually to the keys. This is obviously much more labour-intensive than merely glueing a strip of moulding to the front edge of the key panel before the key levers are sawn out. In the 1830's this moulded decoration was beginning to be supplanted by a facing in plain wood or ivory, although the 1846 Broadwood piano in our collection still has this feature.

In 18th-century France and to a large extent Germany and Scandinavia until the first decades of the 19th century the keyboard continued with the reverse colour-order, using ebony or stained hardwood for the naturals. The accidental keys are often sloped from front to back. The material used was normally a local hardwood, usually stained black, but sometimes baked, with a bone capping. Solid ebony and ivory are rarely found. Italian instruments still continued to be made with boxwood naturals and ebony-capped accidentals until well into the piano era, with other woods used only rarely. German makers used arcading although embossed paper, mouldings, plain veneer and Gothic carved decoration are also found. French harpsichords and some pianos had arcaded keyfronts, but pianos were generally given mouldings in the English style, which strongly influenced that of Paris.

It might be thought strange that the Iberian peninsula has so far received no mention, as there exists a substantial amount of fine Spanish and Portuguese keyboard music from circa 1550-1800, as well as the better-known work of Domenico Scarlatti and his contemporaries Seixas and Soler. Unfortunately, there appear so far to be few, if any, stringed keyboards to have survived from the 16th century, and perhaps a few from the 17th and 18th. Dr. Burney, when in Italy, saw Spanish harpsichords with black naturals and accidentals covered in mother-of-pearl, but instruments such as these have yet to be discovered. A larger number of 18th century Portuguese clavichords, harpsichords and pianos have survived, the keyboards of which have boxwood naturals, dark accidentals and wooden arcades. Some clavichords have vestigially-Gothic decoration carved directly into the end of the key levers.

The distinctive appearances of the various national styles continued into the 19th century, but standardization of the key-covering materials gives an impression of similarity. Ivory became the material of choice for the natural keys, solid ebony for the accidentals, although German and Austrian makers still persevered with bone naturals and ebony-capped accidentals.

There was a gradual disappearance of the little decorative details that make the keyboards of pre-19th century instruments so visually attractive. This was the result of an understandable desire for greater workshop efficiency, when time and money could be saved by the omission of unnecessary elaboration. Decorative scribe lines, chamfered key-heads and arcades disappeared, to re-emerge only with the late 19th century revival of interest in the early instruments and their forgotten or neglected repertoire.

Notes to accompany CD

Thirty-three instruments of the Collection are recorded on the accompanying compact disc. The music has been chosen to illustrate their salient qualities and to provide fuller illustration of the descriptions in the text of the book. Although the pieces are of necessity short, excerpts have been avoided and complete works or movements have been selected. Notes about the various pieces and composers are given below.

1   **English bentside spinet, attrib. Cawton Aston, circa 1700**
Daniel Purcell: Aire in D (from 'Tunes for the Harpsicord or Spinnet', unpublished, Durham University Library)
Small keyboard instruments often seem to possess an incisive quality which goes far to compensate for any lack of volume or dynamic control. The bright and cheerful tone colour of this little harpsichord brings out well the rather chirpy sound of Purcell's tune.

2   **Square piano by Zumpe et Buntebart, London, 1769**
J. C. F. Bach: Allegro assai from 'Six Easy Sonatas' (1785) no. 3 in D
This instrument, an example of the earliest type of commercially produced square piano in England, lacks both volume and dynamic control compared with square pianos of a later vintage. This, however, one tends to forget in performance, since the instrument's vigorous attack, and the pithy, almost strident, tone colour, seem to belie such deficiences.

3   **Square piano by William and Matthew Stodart, London, 1807**
Beethoven: Six Minuets WoO 10, no. 2 in G
There can surely be few dances in the whole of classical music more well-known than this little minuet. English square pianos of the first decade of the nineteenth century often blend effectively the increased dynamic resources with classical purity and restraint. This seems to me to be especially true of this square piano, which therefore allows one to hear this familiar piece afresh.

4   **Square piano by Adam Beyer, London, 1777**
Cimarosa: Sonata in D minor (J. Ligtelijn edition, Broekmans & van Poppel, Amsterdam 1967, Book 1, no. 1)
The limitations of dynamic control, which is such a characteristic of early square pianos, are largely overcome by the so-called 'nag's head swell', a pedal mechanism sometimes found in instruments by this fine builder, which allows the right hand part of the lid to be raised or lowered, thus affecting the volume. The nag's head swell is employed throughout this little sonata in various ways, sometimes by raising the lid a small amount and sometimes fully.

5   **Double manual harpsichord by Jacob Kirckman, London, 1756**
Thomas Gladwin: Sonata VI (from 'Eight Lessons for the Harpsichord' BL. G. 443 e. 8)
The 'Eight Lessons for the Harpsichord' date from the 1750s and are thus exactly contemporary with this instrument. Gladwin's dates are circa 1710 to 1799, and he was well-known as organist and harpsichordist. Burney, in Rees' Cyclopaedia, refers to him as 'a pleasing player in his day, and a worthy man' This sonata, which owes much to the galant style, that was becoming increasingly popular at the time in London, is indeed a pleasing and worthy piece, which demonstrates well the beautiful and lively sound of this quintessentially English harpsichord.

6   **Single manual harpsichord by Joachim Antunes, Lisbon, 1785**
Frei Jacinto do Sacramento: Sonata in D minor
This Portuguese composer's dates are not known, but from his style it seems likely that he was

a contemporary of his compatriot, Carlos de Seixas (1704-1742). The virtuosic keyboard writing is also reminiscent of Domenico Scarlatti. The chromaticism and frequent consecutive sixths emphasize the distinctively pungent flavour of this music and the tone colour of this Portuguese instrument.

7   Italian virginal by Onofrio Guarracino, Naples, 1668
Andrea Gabrieli: Toccata (from Diruta: Il Transilvano)
The free-style toccata was a very popular instrumental form and is thought by some to be a representation of this composer's own improvisations before playing more formal works. The piece makes use of nearly the whole compass of this instrument.

8   Chamber organ by John Avery, London, 1792
Matthew Camidge: Gavotte in A minor ("from a concerto")
The somewhat closed sound of this little organ seems to suit the dark colour of this delightful dance, which is apparently all that remains from a lost concerto. Steven here uses the full range of the pipes, and for this the pedal operated blower is of great importance, for it allows the correct amount of air to be employed for the different combinations.

9   Chamber organ by John Byfield, London, 1766
John Stanley: Voluntary no. V in D
The slow introduction to this work features the open and stopped diapasons, as suggested by Byfield's written recommendations which are pasted to each side of the keyboard. The cornet voluntary, which follows, is interspersed with the echo effects that are characteristic of Stanley's organ voluntaries. For these the combination pedal, which cuts out all the upper registers apart from the four-foot flute, is employed. On this recording Steven Devine uses Stanley's original fingerings which are marked in the music, and the organ itself is hand-blown by William Dow.

10   Harmonium by Alexandre Père et Fils, Paris, 1858
Louis James Alfred Lefébure-Wély: Prelude in A minor
The Parisian organist and composer, Lefébure-Wély (1817-1869) was particularly renowned for his playing of the harmonium, for which he wrote a large number of compositions. The ability of the player of harmoniums to control the supply of wind by the pedal mechanism is a key factor in the expressive possibilities of these instruments, and this is demonstrated here by Steven Devine in his rendition of this slow dirge.

11   Transverse grand piano by Crang Hancock, London, 1779
James Hook: Allegro con spirito from Sonatina in D op. 12 no. 1
Hook's first movement of the D major sonatina is well served by this strange type of spinet-shaped early piano, which Crang Hancock, its inventor, called 'portable grand piano'. Unlike other early English grand pianos of the conventional shape, the instrument is extremely clear and unresonant, which emphasizes the boldness and vivacity of this piece. An unusual feature is that the instrument possesses no means of altering the timbre, since it lacks both sustaining and keyboard shift mechanisms.

12   Grand piano by John Broadwood & Son, London, 1801
Dussek: Rondo in C from Sonatina op. 20 no. 5
Dussek's great love of English pianos, and in particular the rich and resonant instruments built by John Broadwood, is reflected in the many joyous and exuberant works written during the composer's sojourn in England. The 1801 Broadwood has two pedals operating the sustaining mechanism, and the keyboard shift, which, as was the norm in England at the time, can be fixed either on due corde or una corda. The una corda is employed here just once, towards the end of the rondo before the recapitulation of the opening theme.

13   Grand piano by John Broadwood & Sons, London, 1823

Mendelssohn: Venetian Gondola Song in G minor op. 19 no. 6

Mendelssohn was very conversant with English pianos and in fact owned a grand by Broadwood made in 1820. Of the composer's many 'songs without words' the so-called Venetian gondola songs are surely the most atmospheric, and the present instrument, with its delicate almost harpsichord-like tone colour, seems to do justice to this aspect of the above piece. The keyboard shift can be moved to una corda, and this is employed here for the very quiet ending.

14   Grand piano by John Broadwood & Sons, London, 1846

Rossini: Une Bagatelle (from Péchés de Vieillesse, vol. x: Miscellanée pour piano, no. 4)

This scintillating miniature from the last decade of Rossini's life abounds in extreme dynamic markings, from ff to pppp. There is no difficulty in playing loudly on this powerful Victorian grand, but the resonance caused by the light dampers makes very soft playing more of a problem. The characteristic afterglow of sound is evident through the two 'empty' bars near the beginning and towards the end of the piece.

15   Grand piano by John Broadwood & Sons, London, 1859

Tchaikovsky: 'Song of the lark' from 'The Seasons' no. 3, March

This powerful instrument, the largest and most expensive of Broadwood's concert grands at the time, was apparently an example of the model known in the firm as 'The Iron Grand'. This would seem to be a sobriquet well deserved, for the instrument's rigid barring of the soundboard lends a certain toughness and inflexibility to the quality of sound that one can produce. I have chosen 'The song of the lark' for this remarkable instrument, as it seems to reflect so well the rather sad, wintry quality of this haunting piece.

16   Grand piano by Erard, London, 1866

Grieg: 'The bridal procession passes by'

This witty and affectionate evocation of a Norwegian marching band is taken from the composer's 'Scenes of rural life' op. 19. Among the many clever touches in this lovely composition are the way the tune, which can be heard so clearly at the outset, becomes gradually lost under the increased volume as the band approaches the listener, and the strange pianissimo bars that presage this, like the calm before the storm. The full range of tonal possibilities of Erard pianos is demonstrated here, from the delicacy and sweetness of timbre at the opening of the march, to the power and brilliance of the loud passages.

17   Square piano by Muzio Clementi & Co., London, circa 1820

Field: Nocturne no. 13 in D minor

John Field's close association with Muzio Clementi and Clementi pianos renders a contribution by this Irish pianist/composer in a recording such as this a virtual sine qua non. Although recognisably a Clementi piano, this square has a much darker tone colour, particularly in the middle register, than Clementi grands of the same period. The nocturne in D minor, which has 'plaintivo' written at the start of the score, brings out well this aspect of the instrument.

18   Upright (cabinet) piano by Clementi & Co., London, circa 1825

Clementi: 'Six progressive sonatinas' op. 36 no. 1 in C (6th edition)

allegro – andante – vivace

The sonatinas op. 36 were first published in 1797 and went through many editions during the composer's lifetime. In the sixth edition, published in 1820, Clementi made some considerable alterations to the text, particularly with regard to the increased compass of contemporary pianos. There are no changes from the first edition in the first half of the allegro; in the second half, however, after the first four bars, the rest of the movement lies an octave higher in the part for the right hand. The boisterous vivace begins at the original pitch, and only lies an octave higher in the repeated sections. It is the second movement however which provides the greatest contrast. Here, the present piano imparts a truly fragile lyricism to this gentle movement, in which the entire treble section in this edition lies one octave higher.

19   Grand piano by Muzio Clementi & Co., London, circa 1800

Scarlatti: Sonata in D, K. 400

Already in this early grand piano by Clementi we find all the characteristics that are the hallmark of this composer-cum-builder's style – a distinctive lack of resonance compared with most other English makes, a delicate touch and a remarkable clarity reminiscent of contemporary Viennese pianos. The edition used here is from Da Capo Press Vol V no. VII, which itself is a facsimile edition of Breitkopf & Härtel's 1803-1809 Clementi publications, in which the editor explains that twelve of these sonatas 'are originally by Scarlatti but have been touched up by Clementi for the modern taste' *(soient originairement de la composition de Scarlati, (sic) et qu'elles n'aient été que retouchées par Mr. Clementi pour les mettre plus au courant du jour).*

The main alterations have been the addition of the following dynamic markings – cresc., dim., pp, p, f, ff and fz. How much Clementi himself was responsible for all this must remain in doubt, however, since the Scarlatti sonatas were published in this version without Clementi's collaboration.

20   Grand piano by Clementi & Co., London, 1822

Cramer: 'Il Volteggiare' (no. 9 from '25 New and Characteristic Diversions composed for the Piano Forte and dedicated to his pupils')

John Baptist Cramer's close association in England with Clementi, together with the period of this music (the Diversions were published in 1825), make the choice of this grand piano particularly suitable for this lively little study. Very occasional indications for the use of the sustaining mechanism are found in the score, but because of the speed of the piece the so-called 'Harmonic Swell, or Bridge of Reverberation', patented for Clementi pianos in 1821, seemed more suitable. This mechanism therefore has been used throughout, sometimes however in combination with the sustaining pedal and sometimes with keyboard shift to due corde or una corda.

21   Grand piano by Collard & Collard, London, circa 1840

Schumann: Phantasiestücke op. 12 no. 3 'Warum?'

The Collard brothers (Frederick William and William Frederick) still retained in their instruments the clarity and effective damping that were such a feature of the pianos of Clementi & Co., the firm which they inherited in 1832. The present instrument is bichord, which allows the keyboard shift mechanism to move to a single string position – the true una corda. Very few grand pianos have keyboard shift to una corda after this date, because of the danger of damage to a single string by the force of heavy hammers. The una corda can be heard here towards the end of the piece, as the plaintive call of 'why?' is repeated ever more quietly.

22   Fretted clavichord by Georg Friedrich Schmahl, Ulm, 1807

C. P. E. Bach: Presto in C minor Wq. 114/3

C. P. E. Bach's ability to exploit the full resources of the clavichord, the type of keyboard instrument that was so dear to him, is very evident in this piece, which maximizes the use of the compass and demonstrates crystal-clear articulation through the rapid arpeggios and staccato chords.

23   Fortepiano by Sebastian Lengerer, Kufstein, 1793

Mozart: 'Marche funèbre del Signor Maestro Contrapunto' KV. 453a

This effective little elegy was apparently written in the album of Mozart's pupil, Barbara Ployer. The title, one assumes, celebrates the end of counterpoint lessons. The somewhat dry tone colour of the Lengerer seems very apposite for such a piece, and the feeling of desolation is accentuated by the employment of the moderator mechanism through the quiet passages in the second half.

24   Fortepiano by Michael Rosenberger, Vienna, circa 1800
Haydn: Adagio in F Hob XVIII/9
This late classical Viennese fortepiano possesses an exceptionally pure and mellow tone colour, which does true justice to the lyrical quality of Haydn's adagio. Of the instrument's two knee levers, the left one (operated by the left knee) is the sustaining mechanism, and this is employed freely throughout. The right knee lever, the moderator, is reserved for just two very quiet yet highly dramatic chords towards the end of the piece.

25   Portable square piano by Anton Walter, Vienna, circa 1805
Mozart: Adagio from Viennese Sonatina no. 6
This adagio is the penultimate movement of a keyboard version of the Wind Divertimento in C major, K. 439b no. 6. The wind divertimenti date from 1783 and the arrangements for piano appear to be roughly contemporary, although probably not by Mozart himself. They are however ideal pieces for performance on this little instrument, first because of the regard that Mozart had for pianos by this maker, and secondly because, whereas Mozart's piano music is written almost invariably for five octave instruments, most of these arrangements keep within this portable square's compass of 4½ octaves, C-f³.

26   Fortepiano by Johann Fritz, Vienna, circa 1815
Schubert: Six German Dances D. 820
This group of dances was written by Schubert in Hungary in 1824 during his second sojourn with the Esterházy family at Zseliz. The composer's unhappiness during this stay is reflected in much of his music at this time, and these dances are imbued with a certain wistfulness and nostalgia.

The full range of mutation devices is employed here – keyboard shift for the second dance, moderator for the third and sixth, and a range of percussion effects for the loud passages. These last include the bassoon mechanism, and also 'Turkish Music', sometimes on its own and sometimes augmented by combining with the damper mechanism.

27   Fortepiano by Conrad Graf, Vienna, circa 1820
Brahms: Hungarian Dance no. 13 in D
Refer to 1867 Streicher, page 225

28   Fortepiano by Conrad Graf, Vienna, 1826
Beethoven: Bagatelle in B flat, op. 119 no. 11
The deceptive simplicity of this great miniature demands from a piano the maximum of purity and refinement to do it justice. The present instrument is of a slightly later period than the grand piano by Graf used for the first of the two Hungarian dances by Brahms, and possesses a more mellow tone colour. It is also slightly less powerful and lacks the cutting edge of its earlier cousin.

29   Fortepiano by Mathias Jakesch, Vienna, 1832
Hummel: 'Tyrolienne, variée'
These three variations on a Tyrolean air appear in Hummel's great pedagogical work, published in Vienna in 1828, *Anweisung zum Piano-forte-Spiel* ('Instructions on pianoforte playing'). The sparkling quality of the music is greatly enhanced by the gentle clarity of a contemporary Viennese fortepiano such as the present one. Besides the sustaining mechanism, two mutation effects are used – moderator for the final variation, and, right at the end of the piece, the bassoon mechanism for the final chords.

30/31 Fortepiano by Carl Henschker, Vienna, circa 1840

Stephen Heller: Thirty-two Preludes op. 119 no. 21 in G minor and no. 11 in A

The instrument is typical of the later type of Viennese fortepiano, in that the treble is fairly weak and delicate in comparison with the rich sonorous quality of the bass register. Both these characteristics are very evident at the end of each of these subtle little pieces.

32 Fortepiano by Johann Baptist Streicher, Vienna, 1867

Brahms: Hungarian Dance no. 5 in F sharp minor

The thickness of texture which characterizes so much of Brahms' keyboard writing tends to seem more transparent when heard on the type of grand pianos that the composer knew and loved. Conrad Graf was a very conservative builder, and the piano used here for the first of these two Hungarian dances, although of an earlier date than the Graf that Brahms inherited from Clara Schumann, is in all essentials a very similar instrument. The piano used for the second dance appears to be virtually identical to Brahms' own Streicher of 1868. Both the present instruments are true fortepianos; the Streicher, though, has only two pedals – keyboard shift to due corde and sustaining; whereas the older Graf has typically four – keyboard shift to due corde and una corda, bassoon, moderator and sustaining. All these, bar the bassoon, are used in the first dance.

33 Grand piano by Ignace Pleyel, Paris, 1842

Chopin: Contredanse in G flat (1827)

This gentle miniature by Chopin seems well suited to the instrument's characteristic warm and tender tone colour. The exquisite trio section is a mere eight bars long. Although there is no indication that it should be repeated, I have in fact done so here, as one would indeed need to have a heart of stone not to succumb to this temptation.

34 Square piano by Frederick Mathushek, New Haven, U.S.A., 1873

Gottschalk: Ynés

The original manuscript of this piece apparently had the following superscription 'Danza compuesta por L. M. Gottschalk y dedicada á su bella discipula', and a lighthearted feminine capriciousness pervades this little dance, which is based on the habanera rhythm. The massive frame of the Mathushek piano and the high string tension allow the instrument to equal any instrument of the period in power and responsiveness, yet the tone colour is all its own and owes nothing to contemporary grands.

CD recorded by Chris Thorpe at Finchcocks and produced by Steven Devine; the instruments prepared by William Dow and Marcus Weeks.

Bibliography

Afflalg, Winfried, *Conrad Graf*, (die Gesellschaft für Heimatpflege Biberach e. V., Heft 1, 7 June 1995)

Bach, C. P. E., *Essay on the True Art of Playing Keyboard Instruments*, (Versuch über die wahre Art das Clavier zu spielen) translated and edited by William J. Mitchell, (London, 1949)

Basart, Ann P., *The Sound of the Fortepiano: A Discography of recordings on early pianos*, (Berkeley, California, 1985)

Bilson, Malcolm, *Do We Really Know How to Read Urtext Editions?*, (Piano & Keyboard, Part I August 1995, Part II May/June 1996)

Blüthner-Haessler, Ingbert, *Pianofortebau*, (Frankfurt am Main 1991)

Boalch, Donald H., *Makers of the Harpsichord and Clavichord 1440-1840*, third edition, (Oxford, 1995)

Brauchli, Bernard, *The Clavichord*, (Cambridge, 1998)

Brinsmead, Edgar, *History of the Pianoforte*, (London, 1889)

The British Organ Archive, (Central Library, Birmingham B3 3HQ)

The Broadwood Archive, (The Surrey History Centre, 130 Goldsworth Road, Woking, Surrey GU21 6ND)

Burnett, Richard, *English Pianos at Finchcocks*, (Early Music, February 1985)

Burney, Charles, *A General History of Music From the Earliest Ages to the Present Period*, (1789), edited by F. Mercer, two volumes, reproduction of 1935 edition, (London, 1957)

Burney, Charles, *The present State of Music in France and Italy*, (London, 1771)

Burney, Charles, *Music, Men and Manners in France and Italy, 1770* an extended version of the above with Burneys unpublished notes, edited by H. Edmund Poole, (London, 1969)

Burney, Charles, *The Present State of Music in Germany, The Netherlands, and United Provinces, or, The Journal of a Tour through those Countries, undertaken to Collect Materials for a General History of Music*, two volumes, reproduction of 1773 London edition, (New York, 1969)

The Cambridge Companion to the Piano, edited by David Rowland, (Cambridge, 1998)

Clementi, Muzio, *Introduction to the Art of Playing on the Piano Forte*, op. 42, (London, 1801)

Clementi, Muzio, *Twelve Monferrinas for the Piano Forte*, op. 49, (London, 1821)

Clementi, Muzio, *Six Progressive Sonatinas for the Piano Forte*, op. 36, sixth edition, (London, 1820)

Clinkscale, Martha Novak, *Makers of the Piano: 1700-1820*, (Oxford, 1993)

Clutton, Cecil and Niland, Austin, *The British Organ*, (London, 1963)

Cole, Michael, *Adam Beyer, Pianoforte Maker*, (Galpin Society Journal, 48, 1995)

Cole, Michael, *The Pianoforte in the Classical Era*, (Oxford, 1998)

Cole, Warwick Henry, *Americus Backers: Original Forte Piano Maker*, (Harpsichord and Fortepiano Magazine, 4, 1987)

Colt, C. F. (with Antony Miall), *The Early Piano*, (London, 1981)

Cramer, Johann Baptist, *Instructions for the Piano Forte*, (London, 1812)

Cramer, Johann Baptist, *25 New and Characteristic Diversions*, op. 71, (London, 1825)

Crombie, David, *Piano: Evolution, Design and Performance*, (London, 1995)

Czerny, Carl, *Complete Theoretical and Practical Piano Forte School*, op. 500, three volumes, (London, 1839)

Czerny, Carl, *On the Proper Performance of all Beethoven's Works for the Piano*, (Universal Edition 1970)

Czerny, Carl, *Variations on an Austrian Waltz*, op. 203, (London, c. 1825)

Dale, William, *Tschudi The Harpsichord Maker*, (London, 1913)

A Dictionary of Musicians from the earliest ages to the present time two volumes, printed for Sainsbury and Co., (London, 1825)

Dolge, Alfred, *Pianos and their Makers*, (Dover Publications, 1972)

Dussek, Jan Ladislav, *Instructions on the Art of Playing the Piano Forte or Harpsichord*, (London, 1796)

Ehrlich, Cyril, *The Piano: A History*, (London, 1976)

Eigeldinger, Jean-Jacques, *Chopin: pianist and teacher*, (Cambridge, 1998)

Ellis, Alexander J. and Mendel, Arthur, *Studies in the history of Musical Pitch*, (Amsterdam, 1968)

The Finchcocks Collection a comprehensive catalogue of the keyboard instruments of the collection compiled by William Dow, (Finchcocks, 1990, second revised edition 2003)

Fisher, H. A. L., *A History of Europe from the Beginning of the Eighteenth Century to 1937*, (London, 1957)

The Fitzwilliam Virginal Book edited by Fuller Maitland and Barclay Squire, (New York, 1963)

Freeman, Andrew and Rowntree, John, *Father Smith*, (Oxford, 1977)

Gathorne-Hardy, Jonathan, *The Public School Phenomenon*, (London, 1977)

Gleich, Clemens von, *Die frühesten Quellen zur Temponahme bei Mozart*, (Mitteilungen der Internationalen Stiftung Mozarteum 35, 1987)

Gleich, Clemens von, *Harmonie en perspectief*, (Deventer Studiën 6, Deventer, 1988)

Good, Edwin M., *Giraffes, Black Dragons and Other Pianos: A technological history from Cristofori to the modern concert grand*, (Stanford, California, 1982)

Gottschalk, Louis Moreau, *Notes of a Pianist*, (Philadelphia and London, 1881)

Grieg, *Poetiske tonebilleder* op. 3, (Copenhagen, 1864)

Griesinger, G. A. and Dies, A. C., *Haydn: Two Contemporary Portraits*, (*Biographische Notizen über Joseph Haydn* by G. A. Griesinger and *Biographische Nachrichten von Joseph Haydn* by A. C. Dies), translated by Vernon Gotwals, (Madison, Milwaukee, 1968)

Harding, Rosamond E. M., *The Piano-Forte: Its History Traced to the Great Exhibition of 1851*, (revised edition: Cambridge, 1978)

Harley Collection, (British Library)

Haweis, the Rev. H. R., *Music and Morals*, (London, 1876)

The Harmonicon, magazine of articles and music, published by Samuel Leigh, (London, 1823-1833)

Haskell, Harry, *The Early Music Revival: A History*, (London, 1988)

Hasluck, Paul N., *Pianos: Their Construction, Tuning and Repair*, (London, 1905)

Hedley, Arthur, *Chopin*, (London, 1947)

Helmholtz, Hermann, *On the Sensations of Tone*, (Dover Publications, 1954)

Higginson, A. Henry, *Peter Beckford Esquire, Sportsman, Traveller, Man of Letters. A Biography*, (London, 1937)

Hipkins, A. J., *A Description and History of the Pianoforte*, (London, 1896)

Hirt, Franz-Josef, *Stringed Keyboard Instruments 1440-1880*, (*Meisterwerke des Klavierbaus: Geschichte der Saitenklaviere von 1440-1880*) translated by M. Boehme-Brown, (Boston, Massachusetts, 1968)

E. T. A. Hoffmann's Musical Writings: Kreisleriana, The Poet and the Composer, Music Criticism edited by David Charlton, translated by Martyn Clarke, (Cambridge, 1989)

Hollis, Helen Rice, *The Piano: A Pictorial Account of Its Ancestry and Development*, (London, 1795)

Hubbard, Frank, *Three Centuries of Harpsichord Making*, (Cambridge, Massachusetts, 1965)

Hummel, Johann Nepomuk, *Ausführliche theoretisch-practische Anweisung zum Piano-forte-spiel*, (Vienna, 1828)

Kalkbrenner, Frédéric, *Méthode pour apprendre le Piano-Forte à l'aide du Guide-mains*, (Paris, 1831)

Keyboard Music of the 14th and 15th Centuries, edited by Willi Apel, (Stuttgart, 1963)

Kottick, Edward L. and Lucktenberg, George, *Early Keyboard Instruments in European Museums*, (Bloomington and Indianapolis, 1997)

Kuerti, Anton, *To Urtext Is Human: More about Beethoven and Mozart, dots, strokes, slurs and upbeats*, (Piano & Keyboard, September/October 1996)

Kuronen, Darcy, *John Crang Hancock*, a monograph, (Museum of Fine Arts, Boston)

Lelie, Christo, *van Piano tot Forte: Geschiedenis en Ontwikkeling van de vroege piano c. 1450-1867*, (Den Haag, 1996)

Leppert, Richard, *Music and Image: Domesticity, Ideology, and Socio-cultural Information in Eighteenth Century England*, (Cambridge, 1988)

The Letters of Beethoven, translated and edited by Emily Anderson, three volumes, (London, 1961)

The Letters of Mozart and His Family, translated and edited by Emily Anderson, two volumes, (London, 1966)

Loesser, Arthur, *Men, Women and Pianos*, (London, 1955)

Loest, Roland, *Square but grand*, (The Piano Quarterly no. 153, Spring 1991)

The London Pianoforte School, 1766-1860 edited by Nicholas Temperley, 20 volumes, (New York and London, 1985)

Marcuse, Sibyl, *Musical Instruments: A Comprehensive Dictionary*, (London, 1966)

Marmontel, A., *Histoire du piano et de ses origines*, (Paris, 1885)

Maunder, Richard, *Keyboard Instruments in Eighteenth Century Vienna*, (Oxford, 1998)

Meer, John Henry van der, *Um cravo português desconhecido em propriedade particular na Inglaterra*, (monograph on Antunes, c. 1989)

Felix Mendelssohn: Letters edited by G. Selden-Goth, (Random House Inc., U.S.A., 1973)

Milchmeyer, Johann Peter, *Die wahre Art das Pianoforte zu spielen*, (Dresden, 1797)

Mobbs, Kenneth, *A Performer's comparative study of Touchweight, Key-dip, Keyboard Design and Repetition in Early Grand Pianos, c. 1770 to 1850*, (Galpin Society Journal, May 2001)

Moscheles, Ignaz and Fétis, François-Joseph, *Méthode des méthodes de piano*, (Paris, 1838)

Mozart, Leopold, *Gründliche Violinschule*, (Leipzig, 1956)

The Mulliner Book, edited by Denis Stevens, (London, 1973)

Musical Instruments in the 1851 Exhibition, edited by Peter and Ann MacTaggart, (Welwyn, Herts, 1986)

Die Musik in Geschichte und Gegenwart, edited by Friedrich Blume, 16 volumes, (Bärenreiter, 1949-1979)

The New Grove Dictionary of Music and Musicians, edited by Stanley Sadie, second edition, 29 volumes, (London, 2001)

The New Grove Dictionary of Musical Instruments, edited by Stanley Sadie, three volumes, (London, 1984)

Oort, Bart van, *The English Classical Piano Style and its Influence on Haydn and Beethoven: A Dissertation*, (Cornell University, 1993)

Ottner, Helmut, *Der Wiener Instrumentenbau 1815-1833*, (Tutzing, 1977)

Parakilas, James and Others, *Piano Roles: Three Hundred Years of Life with the Piano*, (New Haven and London, 1999)

Pearsall, Ronald, *The Worm in the Bud: The world of Victorian sexuality*, (London, 1969)

Piggott, Patrick, *The Life and Music of John Field 1782-1837*, (London, 1973)

Place, Adélaïde de, *Le Piano-forte à Paris entre 1760 et 1822*, (Paris, 1986)

Plantinga, Leon, *Clementi: His Life and Music*, (Oxford, 1977)

Pleasants, Virginia, *The Early Piano in Britain*, (Early Music, 13/1 1985)

Plumley, Nicholas, *The Harris/Byfield Connection: some recent findings*, (British Institute of Organ Studies: Journal 3, 1979)

Quarterly Musical Magazine and Review, (London, 1818-1828)

Rees, Abraham, ed., *The Cyclopaedia*, (London, 1819)

Reminiscences of Michael Kelly, two volumes, (London, 1826)

Rimbault, Edward Francis, *The Pianoforte, its Origin, Progress and Construction*, (London, 1860)

Robbins Landon, H. C., *Haydn: Chronicle and Works*, five volumes, (London, 1976)

Robbins Landon, H. C., *The Mozart Compendium*, (London, 1996)

Roell, Craig H., *The Piano in America, 1890-1940*, (Chapel Hill and London, 1989)

Rosen, Charles, *The Classical Style: Haydn, Mozart, Beethoven*, (revised edition, Oxford, 1976)

Rosenblum, Sandra P., *Performance Practices in Classic Piano Music*, (Bloomington and Indianapolis, U.S.A., 1991)

Roudier, Alain, *Pleyel au temps de Frédéric Chopin*, Edizioni del Museo del Pianoforte Antico, (Trento, 1999)

Rowland, David, *A History of Pianoforte Pedalling*, (Cambridge, 1993)

Rueger, Christoph, *Musikinstrument und Dekor*, (Leipzig, 1982)

Russell, Raymond, *The Harpsichord and Clavichord*, (London, 1959)

Schenk, H. G., *The Mind of the European Romantics*, (London, 1966)

Skowroneck, Tilman, 'The Keyboard Instruments of the Young Beethoven' article in *Beethoven and his World*, edited by Scott Burnham and Michael Steinberg, (Princeton, 2000)

Spillane, Daniel, *The History of the American Pianoforte, Its Technical Development and Trade*, (New York, 1890)

Starr, S. Frederick, *Bamboula: The Life and Times of Louis Moreau Gottschalk*, (Oxford, 1995)

Streicher, Andreas, *Brief Remarks on the Playing, Tuning and Care of Fortepianos*, (Early Music Facsimiles, Ann Arbor, 1983)

Streicher, Andreas, *Kurze Bemerkungen über das Spielen, Stimmen und Erhalten der Fortepiano welche von Nannette Streicher, geborne Stein in Wien verfertiget werden*, Vienna 1901, (republished in 1987 by *Stichting voor Muziekhistorische Uitvoeringspraktijk*)

Sumner, W. L., *The Pianoforte*, (London, 1966)

Sumner, W. L., *The Organ: its Evolution, Principles of Construction and Use*, (London, 1952)

Sutton, Sir John, *A short account of organs built in England from the reign of King Charles the Second to the Present Time*, (London, 1847)

Türk, Daniel Gottlob, *Clavierschule oder Anweisung zum Clavierspielen für Lehrer und Lernende*, reprint of 1787 edition, (Bärenreiter, 1997)

Tyson, Alan, *Thematic Catalogue of the Works of Muzio Clementi*, (Tutzing, 1967)

Wainwright, David, *Broadwood by Appointment: A History*, (London, 1982)

Wainwright, David, *The Piano Makers*, (London, 1975)

Wegeler, Franz and Ries, Ferdinand, *Remembering Beethoven (Biographische Notizen über Ludwig van Beethoven)*, translated by Frederick Noonan, (London, 1988)

Willetts, Pamela J., *Beethoven and England: An account of sources in the British Museum*, (London, 1970)

Wilson, Michael, *The English Chamber Organ: History and Development 1650-1850*, (Oxford, 1968)

Wythe, Deborah, *The Pianos of Conrad Graf*, (Early Music, 12/4 1984)

Pictorial illustrations index

Music illustrations index

PAGE

General index

A

accidentals
  colour choice 115-16
  keyboard chronology 215, 216
  materials and decoration 217-19
actions
  Anglo-German 200
  Anglo-Viennese 200
  Bartolomeo Cristofori 14-15,
    110, 112
  English 204, 205
  German 206
  glossary definition 200
  harpsichord 206
  single 210
  sticker 39
  Viennese 110, 112, 114, 117,
    151, 152, 211
Adam, John 32
Adam, Robert 32
Addison, Robert 94
advertising
  John Brinsmead and Sons 40-1
  John Broadwood and Sons
    49-50, 56
Agapemone, 'The Abode of Love'
  54
Albert, Prince Consort 57
Alexandre, Jacob 34
Alexandre Père et Fils, harmonium,
  Paris 1858 33, 34, 221
American bias against English
  pianos 43
American square piano 145-8
amplifying devices 125, 126, 140
Anglo-German action 200
Anglo-Viennese action 200
Anton Walter and Son
  square piano, Vienna circa 1805
    119-20, 224
  see also Walter, Anton
Antunes, Joachim, harpsichord,
  Lisbon 1785 24, 26, 27, 221
Antunes, Manuel, grand piano
  1767 26
arcaded decoration 218
Arion 131
Arnaut de Zwolle, Henri 214
attitudes

dancing 95, 96-8
  English music phobia 69, 79-81
August II, elector of Saxony 111
authenticity 197
Avery, John 30
  chamber organ, London 1792
    30, 221

B

Babcock, Alphaeus 147
Bach, Carl Philipp Emanuel, Presto
  in C minor Wq. 114/3 224
Bach, Johann (John) Christian
  Gabriel Buntebart relationship
    49
  Johannes Zumpe relationship 49
  Madame Brillon 169
  square pianos 18
  Zumpe square piano
    performance 49
Bach, Johann Christoph Friedrich
  Allegro assai from 'Six Easy
    Sonatas' no. 3 in D 220
back checks 117
Backers, Americus 34
bad debts 48-9
barless frames 61
barless grands 61
baroque 200
barrel instruments 62, 200
barrel piano 62
baseboard 200
bassoon mechanism 122, 192-3, 200
beak (Schnabel) 110
Beale, Thomas 94
Beale, see also F. Beale and
  Company
beam 200-1
die Bebung 108
Bechstein 43
Bechstein, Carl 145
Beckford, Peter 68-9, 79, 80
Beethoven, Ludwig van
  Bagatelle in B flat op. 119
  no. 11 156-7, 225
  Broadwood instrument gift
    49, 94, 181
  Erard 1803 grand piano 134,
    143, 187

Graf piano loan 125-6
  keyboard shift 188
  Moonlight Sonata 181-2, 187
  Muzio Clementi publishing
    relationship 76-7
  pedal markings 181-3
  Six Minuets WoO 10 no. 2
    in G 220
  Sonata in D minor op. 31 no. 2
    182-3
  tempo 163, 167
bells 121
belly rail 201
bentside 201
  double 114, 204
  triple 211
bentside spinets 15-16
  attrib. Cawton Aston, London
    circa 1700 15, 16, 220
Beyer, Adam 21-2, 180
  square piano, London 1777
    21-2, 220
bichord stringing 188
Billington, Elizabeth 47
'black dragons' 147
Blasser, Thomas, harpsichord,
  London 1744 24, 26
Blunt, Wilfrid 80
bog oak accidentals 218
Böhm, Theobald 204
Bonaparte, Napoleon 134, 136
Bond Street fire 91
bone keys 218
bookcases 84
Bösendorfer 112, 217
boxwood keys 218, 219
Brahms, Johannes 125, 131
  Hungarian Dance no. 5
    in F sharp minor 225
  Hungarian Dance no. 13
    in D 224
brass wires 102-3
'breaking the sound' 151, 195
Breuning, Stephan von 125
bridge 201
  clavichords 107-8
  divided and undivided 102-3
Brillon, Madame 169
Brinsmead, Edgar 39, 40